BIZARRE BEAUTY
THE ART OF WILLIAM HARPER

BIZARRE BEAUTY
THE ART OF WILLIAM HARPER

EDITED BY
GLENN ADAMSON &
MARTHA J. FLEISCHMAN

ARNOLDSCHE

CONTENTS

PREFACE

MARTHA J. FLEISCHMAN

My enthusiasm to produce this book devoted to the art of William Harper was born out of a lifetime fascination with works that are stubbornly original, sometimes disturbing, frequently humorous, and occasionally shocking in content and construction. His ongoing exploration of personal themes, both sacred and profane, continues to offer up discovery at every turn.

Oddly enough, my introduction to Bill Harper's work was made possible through the determination of Pope Paul VI a half century ago. In the wake of the Second Vatican Council, His Holiness was eager to renew a historical bond between contemporary artists, their spiritual journeys, and the ideals of the Vatican Museums with their extraordinary art collections amassed over the centuries. During the 1970s, Pope Paul directed his clerical community to pursue this goal quietly and incognito in New York. They welcomed the support and collaboration of a group of American collectors of disparate spiritual and religious backgrounds and began to assemble, though generous private donations, a new collection of American painting, sculpture, and also the art of outstanding craftspeople. The Committee of Religion and Art in America, as it was known then, was co-founded by my father, Lawrence A. Fleischman, a passionate art collector, connoisseur, and dynamic gallery owner, who was essential in the leadership of this organization. Motivated by a strong desire to place important works of art by American artists into the permanent galleries of the Vatican, he encouraged the philanthropy of like-minded art collectors, and many outstanding paintings and sculptures were acquired for the Modern and Contemporary Art collection, including works by Ben Shahn, John Sloan, and Georgia O'Keeffe. In 1978, in partnership with the Smithsonian Institution, objects for the exhibition *Craft Art & Religion* were expertly selected and displayed within the galleries of the Vatican in Rome, and a symposium of lectures was presented by leading historians and exceptional craft artists of the day.

The Vatican setting for these marvelous objects was remarkable, but the discovery of Harper's creations and eventually an introduction to the artist himself were the most revelatory connection for my own family. With his international visibility in the field, Bill was immediately selected for the

Vatican program, and he enthusiastically participated in this invitational exhibition, creating a Torah pointer for the occasion. Having converted to Judaism the decade before, he found the once-in-a-lifetime exhibition a challenging opportunity. An object at once sacred and personal was made; like many Harper creations, it seems simple at first glance, but it is highly complex in its originality and iconography. The shell of a sea creature, used in place of the traditional pointing human hand, was a daring choice for this elegant enameled object, and an example of the artist's unconventional approach.

Although Harper seemed an unlikely collaborator for our more traditional, historically grounded American art gallery in midtown Manhattan, we subsequently presented three significant Harper exhibitions, newly revealing his work to museums and an array of important new collectors unfamiliar with his art in America and in Europe, such as our adventurous friend Baron Thyssen-Bornemisza. Throughout these years, it was impossible for us to resist acquiring and commissioning new work. We relished adorning ourselves with his jewelry, which never fails to attract excited reactions from friends, as well as perplexed commentary from strangers passing by. This irresistible compulsion continues to the present day.

This book has been a long-term goal and a work in progress for many years. I wish to express my special appreciation to Barbara Paris Gifford, whose original curatorial themes are the framework explored within these pages. Also, great thanks are extended to Glenn Adamson, not only for his perceptive guidance as critic and historian but also for his deft, ambassadorial skills, which were essential in leading this challenging publication project to fruition.

In its exploration of William Harper's lifetime of creativity and its documentation of a most unusual career, our monograph is a journey into the mind of an artist possessed of original and restless expression. *Bizarre Beauty* is also a celebration of my decades-long friendship with the artist himself and of my unceasing admiration for his fearless creative spirit embodied in every one of these works. ◆

TORAH POINTER, 1977

Gold and silver cloisonné enamel on fine silver; 14k gold, sterling silver, copper, shell. 9.75 × 1.75 in. The Vatican Museums, Vatican City

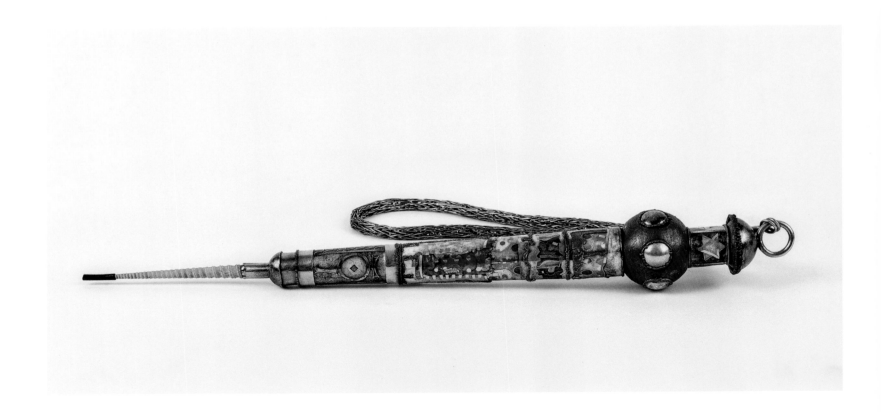

ABRAHAM THOMAS

When holding a work by Bill Harper in your hand, you may feel you are being pulled into an immersive post-apocalyptic world. His intricately assembled objects, ranging from brooches to chalices, treasure boxes to talismans, all possess a deft mastery of materials and a profound sense of experimentation and alchemy.

Harper builds up layers of meaning through a thoughtful juxtaposition of rare and precious materials with utilitarian found objects. Blending the ancient with the industrial, natural world specimens with street flotsam, he creates miniature steampunk environments. Roman glass fragments may sit alongside medical vials of Demerol. Animal bone armatures are ensnared in wires of gold and aluminum. Irregularly shaped pearls embedded within coffee-can lids and plastic bicycle reflectors.

Like a material-culture mixtape, Harper's assemblages feel spontaneous and improvised, combining a frenzied energy with poised contemplation, resulting in freestyle compositions that seem a homage to John Cage's theories on "indeterminacy."

Harper was originally trained in painting, and it shows. He has a supreme talent for applying cloisonné enamel using non-traditional techniques, producing abstract fields of rich color, sometimes milky, sometimes luminous, with hypnotic visual rhythms. They are as much indebted to Kandinsky and Rothko as to Byzantine metalwork.

Harper's objects are deeply personal studies of art history, yet they defy any placement in time. His encyclopedic approach to materiality feels dichotomous—both ancient and futuristic—and jam-packed with endless surprises and curiosities, like some fever dream in which René Lalique is fused with Anselm Kiefer. They could be relics salvaged from the ocean depths of some distant planet. Harper's constructions, made over the course of six decades, continue to fascinate us, offering infinite opportunities to explore each time we revisit these extraordinary worlds. ◆

THE LAST BOOGIE BABY, 2023

Gold cloisonné enamel on fine silver; 18k, 22k, and
24k gold, tourmaline, opal, amethyst, moonstone,
coral, shell, plastic, beetle carapace. 6 × 2 in.

SHAPE SHIFTER
THE LIVES OF
WILLIAM HARPER

GLENN ADAMSON

"My soul is wrought to sing of forms transformed to bodies new and strange!"[1] So runs the first line of Ovid's *Metamorphoses*, that great classical poem of change-in-all-things. It is my first line, too, as I set out to tell the story of William Harper. For, if I had only a few words to describe him, it would be as an Ovid for our times. True, he works in the recalcitrant materials of metal and enamel rather than in verse. Yet he is a kind of poet, whose fantastical ideas spin round acts of transmutation. Look closely at any one of his works or, better, take it in your hand. Feel its certain weight. While precisely fixed in its gleaming materiality—and Harper's compositions are nothing if not carefully judged—it still seems malleable, as if it might begin to dance or otherwise perform. Or as if it might take some new shape unbidden by its maker, just as the nymph Daphne, in Ovid's vivid description, turned into a laurel tree: "Thin bark closed over her breast, her hair turned into leaves, her arms into branches, her feet so swift a moment ago stuck fast in slow-growing roots, her face was lost in the canopy—only her shining beauty was left." That haunting image, immortalized since by countless artists (most famously Gianlorenzo Bernini, in white marble) finds its contemporary equivalent in Harper's jewels, paintings, and other objects. Caught in time, his objects nonetheless retain a plenitude of possibility; they are imbued with the spark of life.

---

1   *Ovid: Metamorphoses*, trans. A. D. Melville (Oxford: Oxford World Classics, 2008), 1.

William Harper with his mother, Margaret Annibel Harper, 1944

If transformation is the essence of Harper's creativity—what happens every time he sits down at his studio workbench, reacting intuitively to what is in front of him, improvising until he has imbued it with vivid animacy—it is also a useful concept in approaching his biography. At every stage of his long career, he has reinvented himself, allowing his creative instincts to carry him into new territory, an ever-evolving dramatic scene. At the same time (and this is true for most great artists, as for great actors), he has remained a recognizable character, with consistent preoccupations and propensities, and a coherent philosophy about what he is up to.

Around the time that Harper was setting out on his career, Susan Sontag wrote her essay "Against Interpretation" (1964). While not necessarily a touchstone for Harper, it aligns with his intellectual sensibility to a remarkable degree, beginning with its epigrams from Willem DeKooning ("content is a glimpse of something, an encounter like a flash") and Oscar Wilde ("it is only shallow people who do not judge by appearances"). Sontag offered a critique of criticism itself, attacking those professional interpreters who make so bold as to give a work of art—that sensuous, ineffable thing—just one particular meaning. In opposition to this academic habit of mind, she called for a kind of writing that clears a space against the chaotic, crowded backdrop of modern life, setting the artwork forth, much as a jeweler might set a multifaceted stone. "The aim of all commentary on art now," she wrote, "should be to make works of art—and, by analogy, our own experience—more, rather than less, real to us."[2]

It is in this spirit that I invite you, now, to walk with me through the densely enchanted thicket of Harper's life and work. My goal is not to explain him, deciphering the output of his psyche as if I had a decoder ring. Rather, I hope to make his achievement as "real" as possible, establishing the historical context in which it has unfolded, reflecting on what it has taken to make his bizarre and beautiful works, as well as what emerges from them. Harper puts everything he has into his work. Glorious to behold, beyond confident in its swaggering elaboration, it is nonetheless shot through with dark strains of insatiable desire and profound melancholy. It is a body of work much like the human body itself, filled with feelings of all kinds, potent, sensitive, vulnerable, ultimately keeping its secrets close. "In place of a hermeneutics," Sontag declared in the famous concluding line of "Against Interpretation," "we need an erotics of art." In Harper's case, nothing else will do.

THE ASPIRING PUPPETEER

He was, by his own admission, a strange little kid. Known then and since mostly as Bill, he was born in 1944 in Bucyrus, Ohio (motto: "The small city in the middle of everywhere"), and spent his first six-and-a-half years out on a farm, without any friends his own age, or, it seems, of any age. His father, William Sr., had served as an Air Force mechanic during World War II, then took up farming, as well as operating a small grocery (put out of business by the arrival of a supermarket), and finally a job at the local post office. In Bill's youth, he was closer to his paternal grandparents, who were also farmers (he has fond, if queasy, recollections of fried chicken dinners prepared from scratch, starting with grabbing a live bird by the ankles), than he was to his own father, who returned home from the war only when his son was eighteen months old —"I was rather afraid of him at first," he says—or to his two brothers, Michael Lee and Jonathon D Harper. He had essentially no exposure to art, and not much else in the way of entertainment, apart from what he could create for himself. It was the sort of situation that, 99 times out of 100, will produce someone with no particular artistic interests. But Harper was in that lonely percentile who, offered no obvious route into the realm of aesthetics, discovers the most promising pathway of all, the one that leads into the interior of their own heads. He drew constantly and made things out of colored paper and bits of wood. "I especially loved carbon paper," he recalled, "when I could get my hands on it, much to the horror of mother, who would find blue tracings everywhere of what I would find."[3] His mother, Margaret Annibel Harper, was a homemaker and an excellent seamstress and made all of Bill's clothing, with some input from him. He remembers clearly a dinner jacket which was "color patterned like ones I saw on Television. I did have rather advanced taste."[4]

To keep himself company, Bill took up some unusually adult cultural interests—opera, classical music—and read fantastical literature like *A Thousand and One Nights* and the mythology of ancient Greece and Rome. As a child of the postwar moment he also watched television, of course, and it was there that he found his first real artistic inspiration: the marionettes of Bil Baird, then hitting the airways in programs like *Life with Snarky Parker* (1950) and the CBS-TV Morning Show. Transfixed, he began making his own puppets, initially as a Cub Scout achievement project. He persuaded his father to construct a simple stage for him, and he began making his own marionettes, based on designs he could find in the local library, with papier-mâché heads built over lightbulbs, bodies of dowel construction, and handmade outfits. By the time he was in the fifth grade, he was presenting miniature theatricals—*Aladdin*, a production he called *Animal Ballet*, and a simple children's show featuring a clown that could blow bubbles—all accompanied by lighting and music, which Harper wrote himself.

He presented these shows to local audiences, at mother-daughter and father-son banquets, elementary schools, PTA gatherings, and children's parties.[5] One year, aged fourteen, he even traveled on his own to the national festival of the Puppeteers of North America, held in Chapel Hill, North Carolina, where he learned to make more complex marionettes with moving eyes, eyebrows, and mouths. He recruited three other kids, one boy and two girls, to serve as his assistants, but it was Bill's show from first to last—"Professor Harper and Company," as he styled the enterprise—and his first real taste of creative expression. His most ambitious production, *Alice in Wonderland*, featured a large cast: "A caterpillar whose eyes were equipped with tiny

Top: William Harper and fellow puppeteers John Weber, Kristine Flocken, and Karen Frey (left to right) in Bucyrus, Ohio, c. 1956.
Bottom: William Harper and fellow puppeteers performing in Bucyrus, Ohio, c. 1956

2   Susan Sontag, "Against Interpretation," *Evergreen Review* 8 (Dec. 1964), reprinted in Sontag, *Against Interpretation and Other Essays* (New York: Farrar, Straus and Giroux, 1966), 95, 104.
3   Oral history interview with William Harper, 2004 January 12–13, Archives of American Art, Smithsonian Institution.
4   William Harper, email to Glenn Adamson, Sept. 17, 2023.
5   Gayl Metzger, "Finds Puppets Fascinating: Youth's Hobby Began 8 Years Ago," newspaper clipping, artist's collection.

lights that could blink red, a Knight of Hearts whose head could come off at the will of the Red Queen, as well as a white velvet covered rabbit, with moveable ears and anatomically correct feet and legs."[6] In retrospect, it is hard not to see these creations as precedents for the vividly imagined, highly articulate characters in his mature artwork.

Bill left off puppetry when he was a sophomore in high school, feeling perhaps that it was kid stuff, but continued making other forms of pageantry: costumes and sets for the drama club, floats for the homecoming parade. He also began taking art classes from a local artist named Alice Tupps, at a studio adjoining her home. The exercises were strictly standard-issue: "Draw a single clay flower pot straight ahead with charcoal, and all the ellipses had to be perfect and it had to be completely symmetrical and the shadows had to be right," as he recalls. "The least creative thing that you could imagine."[7] He applied himself nonetheless, little realizing that this tight, restrictive approach was not what the wider world considered art to be. When he applied to the Cleveland Institute of Art, hoping to become a theater designer, he was dismayed to find himself rejected not once but twice in succession, despite having been a straight-A student in high school.

With the threat of being sent into the Army hanging over his head (the Vietnam draft was years away, but military service was the only alternative to college his father would consider for him), Harper enrolled in an intensive summer course and then managed to get a scholarship to attend a five-year degree program in art education. He'd have studio classes at the Cleveland Institute of Art, but also humanities coursework at Western Reserve University (now Case Western Reserve) and art history sessions taught at the Cleveland Museum of Art. As it transpired, this unusual curriculum proved an ideal combination for a young man who was as intellectually ravenous as he was artistically restless. The collections at the Museum were foundational for Harper, particularly the medieval, African, and Asian holdings assembled by directors William Milliken and Sherman Lee.

At Case Western, Harper fell in with a group of friends of an intellectual cast—primarily Jewish, and primarily from east coast prep schools: "They never seemed to make me feel as though I was not rich."[8] He contributed regular illustrations to a campus literary magazine called *Polemic*, whose editors proclaimed an intent to avoid the "self-flattery" typical of campus publications and instead host challenging political debates (this was, after all, the 1960s).[9] His initial artistic efforts were in painting, but his fellow student Charles Mayer, art editor of *Polemic*, introduced him to enamel, the art form in which he would establish himself and which has remained an important aspect of his expansive repertoire ever since. Rather like the education he was getting, enamel was a hybrid discipline, a craft that was nearly painting, which combined chemistry with decoration, technical control with expressive possibility. Harper was enthralled—and as with every other fascination he has ever had, there would be no stopping him.

William Harper at Case Western Reserve University, c. 1966

6   William Harper, email to Glenn Adamson, Sept. 17, 2023.
7   Oral history interview with William Harper, Archives of American Art.
8   William Harper, email to Glenn Adamson, Sept. 17, 2023.
9   "Polemic Aims for New Heights," *Reserve Tribune*, Sept. 20, 1966, 7.

DEW BOX, 1966

Gold and silver cloisonné enamel on fine silver;
ebony box. 2.5 × 2.5 × 1 in.

THE ALCHEMIST'S APPRENTICE

Kenneth F. Bates, *Perpetual Vine Cup on Stand*, 1965. Transparent enamel (plique-à-jour), copper, silver. Overall: 3 × 4 in. The Cleveland Museum of Art, Bequest of Marie Odenkirk Clark (1972.1195)

To an extent that has often been underestimated by historians, Cleveland was a vital center for American craft—in fact, the most active city in the movement anywhere between the coasts. It was a sophisticated and lively center for the arts generally; Harper spent his pocket money on traveling Broadway shows and concerts at the city's outstanding orchestra, which was located on campus. Most important to him was the Cleveland Institute of Art, which, during Harper's time there (1962 to 1967), boasted an extraordinary range of talents on its faculty: Toshiko Takaezu, then in the most experimental period of her illustrious career as a ceramist and weaver; sculptor Bill McVey; jeweler John Paul Miller and silversmith Frederick Miller (close friends, but no relation); the ceramist Edris Eckhardt, who was also beginning to work in cast glass; and enamelist Kenneth F. Bates. Also in the community were the potters Leza McVey and Claude Conover and industrial designer Victor Schreckengost. This talented group were motivated by friendly competition with one another, especially at the annual May Show, an event without any real parallel elsewhere in the country. Founded in 1919 (and running all the way through 1993), this was a juried exhibition held at the Cleveland Museum of Art. Only those living and working in northeast Ohio were eligible to enter, but practitioners in all disciplines were welcome, and their work was displayed on equal terms, without any distinction between the fine and decorative arts—a hierarchy that was still being rigidly policed elsewhere in the art world. Thanks to this ecumenical atmosphere, as Harper says, "I didn't realize until I was out in the cruel world that I was doing something unacceptable."[10]

While still an undergraduate, in 1966, Harper had a great success of his own at the May Show, winning special mention alongside his own professors (Bates, Takaezu, and John Paul Miller were similarly recognized that year). In Cleveland, no medium shone more brightly than enamels. The prime mover was Kenneth Bates, who had come from Boston to teach in the late 1920s, forging a rare link from the Arts and Crafts era forward to the postwar craft movement. In succeeding decades he trained and otherwise influenced several generations of enamelists, including Doris Hall, Charles Bartley Jeffery, Mary Ellen McDermott, John Paul Miller, Mildred Watkins, and Edward Winter. Their work was regularly exhibited in the May Show and collected by the Cleveland Museum of Art, where Milliken, who in 1930 had acquired an important group of medieval enameled artifacts known as the Guelph Treasure, took a strong interest in the medium.

Another important factor was the presence of the Ferro Enamel Corporation, which produced a wide range of domestic appliances and industrial

10   William Harper, interview with Glenn Adamson, Sept. 14, 2022.
11   Maria F. Ali, *The Century of Progress Documentation Project* (Washington, DC: Historic American Buildings Survey, 1994), Appendix A.
12   Bernard N. Jazzar and Harold B. Nelson, "Painting With Fire: Enameling and the Cleveland School," *The Magazine Antiques*, Oct. 2016.
13   William Harper, interview with Barbara Paris Gifford, 2023.
14   Harper, interview with Barbara Paris Gifford. See Alan Rosenberg and Glenn Adamson, *Rediscovering Paul Hultberg: Abstract Expressionism in Enamel* (Philadelphia: Moderne Gallery, 2021).
15   Oral history interview with William Harper, Archives of American Art; Harper, interview with Barbara Paris Gifford.

goods. (In 1933, they fabricated an entire house in enameled metal for *A Century of Progress International Exposition* held in Chicago, promoted as "an attempt to bring the out-of-date housing industry in line with more efficient manufacturing practices such as those used by the auto industry."[11]) Winter, who had traveled to Vienna to study with the great Secessionist designer Josef Hoffmann, was able to use the kilns at Ferro to create large-scale panels indebted to contemporaneous Abstract Expressionism. Bernard Jazzar and Harold Nelson, the leading historians of postwar enameling, describe the process: "He created the voluptuous curvilinear rhythms using a sgraffito technique, cutting through the enamel with a rake- or comb-like tool before firing."[12]

Harper's response to most of the Cleveland School enamels was typically opinionated: "I thought they looked like Christmas tree ornaments."[13] He felt real affinity only for those artists, like Winter and the relatively free-spirited Mary Ellen McDermott—or outside of the Cleveland context, Paul Hultberg—who adopted a painterly, expressive approach: "I think most good enamels come from people who have the eye of a painter, but have adjusted it."[14] While he respected Bates personally, seeing him as an "immense technician," he found his actual work to be limited by its perfectionism: "I always thought with Kenny that he could have stopped with his prep painting. There was no need really to transfer it because he took no liberties. And once he made it, he knew what the various overlays of color were going to be, and then he just did it."[15]

Early on, Harper found ways to break out of this restrictive *modus operandi*, allowing enamel colors to bleed around the wires of a cloisonné design, or tearing gold foil into rough bits before setting it down as a ground rather than laying it out in the usual tidy patterns. He was simultaneously mastering the craft and testing its boundaries, a relationship to workmanship that has stayed with him ever since. Always exquisitely intricate, his creations are also intentionally disruptive, unpredictable, more than a little

H. Edward Winter, *Plaque: Toccata and Fugue*, 1952. Enamel. Overall: 9.5 × 28 in. The Cleveland Museum of Art, Silver Jubilee Treasure Fund (1952.144)

bit wild. Bates himself recognized this, writing an appreciative note to Harper some years later in which he wrote, with typical good humor: "I'll say irrevocably, you are some kind of genius. I can say that with impunity because I know damned well, I'm not."[16]

THE ABSTRACT CARTOGRAPHER

Personally speaking, 1967 was a big year for Harper. He graduated from Case Western with both a master's degree and a certificate in teacher training, and took up a job as a high school teacher in nearby Parma, Ohio. He also married a fellow student, Riva Ross, converting to Judaism in deference to her family background. In a portent of things to come, in more than one sense, she gave him a sculpture made among the Senufo people of West Africa as a wedding present: "She didn't realize it," he laughs, "but it was a fertility figure."[17] (The couple would have two children, Meredith and Joshua, born in 1971 and 1973.) Harper also had his first one-person exhibition, at the Massillon Museum, a regional Ohio institution.

Creatively, however, this was an uncertain time for him. He was mostly involved with making abstract panels and box lids, stylistically akin to those of Edward Winter or Paul Hultberg, in which the enamel was freely applied like oil on canvas. He would fire the plaques as many as thirty times to achieve an effect of dense, polychromatic overlay. Some of these featured

Paul Hultberg, *Little Johnson*, 1969. Enamel. 48 × 60 in. Collection of Lawrence Hultberg

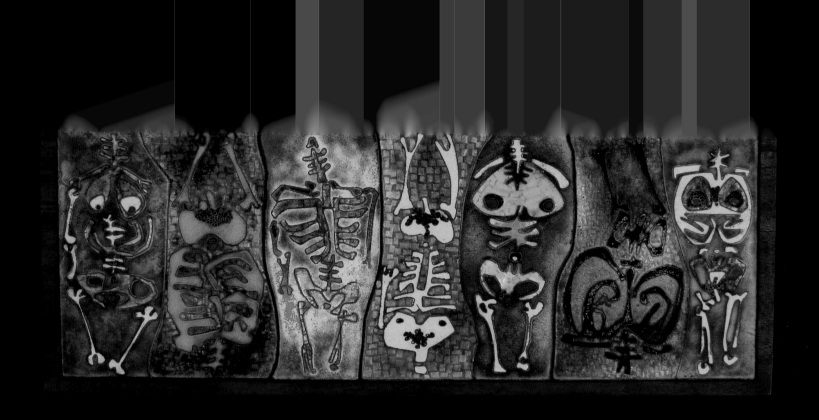

BONE BOX, 1967

Silver cloisonné enamel on copper; silver foil, teak box. 10 × 4 in. Massillon Museum, Sidney S. Cohen Purchase Award (70.109)

figural motifs, as is the case of the *Bone Box* exhibited at the Massillon Museum in 1967, in which skeletal X-rays of figures are rendered using ceramic decals under the enamel, a technique of Harper's own invention. Unfortunately, he lacked access to an industrial facility like the one at Ferro, so these works were limited by the size of his own studio kiln, only about eight by ten inches.[18] He sees them, in retrospect, as somewhat derivative of Abstract Expressionism, "secondary generation—maybe tertiary generation," and he found himself getting rejected at the May Show and "virtually every other [exhibition] that I tried to enter."[19]

Clearly, a paradigm shift was in order. Fortunately for Harper, that is exactly what was happening across America. It was now the late 1960s, and an unprecedented wave of cultural experimentation was breaking across the country: drugs, rock and roll, sexual liberation, and, alongside it all,

16   Kenneth Bates, letter to William Harper, April 1, 1978. Bates wrote this letter just before he appeared in his record-setting fiftieth consecutive May Show; he joked, "Maybe they'll give me a Speedball pen and pencil set," then concluded, "I am not driven like you, and 'may' not have your talent, but Bill, I am shrewd as Hell and don't intend to die in the poor house."

17   Harper, interview with Barbara Paris Gifford.

18   Harper did briefly experiment with a technique used by Paul Hultberg, in which a larger panel is heated on rollers over a series of flames, obviating the need for a kiln.

19   Oral history interview with William Harper, Archives of American Art.

June Schwarcz, *Bowl (#626)*, 1974. Electroplated copper foil, enamel. 5 × 6.25 × 6.25 in.

experimental craft. By personal disposition, Harper was turned off by the counterculture; he did not smoke pot, hated the music (classical was still his thing), and felt no attraction to the messy, uninhibited hippie lifestyle. Even so, he found ways to connect with the electrifying new currents. A crucial moment came in late 1966, when he took his first trip to New York City over the winter break and happened to catch side-by-side exhibitions at the Museum of Contemporary Crafts (MCC) of the assemblage artist Dominic Di Mare and the enamelist June Schwarcz. Di Mare's atmospheric, ritualistic work may well have had an influence—Harper would soon begin making quasi-functional artifacts of similar spiritual implication—but it was Schwarcz who made the most dramatic and lasting impression on him. She had been the breakout star of an earlier group show about enamels at the MCC, in 1959. Her one-person exhibition that Harper saw was one of a series on contemporary American enamelists, including European émigré Karl Drerup (1957), Boston-based historicist Margarete Seeler (1961), modernist jeweler Kaye Denning (1962), and Paul Hultberg (1966), as well one specialist from Italy, Paoli De Poli (1967). Together, these shows attested to the breadth and vitality of current work in the medium, but Schwarcz's power and innovation were unmatched. A physically tiny and personally modest woman, she nonetheless unleashed titanic forces in her objects, which seem to buckle, bend, and flex under the impact of her artistic will.[20]

It would take Harper a few years to digest what he had seen in Schwarcz's work, much less adopt any of her specific methods—notably, electroforming, in which metal is deposited through chemical action over a model. He began using this technique only after he took up a temporary teaching post at Kent State University, in 1970, and had access to the equipment there. In the shorter term, the impact on his work was aspirational rather than technical: "I just loved the roughness of her buildup of the metal in conjunction with the color ... I was amazed how she could use enamel successfully without having it be image oriented. It was simply a marriage of the metal and the enamel."[21] Soon enough, he would be achieving just that sort of alchemical synthesis in his own work.

Harper's initial artistic breakthrough, however—the first work really recognizable as his—led in a rather different direction, more inflected by the era's countercultural energies. When visiting the medieval galleries of the Cleveland Museum of Art, as he so often did, he was unexpectedly overcome by an object-oriented lust for the reliquaries and enameled panels on display. "I suddenly realized how much I wanted to touch them, to caress them."[22] He then made a typically counterintuitive imaginative leap, connecting the experience to some of the more outrageous phenomena of the day, like the revue *Oh! Calcutta!*, with its on-stage nudity, and *Screw Magazine* (founded in 1968), which brought hardcore pornography to a mainstream audience for the first time. "That," he says, "was the threshold I decided to crawl over."[23]

20   See Bernard N. Jazzar and Harold B. Nelson, *June Schwarcz: Artist in Glass and Metal* (Los Angeles: Enamel Arts Foundation/Lucia Marquand, 2019).
21   Harper, interview with Barbara Paris Gifford.
22   Quoted in Sarah Booth Conroy, "Enameled Magic to Touch and to Entice," *Washington Post*, Dec. 4, 1977, H1.
23   Harper, interview with Barbara Paris Gifford.
24   Quoted in Cindy Miller, "Harper is Free From Artist Mold," *Tallahassee Democrat*, May 19, 1974, 7E.
25   Gertrude Stein, *Everybody's Autobiography* (New York: Random House, 1937), 191.

The result was the series *Freudian Toys*, in which he drew an explicit analogy between sex and other forms of play. The first object in the series was made on the spur of the moment for an auction at Penland School of Craft in 1969: a free-form shape, with nude male and female bodies executed in cloisonné enamel, an implied coupling. Harper would later do Plexiglas boxes with naked men on two faces and women on the other two, with a top lid of four faces with adjoining Afro hair, all set into a Plexiglas box. Then there were the *Coins for Hieronymus* (as in Bosch), with faces inspired by the Flemish artist's work on one side and an isolated body part on the other; and the *Dirty Dominos*, of which Harper made four versions. These were reconfigurable compositions populated by male and female genital imagery, as well as nipples and protruding tongues, all rendered in enamel on square Plexiglas plaques. "I wanted people to be able to pick them up and fondle them," Harper recalls, an instinct directly linked to his experience with the surprisingly seductive saints. While entirely of their freethinking time, they were actually relatively sedate in comparison to what was happening in America ("I took the humorous side of the new morality and liberality on sex and nudity, and dealt with it quietly," Harper has said).[24] Nonetheless, these works were quite provocative by the standards of the average craft exhibition. They were kindred to the Funk ceramics being made on the West Coast by artists like Robert Arneson and Patti Warashina, but also a declaration of individual rebelliousness on Harper's part, offset by the refinement of his expertly executed cloisonné.

The sensationalism of the *Freudian Toys*, and their evident connection to contemporaneous Pop Art and graphics, gave Harper his career breakthrough. He had his first shows outside the regional Ohio circuit—a significant example being *Enamels '70*, a survey of the contemporary field held at the Craft Alliance of St. Louis. Here he presented an important if uncharacteristic work: a "lava" chalice clearly reflecting the influence of June Schwarcz, made from spun and electroplated copper, embellished with free-form enamel. It not only won a prize at the exhibition, together with Harper's *Bone Box*, but, somewhat incongruously, made the cover of *Ceramics Monthly*.

As he found wider success and began traveling more often, Harper made one last group of tile-based works, the *Geographies*, which were inspired by the view out an airplane window. He remembered a passage from Gertrude Stein's memoir, in which she described her first plane flight in 1934:

> It was then in a kind of way that I really began to know what the ground looked like ... going over America like that made any one know why the post-cubist painting was what it was. The wandering line of Masson was there the mixed line of Picasso coming and coming again and following itself into a beginning was there, the simple solution of Braque was there and I suppose Leger might be there but I did not see it not over there.[25]

It was with this intriguing analogy between American landscape and French abstraction in mind that Harper made the largest work of his whole career, *A Personal Geography* (1971). The piece incorporated forty-nine two-inch square enamel plaques, which could be rearranged; some of the tiles

Cover of *Ceramics Monthly*, May 1970

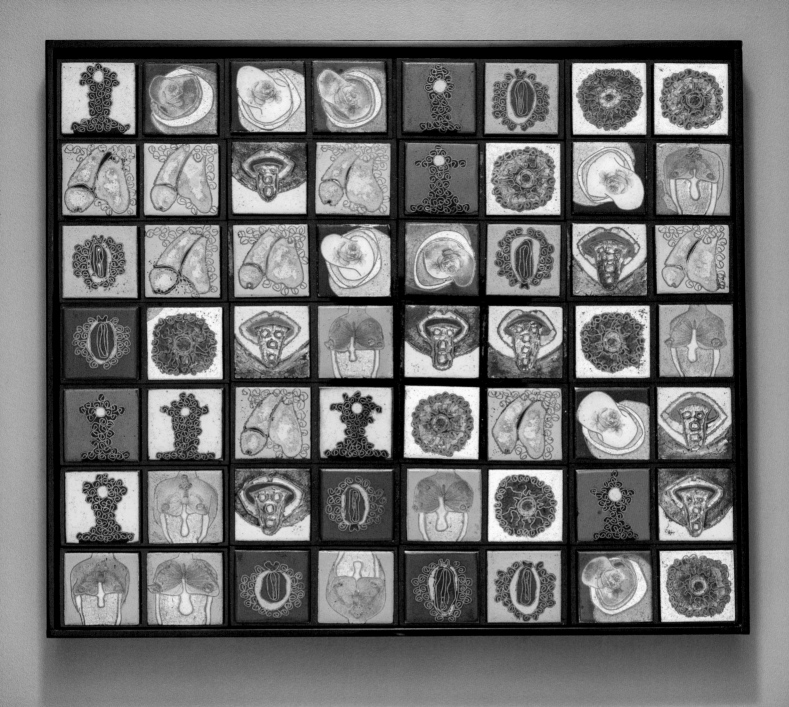

DIRTY DOMINOES #4, 1972

Silver cloisonné enamel on copper; acrylic.
8.25 × 9.25 × 1 in., individual dominoes: 1 × 2.25 in.
Yale University Art Gallery, Enamel Arts Foundation Collection

A PERSONAL GEOGRAPHY, 1971

Silver cloisonné enamel on copper; plexiglass.
1.5 × 16 × 16 in., individual tiles: 2.25 × 2.25 in.

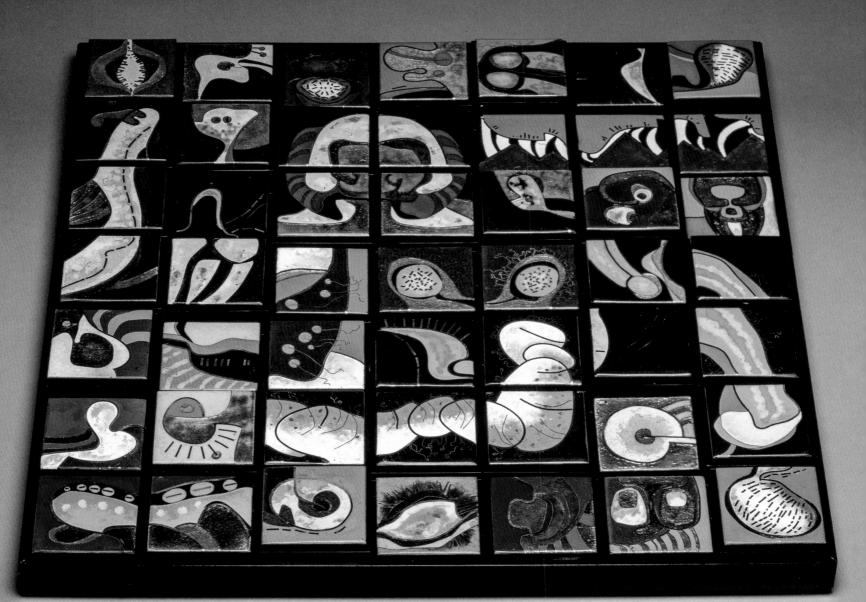

matched up as duets or trios or quartets, making the whole "very musical in feeling." In this case, and in related works like *Strange Gardens* (1973), the landscape is non-specific, as abstract and suggestive as a Rorschach test ink-blot. Other works in the *Geographies* series feature patterns taken from various decorative art traditions—ancient Mesopotamia (the punningly titled *An Ur Geography*), India (*Punjab Geography*), Africa (*Timbuktu Geography*). It's possible to relate these works to prevailing cultural winds; just at this time, artists associated with the Pattern and Decoration movement were beginning to explore vernacular textile and ceramic traditions, seeing them as an underappreciated form of global abstraction.[26] But once again, Harper was working according to his own motivations and methods. As he has said, "In using these patterns, I—for want of a better term—'Harperized' them," and indeed in these works he began to introduce the lush and entrancing visual vocabulary that would become his signature.[27]

THE PAGAN AESTHETE

As mentioned briefly above, Harper had begun visiting Penland in the late 1960s. Though he was there as an instructor, he learned as much as he taught, working alongside some of the craft movement's other leading lights in a collaborative, easygoing atmosphere. "I really could experiment fully with my work in a way that I was not able to during the regular teaching year," Harper has said. "The faculty was encouraged to work right along with the students, to set an example."[28] A particularly fruitful moment came in December 1971—during Penland's off-season—when its director Bill Brown invited seventy-five former instructors to spend two weeks together in an interdisciplinary workshop, modeled on the precedent of Black Mountain College, the famous mid-century avant-garde educational experiment, whose campus had been just an hour south in North Carolina. At this event, Harper fell in with three other adventurous souls: Bob Ebendorf, known for his jewelry ingeniously collaged from found and fabricated elements; Brent Kington, an experienced metalsmith who would have a leading role in the 1970s blacksmithing revival; and Mary Ann Scherr, whose wide-ranging explorations in jewelry included a groundbreaking integration of technology into craft.[29]

Their collaborative give-and-take was an expansive experience for Harper, and it led directly to a new body of work, which had some debt to the work of Di Mare and other artists who were using "tribal" motifs and forms but had as its more proximate inspiration a suggestion from Ebendorf: an ancient Egyptian object called the sistrum, a sacred rattle used in religious observances. Harper liked the idea of integrating movement and sound into his work, and went on to make a series of sistrums and mirrors, now using electroforming as a means to create volume. He sometimes put pebbles

Robert W. Ebendorf, *Man and His Pet Bee*, 1968. Copper, silver, tintype photo, glass beads, brass, aluminum, other found objects. Overall: 6.75 × 4.5 × 0.5 in. Museum of Fine Arts, Boston, The Daphne Farago Collection (2006.150)

26   See Anna Katz, ed., *With Pleasure: Pattern and Decoration in American Art, 1972–1985* (Los Angeles: Museum of Contemporary Art/Yale University Press, 2019).
27   Oral history interview with William Harper, Archives of American Art.
28   Ibid.
29   Thomas A. Manhart, *William Harper: Artist as Alchemist* (Orlando: Orlando Museum of Art, 1989), 10.

FEATHER FETISH, 1974

Silver and gold cloisonné enamel on copper;
electroformed copper, mirror, bronze, feathers.
17 × 5 in.

inside the objects to activate their interiors (much as Takaezu was doing concurrently with her closed forms).[30] The following year, he made three pieces incorporating an uncanny motif, of bird's feet cast in metal—he was inspired by charms he'd seen at Ripley's Believe It or Not!, a newly opened "museum of oddities" in Gatlinburg, Tennessee, not far from Penland.

Soon, Harper was populating his "amuletic" objects with all manner of found ingredients—long tresses of squirrel hair, chipmunk jaws, raccoon vertebrae, snail shells, a snake's rattle, iridescent beetles, and bits of mirror, a common inclusion in African ritual artifacts—all sitting right alongside beautifully wrought enamel and metalwork. In a work called *Fetish Sistrum* (1974) he even incorporated his own brother's wisdom teeth. He later reconstructed his thoughts about the piece: "Well, I love my brother; these are a part of him … using them that way gave them a kind of timelessness that I found very important. They were very personal to me, and hopefully the preciousness of that personal quality would be communicated to the owner and wearer."[31] This relic-based approach distinguished his work from that of other jewelers using found objects at the time, like Ron Ho, Ramona Solberg, J. Fred Woell, or Ebendorf himself. For these artists, the strategy was generally formal in emphasis—introducing adventitious qualities of color and texture into the work—and sometimes political, in a humorous and ironic effect akin to Pop Art.

Harper, by contrast, was after sheer potency. One reviewer wrote that the *Pagan Babies* had "a very refreshing and Congolese flavor, more upbeat than if he had used such old American standbys as bits of dingy industrial waste put together in a typical ironic way, common since the '50s."[32] Though bluntly put, this was perceptive. Harper was purposefully distancing himself from not only respected peers like Ebendorf but also the run-of-the-mill "junk jewelry" with which American craft fairs were awash. African art seemed to offer an alternative model. He had begun to make a more serious study of African art, avidly collecting it and learning about its symbolism. As he later observed, "With African work we have peoples who do not have access to great technology, but they use their minds and the materials that they have at hand to produce art of an extremely high emotional level."[33] At the same time, Harper was well aware of the condescending narrative of Primitivism that had played such a key role in the formation of the modernist avant-garde. It was in full awareness of this backdrop that he used terms like "fetish" in his work, engaging in a self-conscious process of cross-cultural appropriation. His intention was to exalt African art, not only for its formal intelligence (as Picasso had, for example) but also for its spiritual and symbolic depth.

In today's more sensitized cultural climate, this period of Harper's work may raise hackles; it is hard to imagine anyone these days titling an important body of work *Pagan Babies*, as he did in 1977. Yet it is instructive to learn the source of the phrase: it arose in conversation with Bernadette Monroe, wife of curator Michael Monroe (who would soon become one of Harper's most important supporters) and formerly a nun and schoolteacher. She had

30   Glenn Adamson, Dakin Hart, and Kate Wiener, eds, *Toshiko Takaezu: Worlds Within* (New York: Isamu Noguchi Museum and Garden/Yale University Press, 2024).
31   Oral history interview with William Harper, Archives of American Art.
32   Victoria Donohoe, "These 3 artists are so *au courant* that 1969 is *passe*," *Philadelphia Inquirer*, no. 17, 1978, 29.
33   Oral history interview with William Harper, Archives of American Art.

FETISH PIN #1, 1976

Gold and silver cloisonné enamel on sterling silver;
reticulated sterling silver, electroformed copper,
14k gold, pearl, chipmunk jaws. 4.5 × 4 in.

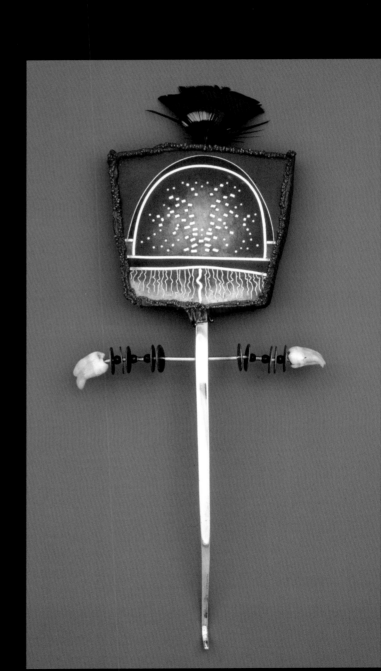

PAGAN BABY #1: GREEN SPIRAL, 1977

Gold cloisonné enamel on fine silver; 14k and 18k gold, pearl, and snail shell. 4.5 × 2.25 in. Dallas Museum of Art, gift of Edward W. and Deedie Potter Rose, formerly Inge Asenbaum collection, Galerie am Graben, Vienna, Austria (2014.33.108)

described taking up collections for the "pagan babies over in Africa that did not have the good Catholic education that they were getting here in America."[34] The phrase immediately appealed to Harper, not because he agreed with the derogatory characterization but on the contrary, because he wanted to invert the logic behind it—siding, as it were, with the pagans.

THE MAGICIAN ADEPT

In a manifesto of sorts published in *Craft Horizons* magazine in 1978, Harper wrote of the works as "idea pieces":

> I hope that all the technical aspects of their existences fall by the wayside, so that the magic and mystery I try to create in them comes through. This magic, this mystery, has to do with giving the viewer something unexpected, a feeling that he/she may be experiencing an object that does not reveal all its secrets. It may be of and about our time, or excavated from an antique time and place, or may be of the future. There is magic in the unknown and I attempt to make objects of the unknown.[35]

Cover of *Step-by-Step Enameling: A Complete Introduction to the Craft of Enameling* by William Harper, 1973

Statements of this kind—whether issued in writing or in the work—had all the more significance because of Harper's ever-increasing prominence in the field. His natural aesthetic inclinations toward elaboration were very much on trend. When the Museum of Contemporary Crafts included his *Rattle for a White Witch* in an exhibition called *Baroque '74* (a cross-disciplinary show that also included the work of jewelers Jamie Bennett, Stanley Lechtzin, Richard Mawdsley, Eleanor Moty, and prodigious blacksmith Albert Paley, among others), he commented, "The current trend in crafts is toward heavy embellishment with emphasis on very elaborate technique. It's a revolt against the very clean, unembellished lines produced by the Danish Modern influence of the 50s and 60s."[36]

Though Harper tended to downplay the importance of raw technique (as in the above-quoted passage), one of the main vehicles of his rise was in fact a how-to book, which he published in 1973. Prosaically entitled *Step-by-Step Enameling*, it was a bestseller not only in the USA but abroad too and immediately made Harper an authority, in demand for workshops and as a teacher. It is indeed an impressive publication, especially considering that he had only been working in the medium for a decade. Not just a clearly explicated primer of processes, it is bracketed at the outset by a brief historical *précis*—from the Middle Ages to Fabergé and Art Nouveau, to Schwarcz and Hultberg—and at the conclusion, a section of experimental techniques like under-enamel collage, his own invention of ceramic decals, and "intentional burnout" through over-firing. "What makes enameling so intriguing," he wrote, "is that it can be freely interpreted, thus continuing to develop and expand as a medium."[37]

It was likely on the strength of this book, as much as the increasing recognition for his work, that Harper finally got a full-time teaching job, at Florida State University (FSU). He, Riva, and their children moved down to Tallahassee in late 1973. (Little did he suspect that he would remain there for over twenty years.) It was a significant appointment in at least two respects, artistically. First, as for so many artists with academic jobs, the steady income freed him to take risks, creatively speaking, and meant that he did not need to earn money through an exhausting schedule of workshops. Second, it expanded his disciplinary horizons, because he was hired to teach not only enameling but also jewelry—not something he had much explored to this point, though his close association with the masterful John Paul Miller in Cleveland at least gave him some indication of the possibilities it might offer in conjunction with enamel. With his customary rapid rate of assimilation, he began teaching himself the relevant skills, staying three weeks or so ahead of the students, and incorporating them into his own work. It was, he said, "like putting warm butter on hot toast."[38] The first wearable pieces he made—among them a series of *Amuletic Beads*, fabricated in precious metals and embellished with lavishly varied polychrome enamel, and two related *Magician's Hoops*, neckpieces built on geometries of wire—attest to his immediate confidence in his new discipline.[39]

Meanwhile, Harper was making an impression at FSU, both for the outlandish nature of his work and his outspoken personality. He was often featured in the *Tallahassee Democrat*, which tended to portray him, perhaps fairly, as a cosmopolitan outsider rather than a part of the community. "Humility is not one of William Harper's virtues," one article began, then quoted him as saying, "It may not be very modest, but I think I'm one of Tallahassee's best-kept secrets."[40] That, too, was true enough. Even as interest in his work was rising on the national stage, he rarely made a sale locally. He has said that his relationship with the other art faculty could be awkward, because he was the only one regularly showing in museums around the country but also worked in a supposedly minor medium. His peers tended to regard him with a strange combination of envy and condescension.

Bill and Riva set themselves apart further through their choice of home—a dramatic modernist structure commissioned from the local architect Paul Anthony, totally open-plan, without drapes, featuring a glass-enclosed plant conservatory as its dramatic centerpiece, all "plunked down into Ralph Lauren-ville," as Harper puts it.[41] The house was filled with their growing collection of African art, Persian rugs, and works by Harper's peers, sometimes obtained as trades. Eventually this repository came to include works by a stellar cast of craft movement pioneers: textiles by Lenore Tawney, Neda Al-Hilali, Diane Itter, Gary Trentham, Dominic Di Mare, John McQueen, and Françoise Grossen; an early glass cylinder of Dale Chihuly's; ceramics by Graham Marks, Toshiko Takaezu, Paulus Berensohn, Richard DeVore, and Paul Soldner; and, of course, enamel vessels by June Schwarcz. The dining chairs were by Marcel Breuer and the dinnerware by Michigan ceramist John

34   Harper, interview with Barbara Paris Gifford.
35   William Harper, "The Magic of Cloisonné," *Craft Horizons* 37, no. 6 (Dec. 1977), 56.
36   Julian Veal, "Return to Basics a Must, Top Ranked Artist Insists," *Tallahassee Democrat*, undated clipping (c. 1974). See also *Baroque '74* (New York: Museum of Contemporary Crafts, 1974).
37   William Harper, *Step-By-Step Enameling: A Complete Introduction to the Craft of Enameling* (Racine: Western Publishing Company, 1973), 68.
38   Robert Cardinale and Lita S. Bratt, *Copper 2: The Second Brass/Bronze Exhibition* (Tucson: University of Arizona, 1980), 54.
39   These necklaces were partly inspired by a set of Chinese cloisonné enamel beads that Harper had seen at the Victoria and Albert Museum in London, on a trip funded by the National Endowment for the Arts.
40   Ellen Templeton, "Why Keep Talent a Secret?," *Tallahassee Democrat*, Jan. 15, 1978, 12E.
41   William Harper, interview with Glenn Adamson, July 13, 2023.

AMULETIC BEADS #3, 1976

Gold and silver cloisonné enamel on fine silver
and fine gold; 14k gold. Diam.: 1.25 × 7 in.
Smithsonian American Art Museum, Gift of
Dr. and Mrs. Matthew M. Cohen (1986.55)

Stephenson.[42] One room was devoted to Harper's studio—he has always worked at home. Altogether, it was an extraordinary environment and, despite the very Floridian touch of the indoor hanging garden, quite out of keeping with what Tallahasseeans expected of their neighbors.

The same was true, of course, of Harper's jewelry. Riva, after some initial hesitation, wore it boldly around town, making her a conspicuous presence in the local supermarket.[43] This raises an interesting issue. Harper has often said that, when making jewelry, he does bear wearability in mind. But in practice, this has been more a creative parameter than a primary artistic intention. The small scale and established format of a necklace, brooch, or pin demarcate an arena within which he can freely invent. But he has never had his work photographed on the body, is quite happy to see it displayed in a gallery or museum case, or treated as "table pieces" to be picked up and closely examined.[44] A little later in his career, by which time the 1980s fashion for "power dressing" had made his high-intensity jewelry seem at least a little more mainstream, he commented, "My work is not bought by the casual shopper. Someone doesn't buy one of my pieces to match a dress. Usually it's the other way around—they buy a dress to match a piece … On the other hand, a really good painter doesn't sit down and do a painting to match the sofa and the carpet."[45]

What it comes down to is that Harper does not, like many of his peers, care all that much about riffing on or otherwise enhancing a wearer's personality—in fact, he never works on commission and has no specific owner in mind when he creates a piece. The metalsmith Carrie Adell once made a perceptive comment about this in a review of Harper's jewelry; a woman wearing one of his pieces may be "herself a walking warehouse of visual and emotional associations," she wrote, "but the work tells more about the maker as an artist and a human being. The work stands for itself, and for its process of creation."[46]

The relationship between Harper and his potential audience is, then, not what we might expect of a jeweler. Far from making accoutrements, each of his pieces is an independent microcosm, a world unto itself. The anthropologist Alfred Gell theorized the well-crafted artwork as a sort of trap for the mind: "It embodies intentionalities that are complex, demanding of attention and perhaps difficult to reconstruct fully."[47] This is a good way of understanding Harper's work and, indeed, an idea that he has often voiced himself. In 1978, for example, he spoke of wanting to "catch and hold the viewer; the more one has to look at, the more he wants to see. The more he sees, the more he is forced to look. This complexity has provided the impetus in the search for an interaction of surface and form in my work in enamel; to hold the viewer while eyes explore the many secrets to be found."[48]

A greenhouse, right, serves as the main entrance and hallway of the Harper's home. The dining room, above, features a smoked glass table and museum cane chairs. The Harper home is a showcase for their collection of African masks, Oriental rugs, prints and other artwork. Privacy is theirs on a wooded lot.

William Harper's home in Tallahassee, Florida. Images courtesy of the *Tallahassee Democrat*, June 26, 1976.

42   William Harper, email to Glenn Adamson, Sept. 18, 2023.
43   Templeton, "Why Keep Talent a Secret?"
44   Quoted in Sabine Ehlers, "In Search of A Lost Art," *Tampa Tribune-Times*, Nov. 17, 1974, 10.
45   Uncited clipping, May 24, 1987, artist's collection.
46   Carrie Adell, "William Harper," *Metalsmith* 7, no. 4 (Fall 1987), 54–55.
47   Alfred Gell, "Vogel's Net: Traps as Artworks and Artworks as Traps," *Journal of Material Culture* 1, no. 1 (Mar. 1996), p. 37.
48   Quoted in Dorothea T. Apgar, "Jewels for the Mind," *[Baltimore] News American*, Mar. 2, 1978, B1. For a similar comment, see Harper, "The Magic of Cloisonné," 55.

The same year that Harper wrote those words, he began a small but crucially important body of works that perfectly embodied them while also establishing a new artistic lexicon that has dominated his work to the present day. These were his *Albino* and *Mystery* series, in which passages of abstract enamel are asymmetrically framed within linear wire elements. Pearls and other semiprecious stones (like quartz and moonstone) complete the inventory. The ingredients are conventional enough—in fact, these were among the first works in which Harper made conspicuous use of gold, that most traditional of materials—but they are arranged in a wholly new way, dynamic, unpredictable, and improvisatory in a way that even the *Pagan Babies* had only gestured towards.

It comes as no surprise, perhaps, that when making the *Albino* pieces, Harper was looking closely at the early works of Cy Twombly: big, bare compositions with just a few scribbles of pigment and pencil over a white gesso ground. Harper remembers asking himself, "How could this man do this, and why do I like it so much?" and relatedly how he might use opaque white enamel in an equally active manner—so that it did not look like "the front of a refrigerator," as he puts it.[49] Another innovation in the *Albino* series has to do with its developmental logic, with the central form becoming successively more pronounced from one piece to the next, becoming "obviously a cross, without being a crucifix," as Harper puts it, "without looking like it needs Jesus to finish it."[50] This was, after all, the disco era; crosses and Stars of David were bouncing up and down on daringly bared chests across America. This struck Harper as vaguely hilarious. Was his newly adopted métier of jewelry losing all religious and spiritual significance? If so, what did that mean for his own work? Harper would soon answer that question, in a body of work that was more complex and profound than anything he had yet made.

49   Harper, interview with Glenn Adamson, Sept. 14, 2022; Harper, interview with Barbara Paris Gifford.
50   Harper, interview with Barbara Paris Gifford.

Cy Twombly, *The Age of Alexander*, 1959–60. Oil, crayon, and graphite on canvas. 118 × 196.25 in. The Menil Collection, Houston, Gift of the artist; 1994-29

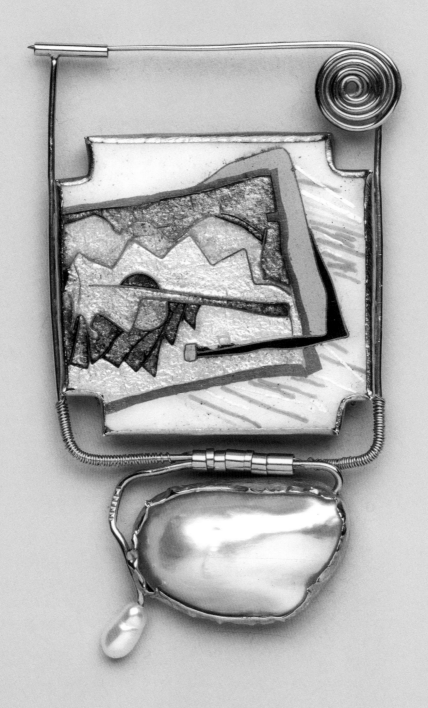

ALBINO I, 1978

Gold and silver cloisonné enamel on copper;
sterling silver, 14k and 24k gold, pearl. 4 × 2.5 in.
Philadelphia Museum of Art, Gift of Mrs. Robert
L. McNeil, Jr., 1994-92-2

THE SKEPTICAL THEOLOGIAN

Harper finished the 1970s on a high. He had begun exhibiting with Helen Drutt Gallery in Philadelphia, the most adventurous and influential craft gallery on the east coast. This was the first time he had representation commensurate with his ambition, and he responded with two knockout shows of the *Pagan Babies* and more recent work, in 1978 and then 1979 (the latter exhibition began at FSU, then traveled to Drutt's space).[51] Also in 1979, Harper had his first international solo show, at Electrum Gallery in London, Britain's leading venue for contemporary jewelry. Harper had been to the city twice already on grant-funded trips but was unable to attend. Wendy Ramshaw, leading light of the London jewelry scene, wrote him an encouraging letter about it, saying that "there was nothing lacking in the display." Unfortunately she and her partner, David Watkins, were the only ones to buy a piece; as Ramshaw noted, "Things are very slow in this country and people are even less adventurous than usual. It is the wrong time to be experimental and exciting—more to be sober, tasteful and not too expensive."[52]

The banner year of 1979 had, as its crowning achievement, an exhibition at the Renwick Gallery, Smithsonian Institution, in Washington, DC. Just five years on from its opening, it was initiating a series of one-person shows. Harper would be the second artist so honored (the first was Albert Paley). The exhibition, curated by Michael Monroe, opened in late 1977—as it happened, immediately following a presentation of Fabergé masterworks at the city's National Geographic Society, making the vivid contemporaneity of Harper's approach to enamel all the more evident. It was a stunning achievement and catapulted Harper to national fame. A review by prominent critic Sarah Booth Conroy was rhapsodic and aligned clearly to the artist's own thoughts about his work: "The eye rejoices in the richness of the colors while trapped by the strange pathways of the designs."[53] Strangers sent Harper interesting findings thinking he might be interested in using them for his jewelry, including, in one case, a packet of cat's whiskers.

Concurrently with the retrospective, Renwick Gallery director Lloyd Herman was organizing a project for the Vatican in Rome, with a concept as simple as it was ambitious: a group of contemporary craft artists would be invited to make ecclesiastical objects to set aside the great medieval and Renaissance artifacts in its collections.[54] Harper was an obvious choice for the project, though when invited to participate, his response was anything but self-evident: for the epicenter of the Catholic faith, he made a Torah pointer (see p. 7). This was all the more ironic given that he was a relatively recent (and completely non-devout) convert to Judaism—an example of Harper's playful, jousting relationship to religion, which would soon occupy a central role in his work.

---

51   Elaine Varian and Albert Stewart, *William Harper* (Tallahassee/Philadelphia: Four Arts Gallery, Florida State University/Helen Drutt Gallery), 1980.

52   Wendy Ramshaw, letter to William Harper, undated, c. 1979.

53   Conroy, "Enameled Magic to Touch and to Entice," *The Washington Post*, December 4, 1977, H1.

54   See *Craft Art and Religion: Second International Seminar* (Washington, DC: Smithsonian Institution/Committee of Religion and Art of America, 1978). Speakers at the event included Sam Maloof, Brent Kington, and Paul J. Smith, among others.

PRESIDENT'S COLLAR, 1982

Gold, silver cloisonné and champlevé
enamel on fine silver; 14k and 24k gold,
silver, glass. 18.5 × 8.75 in. Yale University

GOBLET, 1981

Silver and gold cloisonné enamel on silver forms; 14k gold. 6 × 6.5 × 6.5 in.

The Vatican project also presaged two big opportunities for Harper. The first was a one-off commission, entirely singular within his career. He was invited to enter a competition to make an ornamental collar for the President of Yale University, A. Bartlett Giamatti, to wear at annual commencement. It was a replacement for one made by Tiffany & Company in 1905, which had been stolen from a campus storeroom. Harper submitted a finished design drawing—the only time in his career he ever made one—and was chosen over his Penland colleagues Bob Ebendorf and Mary Ann Scherr, as well as the Danish-born Hans Christensen, the eminent modernist silversmith based in Rochester. "I would've given it to Hans Christensen instead of me, his forms were absolutely beautiful," Harper says, but it is easy to see why he got the nod: he had the perfect vocabulary and technical repertoire to rival the elaboration of the lost Tiffany collar. He also provided an appropriately heraldic symbolic scheme, with "Hebrew characters referring to the biblical sacred lots cast to ascertain divine will" and the university motto, *Lux et Veritas*, all picked out in cloisonné.[55]

The other sequel to the Vatican commission was of more long-lasting consequence, as it led to Harper's involvement with the storied Kennedy Galleries, one of New York City's oldest and most respected art dealers. Founded over a century earlier, in 1874, Kennedy was now under the leadership of Lawrence A. Fleischman, whose primary expertise was in American paintings. He was also, however, a knowledgeable collector of antiquities and decorative art and closely involved in the Vatican exhibition (he had been made a Papal Knight of the Order of St. Sylvester in 1978). It was in this connection that he became aware of Harper's work. Given his wide-ranging interests, it is not surprising that he was intrigued; what is more surprising was that he offered Harper a show in his gallery. In a space where visitors typically saw paintings by the likes of Winslow Homer and Edward Hopper, they would now encounter one of the world's most avant-garde jewelers.

That suited Harper just fine. By this time, he was eager to break out of the confining circuit of the craft world, which even the Renwick show had not done for him. "I don't even like the word 'craft' anymore," he said dismissively, in 1981. "It reminds me of making sandals."[56] The wholly unrelated context of Kennedy Galleries offered him a welcome chance to show work entirely on its own terms. He rose to the challenge with two astonishing exhibitions. First, in 1981, came *The Art of William Harper* (to which we have nodded in the subtitle of the present volume). It included over fifty pieces, including impressive developments of Harper's earlier bead necklaces— among them, two versions of a design called *Bib of Charms*, which put his hyperactive ornamental imagination on lavish display. In addition there was a variation on the Torah pointer that Harper had made for the Vatican. While preparing for the exhibition, he also made a drinking goblet as a commission for Fleischman, with a mercury-gilded interior, elaborately engraved exterior, and replaceable enameled roundels—one set for each of the four seasons.

---

55 "Giamatti of Yale to Wear a New President's Collar," *New York Times*, May 16, 1982, 52. The collar is now in the Yale University Art Gallery collection; see Erin E. Eisenbarth, *Baubles, Bangles, and Beads: American Jewelry from Yale University, 1700–2005* (New Haven: Yale University Art Gallery, 2005).

56 Helen Cullinan, "Harper Dazzles in N. Y. Exhibit," *Cleveland Plain Dealer*, June 28, 1981, 24.

More indicative of his future direction, however, were examples from his *Mystery* series and a subsequent project called *Nine Sketches*. The works were miniature essays in associative thinking, in which he tested the communicative possibilities of his abstract syntax in enamel. In 1975, Harper had been able to visit Japan as part of a trip organized by the American Craft Council. As for so many artists and craftspeople, the country had a profound impact on him. His deepest impression was of temple moss gardens, which conveyed a powerful spiritual resonance with extraordinarily minimal means. In the *Mystery* series, he tried to do something comparable. Like the *Albinos*, the brooches feature an intense passage of abstract enamel with a gold wire surround; they are like windows into some completely alien environments. He gave them their collective title because even he couldn't quite understand what he'd done at first: "It's a mystery why I called them mysteries and what they're about."[57] In the *Nine Sketches* he further particularized the premise while deepening the air of enigma. Each work in the series was devoted to a material that gives rise to strong sensations, visual, olfactory, or gustatory: cobalt, cinnamon, sapphire, incense, saffron, pistachio, hoarfrost, tongue, fungus. These themes are not literally depicted in the pieces; rather it is as if Harper had distilled their essences and were stirring them into the alchemical pot of his process. The effect is almost hallucinatory, a quality that is paralleled by the other titles he was using at this time, which refer to drugs (opium and nightshade), supernatural presences (ghosts and specters), and performative genres (Japanese kabuki theater and African-American boogie music), all pathways to altered mental states.

This may be a good point to intervene in the narrative—just as Harper himself often has. You will have noticed, by now, that his custom is to work in more or less discrete and titled series. These function for him somewhat like theatrical productions (one thinks again of the puppet shows of his youth), with their own *dramatis personae* and sometimes dramatic arcs, too. Occasionally, however, he interrupts himself and makes one or a few isolated works. These are, in his mind, explicitly experimental: the goal might be to explore a compositional idea or perhaps a new color combination—he employs over 200 enamels, and, in juxtaposition with gemstones and other materials, his palette is effectively infinite. Harper notes that in 1984, he was fortunate enough ("and patient enough") to attend a revival of Robert Wilson and Philip Glass's famous postmodern opera *Einstein on the Beach*, which is fully five hours long and structured into five main acts. In between are shorter bits of linking material that Wilson, rather fetchingly, called "knee plays." Harper was intrigued by the similarity to his own interlude works, which serve as connective tissue between longer series. He has used the same phrase to describe them since, defining them as "one-off works that are complete unto themselves, but also have both physical presence and content suggestions of what might follow, and yet be perfectly able to stand alone."[58]

57   Oral history interview with William Harper, Archives of American Art.
58   William Harper, email to Glenn Adamson, Sept. 25, 2023. Among the works that Harper considers to be "knee plays" are *Wizard* (1979), *Transfigured Mystery* (1979), *Harlequinade* (1980), *Robes 1* and *2* (1981), *White Witch* (1984), and more recently *Flotsam I, II,* and *III* (2007), *Solar Mystery* (2008), and *Aurora Disc* (2015).

BIB OF CHARMS II, 1980

Gold and silver cloisonné enamel on copper;
14k and 24k gold; sterling silver, moonstone.
16.5 × 12.75 × 1.25 in., chain: 27 in.

PINK MYSTERY, 1978

Gold and silver cloisonné enamel on copper;
14k gold, sterling silver, pearl, glass. 3.5 × 2.75 in.

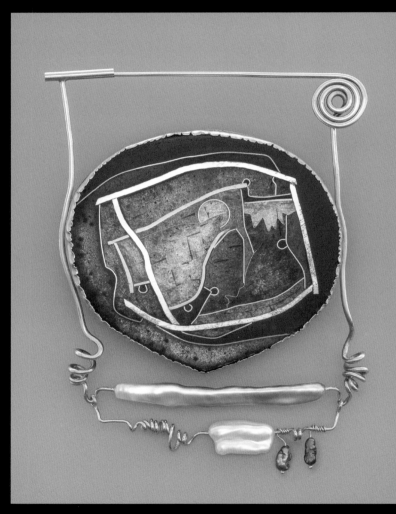

GREY MYSTERY, 1979

Gold and silver cloisonné enamel on copper;
14k gold, sterling silver, bronze, copper, pearl.
5 × 3 in. Yale University Art Gallery,
Janet and Simeon Braguin Fund

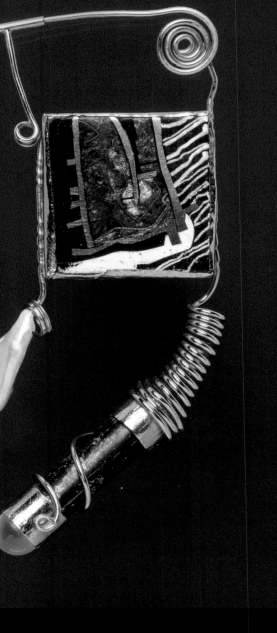

NINE SKETCHES I–COBALT, 1980

Gold and silver cloisonné enamel on copper;
14k and 24k gold, bronze, pearl, antique glass,
moonstone. 3.25 × 2 in.

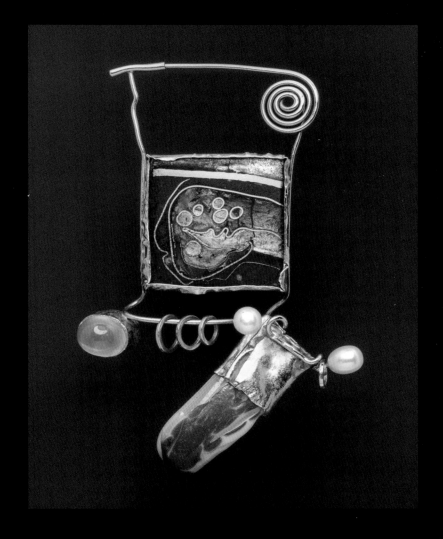

NINE SKETCHES VIII–TONGUE, 1980

Gold and silver cloisonné enamel on copper;
14k and 24k gold, pearl, glass, moonstone, 3 × 2 in.

Back to the story, now: Harper's second show at Kennedy, staged a year later in 1982, was still more ambitious and heightened his creative engagement with religion to a fever pitch. Building on the compositional template he'd already established, he now added an allegorical layer, rich in historical and narrative allusion. The show was called *Saints, Martyrs and Savages* and was comprised of works relating to each of these three ideas. In an artist's statement (republished in full in this volume), Harper posed a rhetorical question: "At what point does the hope for supernatural protection stop, and the desire for individual adornment begin?" At stake here was a fundamental question not just about jewelry but about the nature of human belief itself. Is it ultimately bound up with transcendence, a leap of faith that takes us out of the earthly realm? Or, on the contrary, an instinctive matter, grounded in the natural body, and in personal identity?

Harper did not claim to resolve this difficult philosophical quandary, of course, instead treating it as the departure point for a deeply searching, poetic body of work. It would not be an exaggeration to say that in this second exhibition at Kennedy Galleries he arrived at his mature idiom, the paradigm in which he still operates today. A crucial new aspect was that of characterization. Rather than abstract themes, his pieces now manifested one or multiple personae, real or imagined. This makes them instantly relatable—it's impossible not to think of the puppets he made when he was a teenager—while also allowing for new dimensions of psychological and mythical content. The *Martyrs*, with their haunting expressions and pared-down, archaic settings, and the *Savages*, with their animalistic demeanors and ritualistic found objects, demonstrate the expressive potential and range. (Harper's new artistic strategy is telegraphed most clearly, however, in the *Saints*, which hearken back to that moment of sensual revelation he'd had in Cleveland, while also (as Cynthia Hahn and Ugochukwu-Smooth Nzewi explain in their contributions to this book) triangulating between medieval and African art. Some of the works have removable faces—tacitly suggesting that religion is often worn like a mask—and charms hanging from their bodies, in a manner that feels distinctly un-Christian. The conceptual fusion of St. Sebastian, who was slain in an onslaught of arrows, and Congolese Nkisi Nkondi figures, penetrated with nails, is the most striking instance of the cross-cultural hybridity in the series, but the same syncretic thinking runs through all of Harper's *Saints*, and indeed much of his work since.

Witness the *Archangel Shiva Sebastian*, in which three different entities from two different religions are compounded into a single representation. Harper used enamel to capture the figure's staring visage—its wildly asymmetrical eyes are perhaps a nod to Picasso—and also to render the figure's lavish garment, which has the sweeping contours of a Catholic chasuble but the jewel-like tones of Indian textiles. (While Harper had not been to India at this point, he would travel there in 1989 and was keenly interested in its decorative art traditions.) Below this, a cosmic spiral stands in for a body. The composition is completed by a cluster of charms including an insignia recalling a Hamsa, an apotropaic sign of the hand used to ward off the evil eye. As Harper points out, divinities like Shiva have historically appeared in many guises. Christian saints, similarly, have long been inventively portrayed by artists: Mantegna's St. Sebastian could have been carved from a block of granite, while Guido Reni imagined him as a sexy, languorous pin-up.

JABBERWOCK (KNEE PLAY), 1976

Gold and silver cloisonné enamel on fine silver;
14k gold, mirror, animal claw

THE ARCHANGEL SHIVA SEBASTIAN, 1982

Gold cloisonné enamel on copper and fine silver; 14k and 24k gold, sterling silver, copper, pearl, shell, moonstone, tourmaline. 8.25 × 4 in.

SELF-PORTRAIT OF THE ARTIST AS ST. SEBASTIAN, 1987

Gold cloisonné enamel on fine silver and fine gold;

In a sense, then, Harper's extraordinary jewel sits within an art historical lineage of constant re-imagination. But his assimilation of multiple religious iconographies and, above all, his daring idea that this whole transcultural sweep can be compressed into a small, precious object that bespeaks a contemporary mode of thinking and believing? This was something genuinely new.

THE DICHOTOMOUS SOUL

Ironically, Harper's most artistically accomplished exhibition to date was a commercial failure. The first show at Kennedy had sold well, despite the fact that it was such a complete departure from the galleries' usual offerings. Whether it was because of the extreme avant-gardism of the new work, though, or (just as likely) because Fleischman already placed Harper's works with many of his clients, there were few sales from *Saints, Martyrs and Savages*. The partnership ended, but very amicably. The Fleischman family has continued to collect and support Bill's work ever since, presenting an exhibition of his artist's books in 1998; Martha Fleischman, Lawrence's daughter, has been the animating force behind the present volume.

As for Harper, like any true avant-gardiste, he was untroubled by the reception to his new work and forged right ahead, continuing to explore the subject of Christian saints. In 1985, he created a suite of four pieces depicting Teresa of Ávila—the nun so memorably portrayed by Bernini for the Cornaro Chapel, Santa Maria della Vittoria, in Rome—which traces her spiritual "ecstasy," beginning with a representation of highly stimulated confusion and ending with a phallic pearl plunging downward into a bed of vibrant red. Harper has clearly explained what is going on here: "The titles essentially are a free-form poem that basically are the stages of an orgasm, and each one is meant to build towards that quality, to the fourth one, which is obviously the climax."[59] Yet there is nothing especially explicit about the designs—if you wore one around town, no one would recognize it as pornographic. Harper was exploring themes of sexuality in his characteristic way, at once highly charged and beguilingly elliptical.

One of the remarkable features of the first work in the *Ecstasy of St. Teresa* series is the inclusion of a broken bicycle reflector. He had first included this unusual material in his work in 1979, in a piece called *Transfigured Mystery*—he has said the idea came from noticing the similarity of its surface texture to that imparted by a rolling mill. (He was extremely tickled when a potential buyer assumed the red material was garnet; Harper explained it was just plastic, and "that killed that sale right away."[60]) But what really captivated him about this gleaming plastic trash was the way it established a tension within the object. He had long been interested in breaking down the opposition between the precious and the non-precious, a key dynamic in the *Pagan Babies* and other found object jewelry he had made in the 1970s. Now, he saw

---

59   Oral history interview with William Harper, Archives of American Art.
60   Harper, interview with Barbara Paris Gifford.

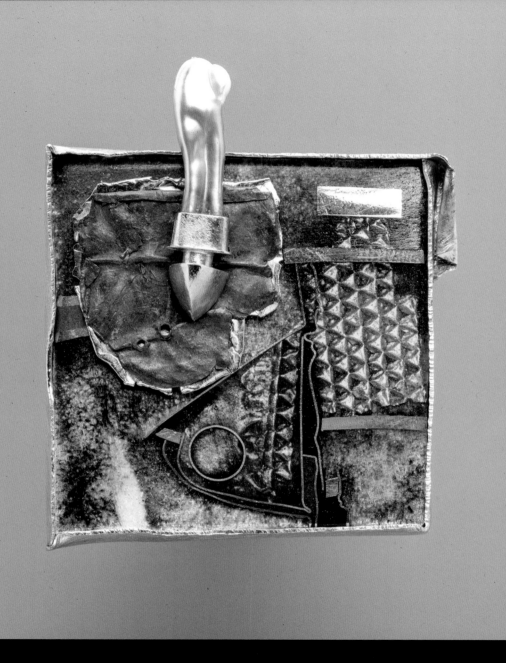

THE ECSTASY OF ST. TERESA II
... AND THE DARKNESS OF THE

THE ECSTASY OF ST. TERESA III
... AND SHE WAS FILLED WITH THE RADIANCE OF HIS LIGHT ..., 1985

Gold cloisonné enamel on fine silver and fine gold;
14k and 24k gold, sterling silver, shell, rutilated quartz,
moonstone, shark tooth. 3.25 × 2.25 in.

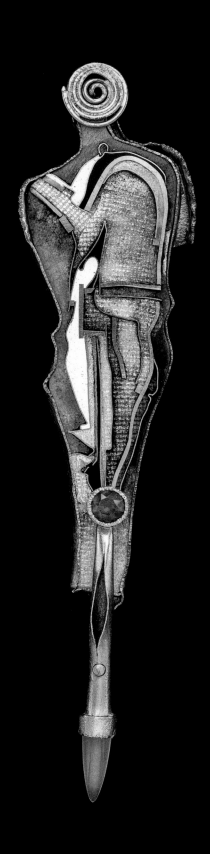

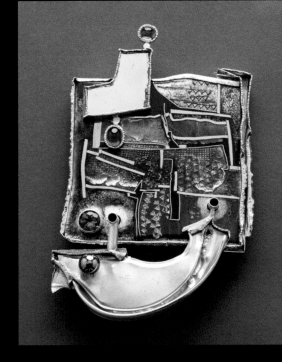

THE WHITE HERMAPHRODITE, 1987

Gold cloisonné enamel on silver; 19k and 24k gold,
rose quartz, rhodochrosite. 7.5 × 1.5 in.

PENTIMENTI #10: STIGMATA, 1987

Gold cloisonné enamel on fine silver and fine gold;
14k and 24k gold, lead, sterling silver, peridot,
tourmaline, shell, tooth, plastic. 4 × 2.75 in.

that this was only one of several dichotomies structuring his work. He set out to explore them all, and all at once.

A pivotal example of this polyvalent dialectical method is *The White Hermaphrodite* (1987). As suggested by the title, the piece has at its heart the transgression of the gender binary. Harper had been reading about hermaphrodites in ancient Egypt, who were considered to have oracular powers, and was interested in the idea that freedom from the static opposition between male and female might somehow empower one to cross the boundary between present and future: "This creature represented perfection through a reconciliation of opposites [...] the Hermaphrodite can cast off sterility and predict its own ability to self-procreate. It points the way to transformation and ultimate perfection."[61]

A lot to put into a piece of jewelry. But Harper's intention was never didactic, as if he were drawing a diagram. On the contrary: it is vital that the subject matter of a piece like *The White Hermaphodite* remains hidden, submerged below the horizon of legibility. There are certainly clues scattered throughout: the constant disruption of symmetry, the sinuous enamel, and the faceted red stone marking the figure's nether regions all suggest an ambiguity between singularity and duality. But this content remains latent, acting like an interior energy source and emanating as an impression of involved, hard-to-define intricacy, much as a perfume scent wafts forth from a beautiful blossom. The instinct that had guided Harper when he was making his *Nine Sketches* (the pieces based on cinnamon, pistachio, and so on) was still with him, but it had now matured into a fully-fledged, open-ended artistic methodology. A good word to describe the approach would be "hermetic" (etymologically derived from the name of the god Hermes), meaning both "secretive" and "occult." Harper's pieces remained exquisite as specimens of craft, innovative as jewelry, sophisticated as abstraction. Now, they were also tantamount to magic spells, whose effects—like the enchantments in fairy tales—might become clear only with the passing of the years.

Harper's steady maturation as an artist was now rewarded, thanks in no small part to a trip he took to the Orlando Museum of Art in 1987, where he lectured in conjunction with the traveling show *The Eloquent Object*. He formed two important connections in the city: first, to the museum's curator Tom Manhart; second, to Norma and Bill Roth, who would be his most active collectors in subsequent years. In the latter case, it was love at first sight. After the Roths heard Harper give his artist's talk at the museum, they promptly invited him to stay at their home in nearby Winter Haven and bought seven pieces on the spot. They would ultimately acquire about fifty examples of Harper's jewelry, plus dozens of paintings, works on paper, and sculptural objects. Manhart, meanwhile, organized a full-scale retrospective for the Orlando Museum of Art in 1989. The show traveled to an impressive eight further venues, including the American Craft Museum in New York and museums in Norway, Germany, and France. Manhart wrote an excellent essay for the accompanying catalogue, providing the most complete account of Harper's work to that date. Among the many glories of the show were Harper's *Pentimenti*, the title taken from a term of art that refers to the visible traces of the earlier state of a painting. This transmutation of a nominally

---

61   Quoted in Manhart, *William Harper: Artist as Alchemist*, 14.

accidental effect into a purposefully generative tactic further attests to the importance that the principles of multiplicity and contradiction were assuming in his work.

In 1990, Harper began showing in New York City again, initially at Franklin Parrasch Gallery in a show called *Self-Portraits of the Artist, Sacred and Profane.* This was another significant milestone, a logical extension of the character-based work that had emerged in the 1980s. Harper now put himself in the frame, exploring his own identity as a kind of layered palimpsest. In two pieces included in the Orlando show, he had cast himself as St. Anthony—who appealed to him because of the story of his temptation by demons—and, in a recurring appearance, as St. Sebastian. At Parrasch, he represented himself in multiple other guises: as the Hindu goddess Kali; as a haruspex, a Roman seer who read entrails; and, self-referentially, as one of his own *Pagan Babies.*

Another group of self-portraits in the Parrasch show represented Harper's experience of migraine headaches, which had plagued him for years, sometimes incapacitating him for two weeks at a time. The pieces are appropriately brutalist, conspicuously lacking his usual polychrome enamel, with faces made from smashed metal caps of fluorescent lighting tubes, an "O of agony, like a crying mouth" in the dead center.[62] (Harper had first introduced this motif in his self-representation as St. Anthony.) In a sense, these works symbolize the interruption of Harper's creative process—"they're the antithesis of what jewelry is supposed to be," he said, "I think that's their power"—yet their very existence attests that even such a horrific, abyssal experience can be transmuted into art.[63] As the critic Jane Addams Allen, founder of the *New Art Examiner,* wrote in the accompanying publication, the pieces thus perfectly embody "the dichotomy between the pain of introspection and the ecstasy of revelation that lies at the heart of the creative process."[64]

At this otherwise triumphal moment, Harper was beset with another grave health problem: he suffered a double retinal detachment, in 1990. He was left with only partial sight in his right eye, and none at all in his left. This was both eerie—in his first self-portrait as St. Anthony, he had shown himself as having only one eye—and also extremely upsetting, as he faced the possibility that he might become entirely blind (a terrifying prospect, like Beethoven going deaf in mid-career). He was sidelined from enamel and jewelry work for a time and returned to painting, the first medium he had explored. The state of his mind at this dark hour is captured in the harrowing *Self-Portrait of the Artist, Living in Fear of Losing his Sight—Unable to Sleep,* which has the deeply fissured texture and gripping existentialism of an early Jean Dubuffet, an artist who would become extremely important to Harper a little later in his career.

Fortunately, the worst did not happen; Harper retained vision in one eye and was able to return to work. Further exhibitions at Parrasch followed and, then, representation by Peter Joseph, a Manhattan investment banker and collector who had opened an ambitious gallery for furniture in 1990.

62   Cynthia Parks, "A Potent Artist's Power Jewelry," uncited clipping (1991), author's collection.
63   Oral history interview with William Harper, Archives of American Art.
64   Jane Addams Allen, "Mythmaker for a Culture," in *William Harper: Self-Portraits of the Artist, Sacred & Profane* (New York: Franklin Parrasch Gallery, 1990).

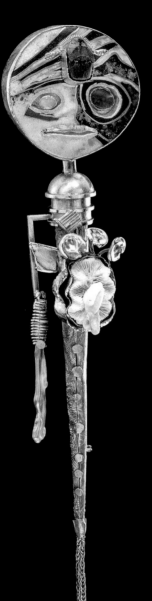

SELF-PORTRAIT OF THE ARTIST AS A HARUSPEX, 1990

Gold cloisonné enamel on fine gold and fine silver; 14k and 24k gold, sterling silver, opal, pearl, coral, shell, carapace. 11.5 × 2.5 in. Smithsonian American Art Museum, Gift of the James Renwick Alliance and Museum Purchase through the Smithsonian Institution Collections Acquisition Program

SELF-PORTRAIT OF THE ARTIST WITH A MIGRAINE III, 1988

14k gold, sterling silver, aluminum, synthetic ruby, pearl. 10 × 2 in.

SELF-PORTRAIT OF THE ARTIST AS A PAGAN BABY, 1990

Gold cloisonné enamel on fine gold and fine silver; 14k and 24k gold, citrine, garnet, carapace. 4.25 × 3.75 in.

This intervention marked a decisive (if temporary) turn in the careers of several leading designers like Wendell Castle and Gaetano Pesce. Joseph also showed the wrought iron furniture of Albert Paley, whose paths had so often crossed with Harper in the past. Even so, adding a jeweler to the mix was an experiment: as he had been at Kennedy Galleries, Harper was an odd man out.

He responded to the opportunity with yet another sensational exhibition outing, bifurcated into two parts: *Jasper's Variations and Fabergé's Seeds*.[65] One of Joseph's gallery team, Carole Hochman (who has since had a distinguished career at Barry Friedman, Ltd., and its successor gallery, Friedman Benda), aptly noted of the show, "It's basically his homage to Jasper Johns and his anti-homage to Fabergé."[66] Harper might have shared a medium with the great Russian purveyor of precious objets d'art—it was when he began showing with Joseph that he started using 18 karat gold—but his artistic sensibility was completely aligned with Johns, as the art critic Arthur Danto explained in an accompanying essay (reprinted in the present volume, alongside a later, previously unpublished text about Johns by Harper himself). Also included in the publication was a fascinating textual experiment in which Harper responded to Johns's famously terse summary of art-making: "Take an object, do something to it, do something else to it." In response, Harper composed an elaborate set of instructions-to-self, including the dizzyingly postmodern lines, "'Paint' paint from a painting; 'Paint' enamel from a painting from a painting. 'Quote' yourself; 'quote' someone else quoting himself ... Find Beauty through the Gesture."[67]

Partly on the strength of his connection to Peter Joseph, and partly because he'd finally had enough of academic life as the exponent of a supposedly minor art form, Harper quit his job at FSU and moved north to New York City in 1995. That year, he also presented two further exhibitions at the gallery. The first was a small display of earrings, a genre he had not much explored, with the nice title of *Ear Follies*, the second a larger exhibition, dedicated to the spirit of Sergei Diaghilev and his Ballets Russes (a topic explored in depth in Mary E. Davis's contribution to this book). This engagement with the theme of dance led to a further series of works inspired by the work of choreographer Twyla Tharp, sold to benefit the American Ballet Theater, where Joseph was a leading patron. Harper responded with a typical creative explosion, making in rapid succession five major brooches and two neckpieces. All were based on the geometrical figures of square, circle, diagonal, and spiral, from which Tharp's dances were built, and executed in a reduced modernist palette of black, white, and red. One of the brooches was acquired by the prominent Virginia-based collectors Sidney and Frances Lewis and subsequently donated to the Museum of Arts and Design in New York.

Sadly, this was to be Harper's last collaboration with Joseph, who was diagnosed with cancer shortly after and forced to close his gallery; he died in

---

65   This first show at Peter Joseph was the first time I myself experienced Harper's work, while I was working as an intern at the American Craft Museum. It absolutely blew my mind, dramatically expanding my conception of what jewelry could do, and be. The present essay is in some ways an attempt to make sense of that experience, three decades later.

66   Quoted in Mark Hinson, "Tallahasseean Has Fifth Avenue Show," *Tallahassee Democrat*, Dec. 11, 1994, 3.

67   William Harper in *Jasper's Variations and Fabergé's Seeds* (New York: Peter Joseph Gallery, 1994).

SELF-PORTRAIT OF THE ARTIST, LIVING IN FEAR OF LOSING HIS SIGHT – UNABLE TO SLEEP, 1993

Mixed media, acrylic paint on paper; plywood panel. 6 × 8 ft.

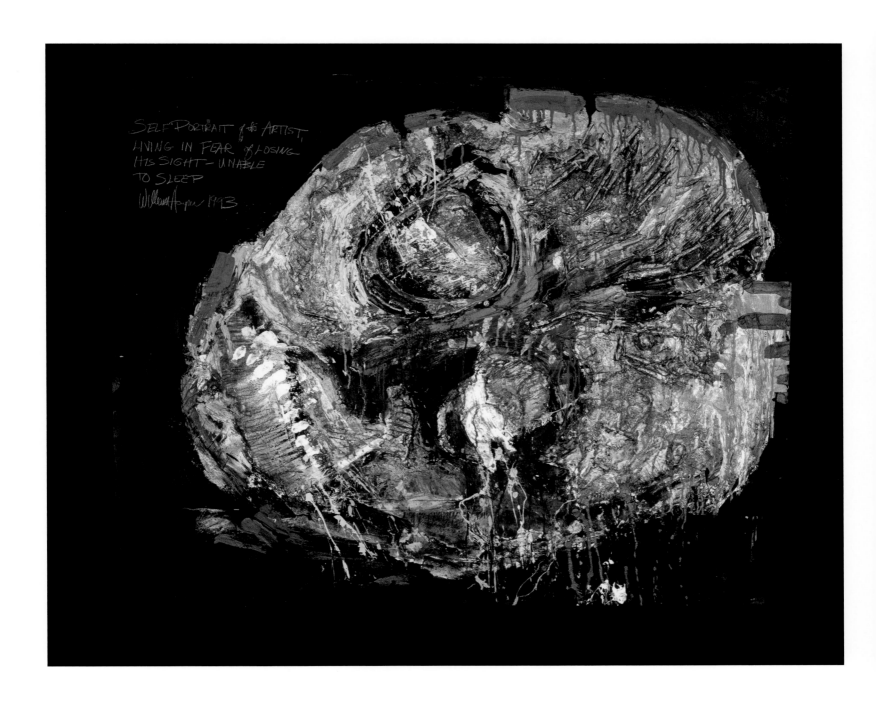

FABERGÉ'S SEED #5, 1992

Gold cloisonné enamel on fine silver; 14k and
24k gold, sterling silver, pearl. 5 × 2.25 in.

**SHOVE CAUSES A PUSH
(NECKPIECE FOR TWYLA
THARP MOVEMENT),** 1995

Gold cloisonné enamel on fine silver; 14k and
24k gold, sterling silver. 16 × 15.5 × 2.75 in.
Museum of Arts and Design, New York, Gift of
Wendy Evans Joseph, 2001

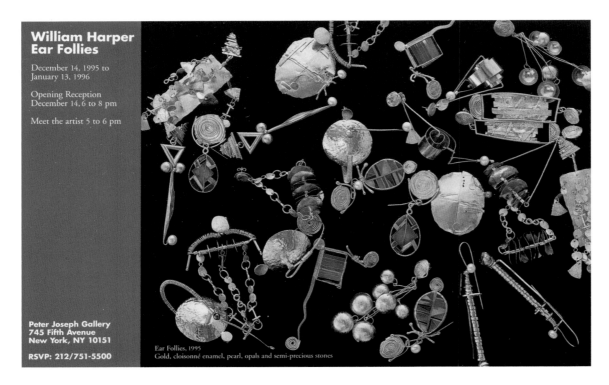

Flyer for *Ear Follies*, Peter Joseph Gallery, 1995

1998. In theory, this could have left Harper somewhat adrift in his new home. In practice, he had no shortage of support from his long-term clients, or opportunities to exhibit his work with gallerists such as Ruth Siegel and Franklin Parrasch, both in New York, and Susan Cummins, in Mill Valley, California. For the first time in his long career, he was able to devote himself single-mindedly to making his art.

A PAINTER MADE GOOD

Harper's move to New York City happened to coincide with an exhibition at The Metropolitan Museum of Art entitled *Pages of Perfection*, a loan show of Islamic manuscripts from the Institute of Oriental Studies in St. Petersburg, Russia. It was, most agreed, a revelation. As Holland Cotter wrote in his review in the *New York Times*, these books were "portable, meant to be passed from hand to hand, greeted with murmurs of admiration, read aloud from, cherished in private" yet at the same time "enormous in breadth: from botany to astronomy, from military history to erotica, in forms from poems to psalms and prayers. And it is not too much to say that within their pages the very soul of a culture is distilled."[68]

It's hard to imagine anything that would have been more stimulating to Harper's fertile imagination. "I was so overjoyed at examining them closely," he says, and was sufficiently enraptured that he initiated a wholly new body of work, applying himself to the laborious but gratifying project of making books. Presented in 1998 under Martha Fleischman's aegis at Kennedy Galleries—the installation was designed by Harper's son, Joshua, a practicing architect—they were a welcome break from jewelry, an opportunity to stretch out. Collaged like his early jewelry, densely populated with expressionistic marks like his paintings, the books are large-scale objects, bound in small coffers which open to reveal a hinged, accordion-style wooden framing system, into which are inserted a series of pages—actually painted wooden panels rather than paper. To leaf through them is to encounter a boiling stew of art history, found objects, and long inscriptions, like this one from the book *Beasts and Demons of a Strange and Savage Mind*:

> I am a sponge. The Creatures in [a] Bosch painting can spark my desire to make strange jewels. My intense LUST for the Art of Africa can often drive me crazy—to look at it and really see its MAGIC, MYSTERY, and POWER … The thrill of experiencing with all my senses all those miraculous objects drives my desire to own them. I covet! And so it is with so much creative genius of artists and craftsmen, named and unnamed, over the centuries. I collect the thrill of the memories in probing their power and revisit them in the Garden of My Mind.

The confessional tone, here, offsets the sheer extravagance of the book itself, a tome that seems to be physically made of stray impressions: bits of torn paper, butterflies, Moët & Chandon champagne foil. This associative method is also seen in the books' contents, which are often organized in the manner of a medieval compendium or bestiary—apparently orderly but bursting with invention. His two-volume *Pages of Saints*, for example—a return to the theme that Harper had explored intensely in his jewelry some years earlier—has a scholarly air, with quotations borrowed from various historical sources. Yet a current of vivid fantasy runs throughout the book: "If I couldn't find a Saint to go with the letter," he says, "I simply made one up."

Michael Monroe, in the accompanying publication to the Kennedy show, rightly described the books as "adventures into hidden realms," and they do indeed offer a journey into the hitherto uncharted territory of Harper's mindscape.[69] Nor was this diaristic quality confined to Harper's books. In general, his work, like that of his hero Jasper Johns, was becoming more interiorized, biographical, thickly encoded. The books developed side by side with containers for his jewelry that he calls "casks," which bristle with nails, wire, keys, and other miscellaneous findings. These featured prominently in another exhibition that Harper had in 1998, concurrently with the one at Kennedy: *The Barbarian's Trapeze and Other Jewels*, at Primavera Gallery in New York. "The two shows complemented each other," Harper notes, "but in totally different media."[70] They are indebted to African objects and medieval caskets but also to the work of the assemblagist Joseph Cornell.

68   Holland Cotter, "Islamic Manuscripts, Out of Hiding at Last," *New York Times*, Oct. 1, 1995. See also *Pages of Perfection* (St. Petersburg: ARCH Foundation Electra/Institute of Oriental Studies at the Russian Academy of Sciences, 1995).

69   Quoted in Michael Monroe, "William Harper: Volumes of Souls," in *William Harper: Volumes of Souls* (New York: Kennedy Galleries, 1998), 3.

70   Harper, email to Glenn Adamson, Sept. 18, 2023.

PAGES OF SAINTS, VOL. II, 1996–98

Mixed-media collage on board with wood, silk, plexiglass,
steel, and mixed-media assemblage. 16 hinged panels,
each 16 × 10.5 in., overall length: 170 in.

SAINT

DILIA

— BORN BLIND —
HER SIGHT WAS
RESTORED THROUGH
A MIRACLE... PRAY
TO HER FOR BLINDNES
AND OTHER
EYE DISEASES

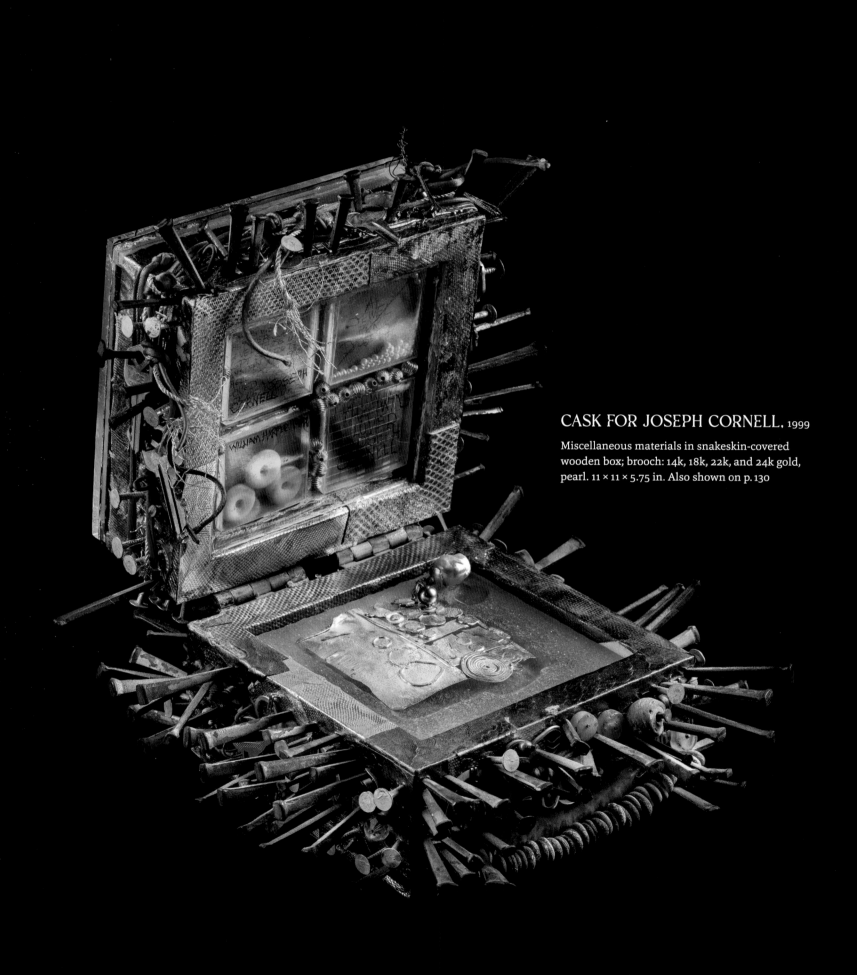

CASK FOR JOSEPH CORNELL, 1999

Miscellaneous materials in snakeskin-covered
wooden box; brooch: 14k, 18k, 22k, and 24k gold,
pearl. 11 × 11 × 5.75 in. Also shown on p. 130

One thing that many of Harper's artistic heroes have in common—Johns, Twombly, Cornell—is that they were homosexuals, in a period when it was both illegal and dangerous to be so. Harper's own sexuality has made him sympathetic with these figures and the way they encode their desires in complex and subtle ways into their art, "like a locked-up puzzle with no key."[71] The 1998 book *Caravaggio's Closet*, which features an especially homoerotic picture by the great (and gay) Baroque painter on its cover (*Youth with a Ram*, 1602, now at the Capitoline Museum), seems in retrospect like a bold declaration of intent. He'd had isolated same-sex encounters in his youth, and after 2002, when he and Riva divorced, he came out as bisexual. Today, he is happily married to William Benjamin, affectionately known to one and all as "Big Bill." While it would be far too literal to read any of Harper's work as a simple expression of queer pride—as we have seen, his treatment of identity has always been multifaceted and intentionally elusive—it is certainly possible to see in his work the reflection of his experience of being part-closeted, and an association of eroticism with the illicit, the underground.

The earliest work that addresses these issues clearly, albeit obliquely, is a double homage to Twombly and Cornell from 1994. A rectangular patch of enamel—a stand-in, perhaps, for the photographs that often feature in Cornell's work—sits within a pinwheel of tourmaline, coral, agate, opal, and pearl. Its overall quality, like that of Twombly's paintings, is at once sketchy and elegant. In subsequent pieces, Harper makes more specific reference, though again the correspondences are only suggestive. Harper's response to *Poems to the Sea* (a suite of twenty-four drawings that Twombly made in July 1959, reportedly in a single day) bears little resemblance apart from the nervy draftsmanship of the wirework. *Cy's Petals of Fire*, similarly, alludes to the intense color of a 1989 painting of that title through its inclusion of blaze-red enamel and coral. But it has a totally different composition, featuring a wayward spiral of vegetal and geometric ornament. If anything, Harper's take on Twombly shows the difference between the two artists' sensibilities: it's a fascinating contrast of two furtive and fertile imaginations, one joyously luxuriant, the other soberly restrained.

Something similar can be said of Harper's more recent *Dubu* works, made over a two-year period in 2017–18. Like the use of "Cy" in the titles of the Twombly works, the cheeky truncation of Jean Dubuffet's name indicates an attitude of familiarity, intimacy even, but also a playful desire to transform. A little surprisingly, maybe, Harper is not all that interested in the *Hourloupe* cycle, Dubuffet's most recognizable works, which feature strongly contoured black and white shapes, further embellished with blue and red. This idiom would have been easy enough to replicate in cloisonné, but Harper is much more partial to the earlier drawings and paintings, antic and textural, and made more explicitly in relation to so-called "outsider" art. He knows full well that, as with the modernist cult of African art, Dubuffet's work has a tacit paternalism in it. But appropriation is exactly what Harper doesn't do. Instead he skirts round the things he loves, admiring them askance. He's not an outsider artist, nor is he emulating one; "I'm an insider artist, playing hooky."[72]

71   Harper, interview with Glenn Adamson, Sept. 14, 2022.
72   Ibid.

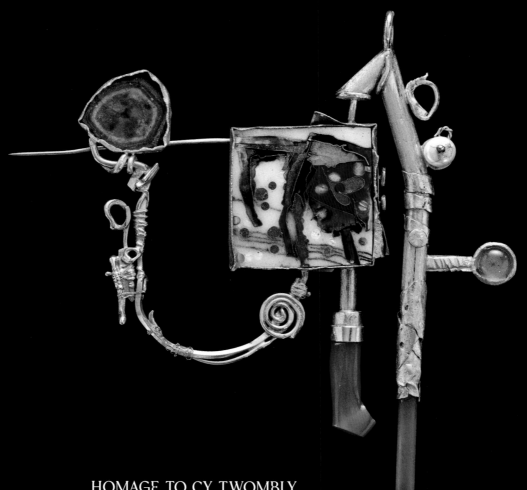

HOMAGE TO CY TWOMBLY
AND JOSEPH CORNELL, 1994

Gold cloisonné enamel on gold and silver;
14k, 18k, and 24k gold, sterling silver, tourmaline,
coral, agate, Mexican opal, pearl. 7 × 5.5 in.
The Metropolitan Museum of Art, Gift of Donna
Schneier, 2007.384.18a

ROYAL DUBU I, 2017

Gold cloisonné enamel on fine gold and fine silver; 18k, 22k, and 24k gold, tourmaline, pearl. 4.5 × 4 in.

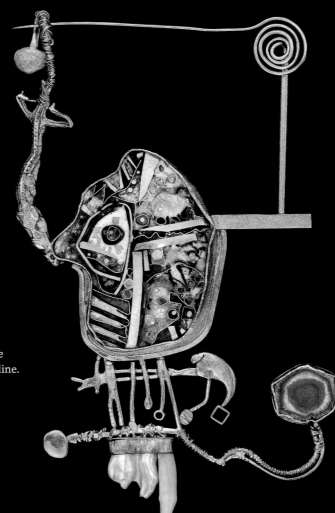

THE ALBINO DUBU, 2017

Gold cloisonné enamel on fine gold and fine silver; 18k, 22k, and 24k gold, pearl, tourmaline. 4.75 × 4 in.

The earliest works in the *Dubu* series have rangy compositions, loose yet compartmentalized. Their expansiveness is like that of Dubuffet's cityscape paintings, such as *Business Prospers* (1961), but without the foreboding sense of claustrophobia. *Royal Dubu I* and *II* are more spacious, giving us big pools of colorful enamel to lose ourselves in. The enamel jewels are set into the pieces off-kilter, evoking Dubuffet's clusters of furious mark-making. Only one piece in the series—*The Albino Dubu*—refers to a specific work (*Nez Long et Chaise Septembre*, also from 1961); it is also, of course, a callback to Harper's breakthrough series of the late 1970s. Even in this case, he's made the image his own, transmuting the half-slaphappy, half-menacing character into his own idiom. Three pearls descend like snaggled teeth—or is it the albino's nose, mouth, and chin?—while the figure's eye becomes a single, staring stone.

Harper's engagement with the art of Twombly and Dubuffet is in many ways emblematic of his later work. His magpie instinct to gather stray new impressions and feather his own creative nest with them remains undiminished, yet it has brought him full circle. When Harper was first learning how to work with enamel, he often understood it in relationship to his previous work in oil on canvas; from that point on, he would often speak of himself, with a hint of self-mockery, as a "painter gone bad." That, of course, is in the eye of the beholder. How many museumgoers faced with a work by Twombly or Dubuffet exclaim indignantly, "But my kid could do that!" (Twombly once lived and worked in a palazzo in Rome, where he allowed his young son to draw on the plaster walls; even his admirers noted a strong similarity.) Harper, similarly, having completely mastered his discipline, feels entirely at liberty to disregard its proprieties. He remains a painter at heart, driven above all by curiosity, an instinct to gather and react in the moment, even as the artwork takes shape in front of him.

Many of the works Harper has made since 2000, like the marvelously various *Flotsam* series, put this improvisatory process at the forefront; like his *Pentimenti* of the 1980s, their emphasis is on second thoughts, secondhand usages. In the *Quarantine* series, which he made during the Covid pandemic lockdown (a uniquely political body of work, examined by Toni Greenbaum in her essay for this volume), one can see Harper's hyperactive, effortlessly inventive mind at work. Even when a case of Guillain-Barré syndrome robbed him temporarily of the fine motor control required to make jewelry, he remained prolific, creating a voluminous output of drawings, including the related series *Ancient Manuscripts* and *Ancient Tapestries*. In these visionary works, most of which were executed within the span of a single day, Harper reprises his persistent themes of satirical self-portraiture, jubilant sexuality, and historical allusion. The mark-making ranges from thick accretion to feather-light traces, sometimes recalling the artful scribbles of early Twombly; some feature elements of collage, including netting, cut-out letters, and flattened tangerine peels. Other works made at this time are executed in a Pointillist style with felt-tip marker, a time-consuming process that nonetheless crackles with energy on the page.

Like so many artists in their later careers—Titian, Monet, and Bonnard spring to mind—Harper is working with complete confidence, a fluid freedom of gesture that is only available to the most practiced hand. In the drawings, and in many of his newer jewelry pieces, he has revisited themes from earlier moments in his career, approaching them with a new freedom.

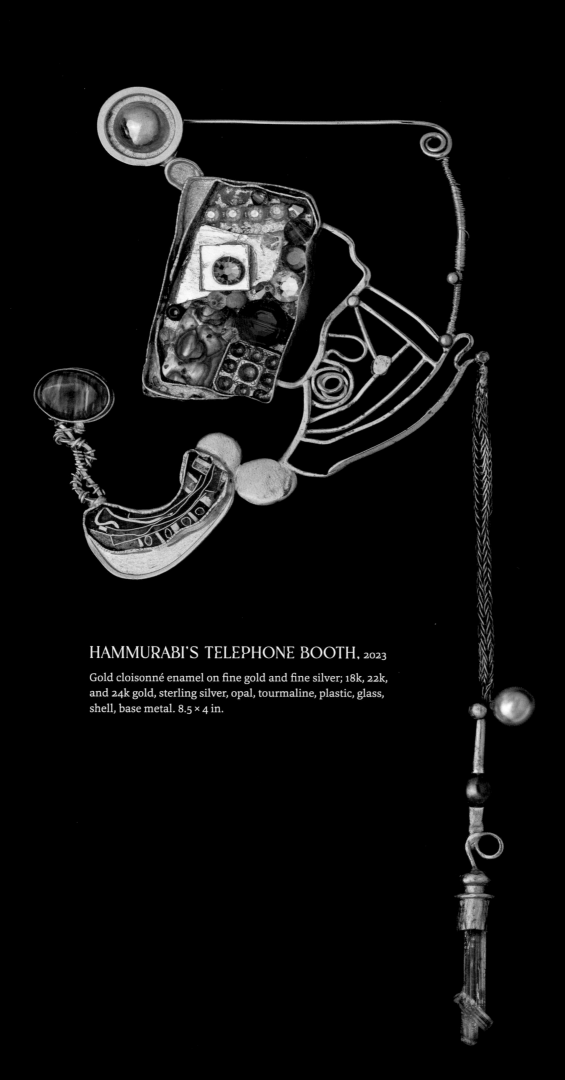

HAMMURABI'S TELEPHONE BOOTH, 2023

Gold cloisonné enamel on fine gold and fine silver; 18k, 22k, and 24k gold, sterling silver, opal, tourmaline, plastic, glass, shell, base metal. 8.5 × 4 in.

DOUBLE SELF-PORTRAIT OF THE ARTIST
WITH AN EXTRA EYE

DOUBLE SELF-PORTRAIT OF THE
ARTIST WITH AN EXTRA EYE, 2022

Watercolor on collaged paper. 24 × 18 in.

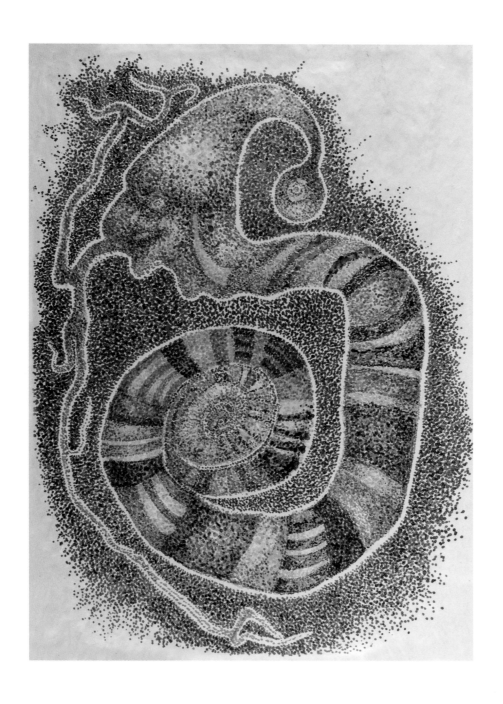

MAN/SERPENT DEVOURING
HIS OWN TONGUE, 2022

Colored marker on paper. 27.25 × 19.25 in.

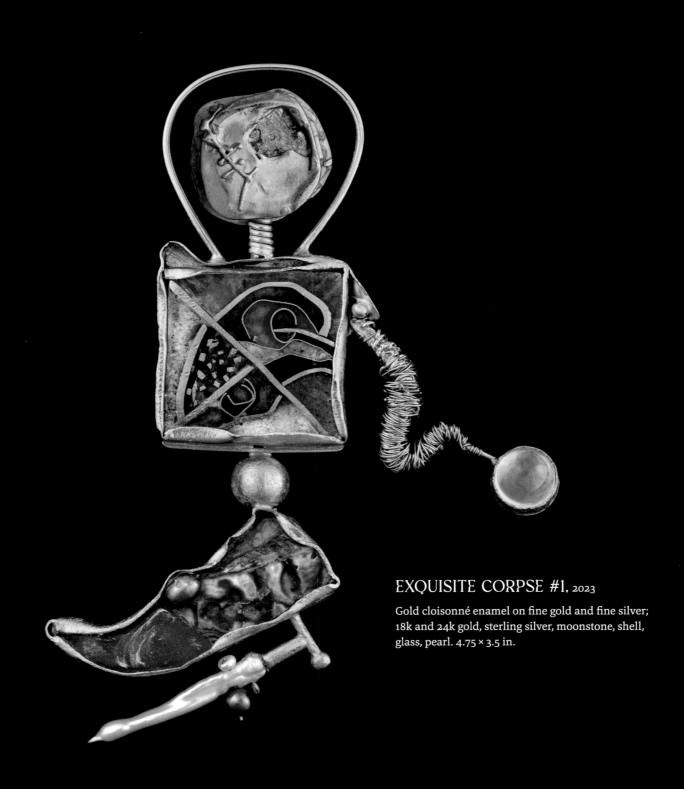

EXQUISITE CORPSE #1, 2023

Gold cloisonné enamel on fine gold and fine silver;
18k and 24k gold, sterling silver, moonstone, shell,
glass, pearl. 4.75 × 3.5 in.

As this book was going to press, he was just finishing off two complex allegorical works, one of which bears the rather wonderful title *Hammurabi's Telephone Booth*, as well as a series of pieces based on the famous Surrealist game "exquisite corpse," in which artists successively complete portions of a single image, in the hopes of arriving at unbidden psychic juxtapositions. Harper, the shape-shifter, is by now so multivalent in his instincts that he can do this all by himself. The compositions are willfully disjunctive, and yet they feel like encapsulations of his career thus far: one can see in them the fleeting impressions of the innumerable characters, gestures, and ideas that have graced his artistry over the decades.

It is almost too tedious to repeat that jewelry is an art form, with nothing inherently minor about it. As Harper has amply demonstrated over the course of his long career, it can bear just as much complexity as painting can, achieve just as much expressive range. That we see this comparatively rarely is not a limitation of the discipline itself but rather the biases that are typically brought to it. Many jewelers have vigorously contested that bigotry of low expectations, but very few with Harper's daring, nuance, and intellectual depth while operating entirely independently of what jewelry normally looks like or "should" be. He has escaped any imposed framework of disciplinary relevance by the deceptively simple yet almost impossible-to-achieve means of establishing his own.

The last time I visited Harper in his studio, his workbench was populated with fragments in various states of completion. Precious stones glowing with inner light sat in near orbit, as if they'd been pulled into his domain by gravitational attraction. The still unfixed configurations, informal to the point of almost seeming haphazard, were nonetheless tantalizingly close to genius. There was little doubt that, before he was done, they would be consummated, becoming something beautiful, bizarre, never before seen. The next time I visit him, I know it will all have changed, and yet—one last dichotomy—it will still be just the same. For, if there's one thing we can say for sure about Bill Harper, it's that his wonders will never cease. ◆

William Harper's jeweler's bench, NYC, 2023

"

THERE IS MAGIC
IN THE UNKNOWN AND
I ATTEMPT TO MAKE
OBJECTS OF THE
UNKNOWN.

COIN FOR HIERONYMUS:
THE THIEF-FACE AND NIPPLE
(front and reverse), 1972

Silver cloisonné enamel on copper;
electroformed silver. 2 × 2 × 5 in.

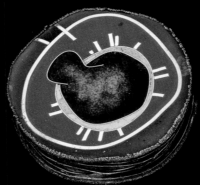

PROSTITUTTI PUZZLE, 1972

Silver cloisonné enamel on copper; plexiglass.
7 × 7 × 4 in.

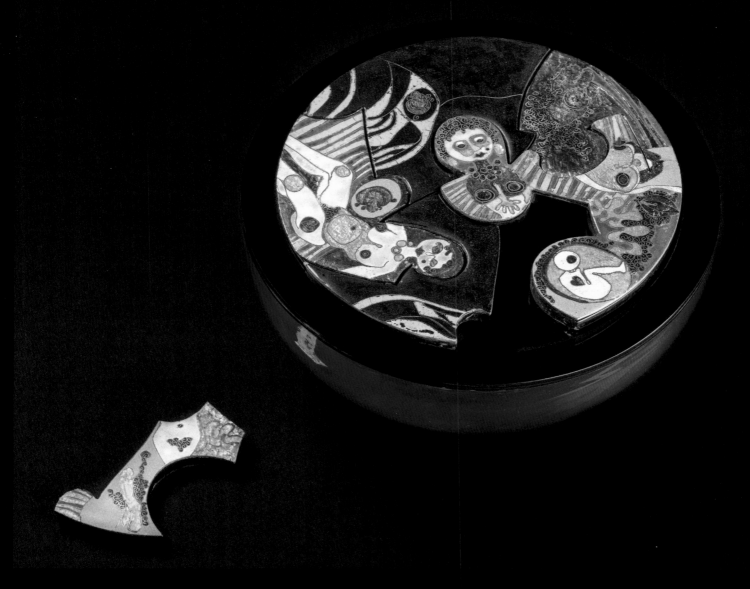

BIRD, 1972

Silver cloisonné enamel on copper;
ceramic decals, plexiglass. 3 × 3 in.

ALLIGATOR BUTTON, c. 1972

Silver cloisonné enamel on copper with
silver electro forming

RAIN RATTLE, 1972

Silver cloisonné enamel; electroformed copper, mirror, antler

GARDEN RATTLE, 1973

Gold and silver cloisonné enamel on copper; electroformed silver, mirror, pebbles, cast bronze.

RATTLE FOR MEDUSA, 1973

Silver and gold cloisonné enamel; silver electro-
plating, cast bronze, mirror, pebbles. 5.25 × 2.25 in.
The Cleveland Museum of Art, The Mary Spedding
Milliken Memorial Collection, Gift of William
Mathewson Milliken (1973.79)

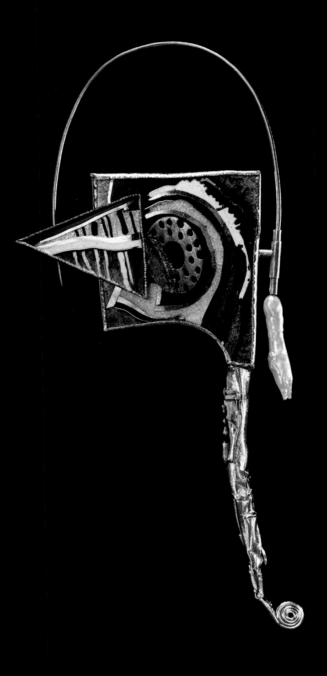

FETISH PIN #3, 1974

Gold and silver cloisonné enamel on sterling
silver; electroformed copper, bone, pearl.
5.25 × 2.25 in.

FOSSIL, c. 1972

Gold cloisonné enamel on fine silver;
14k, 18k, and 22k gold, pearl

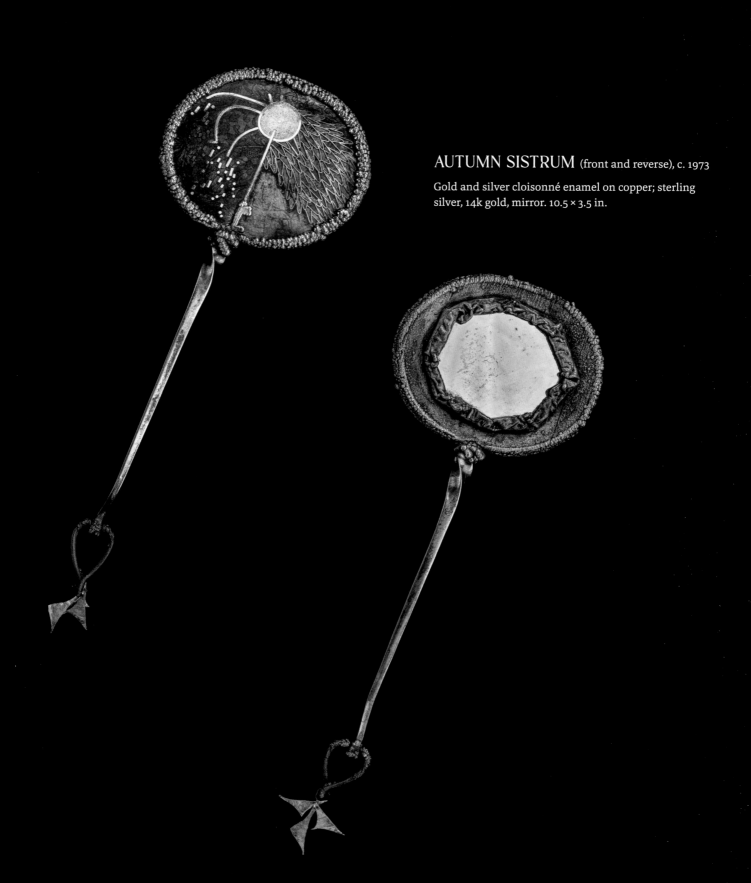

AUTUMN SISTRUM (front and reverse), c. 1973

Gold and silver cloisonné enamel on copper; sterling silver, 14k gold, mirror. 10.5 × 3.5 in.

PUNJAB GEOGRAPHY, c. 1975

Plexiglass frame; fine gold and silver cloisonné
enamel on copper. 3.25 × 6.75 in., individual tiles:
1 × 2.25 in.

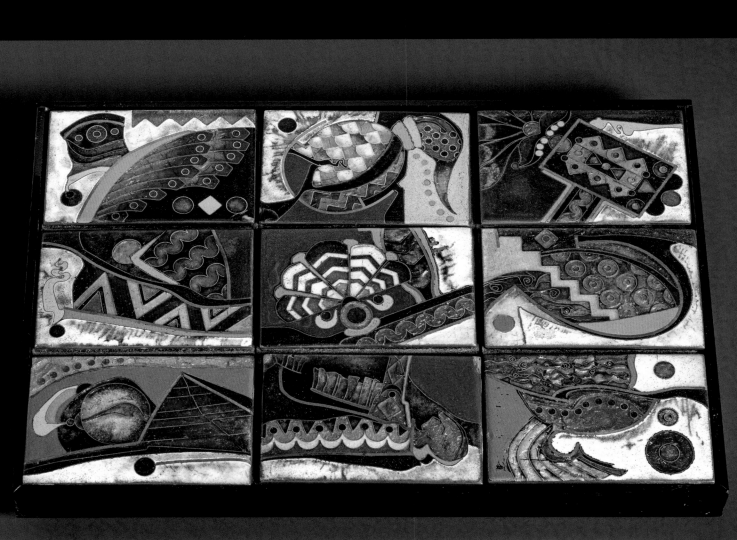

HAIR FETISH, 1974

Gold and silver cloisonné enamel on copper;
electroformed copper, mirror, hair. 16 × 7.5 × 3 in.

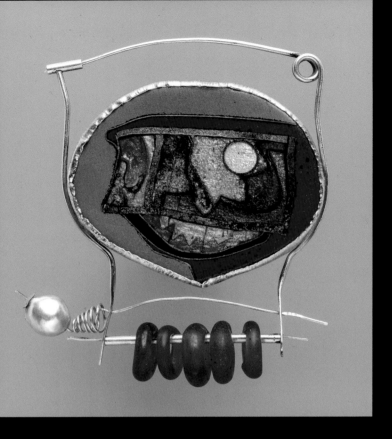

MYSTERY PIN, 1976

Gold and silver cloisonné enamel on copper;
14k and 18k gold, sterling silver, pearl, antique
African glass. 3 × 2.75 in.

MYSTERY PIN #2, 1976

Gold and silver cloisonné enamel on copper;
14k and 18k gold, sterling silver, bronze, pearl.
2.25 × 2.25 in.

PAGAN BABY #4: THE SERPENT, 1977

Silver and gold cloisonné enamel on copper; 14k
and 18k gold, sterling silver, fresh and saltwater pearl,
shell, rattlesnake rattle. 5.7 × 2.8 × 0.7 in. The Museum

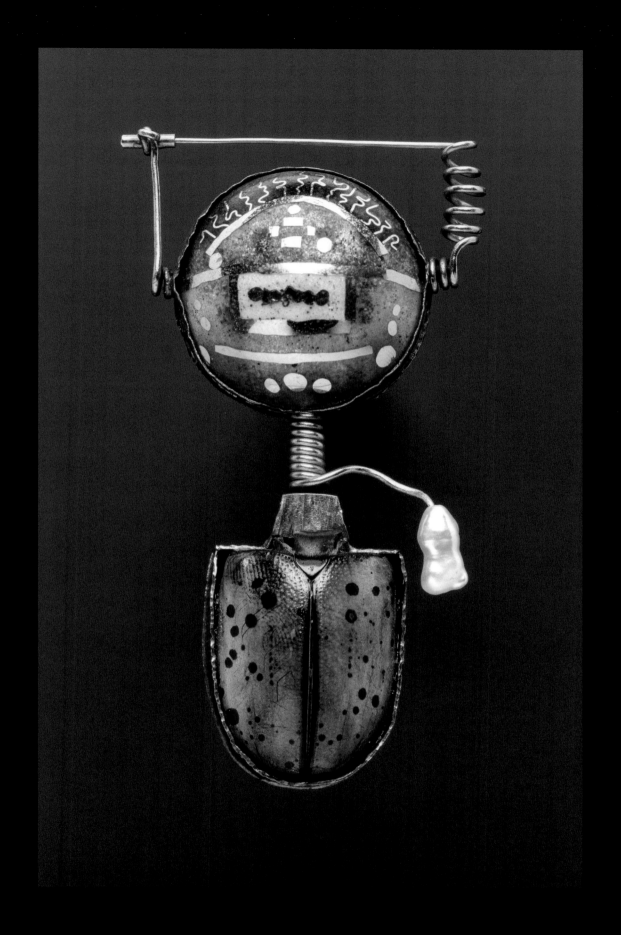

PAGAN BABY #6: THE SCARAB, 1977

Gold cloisonné enamel on fine silver; 14k, 18k, and
24k gold, sterling silver, carapace, freshwater pearl.
3.25 × 1.75 in. The Museum of Fine Arts, Houston,
Helen Williams Drutt Collection, Museum Purchase
funded by Caroline Wiess Law Foundation (2002.3800)

PAGAN BABY #10: ORANGE SCARAB, 1978

Gold cloisonné enamel on fine silver and fine gold; 14k gold,
sterling silver, bronze, pearl, garnet, beetle carapace.
4 × 2.25 in. Philadelphia Museum of Art, Purchased with funds
contributed by The Women's Committee and the Craft Show
Committee of the Philadelphia Museum of Art in memory of
Diana Rogers Dripps Dorrance, 1991

EAR PAGANS IV: NEPTUNE, 1978

Gold cloisonné enamel on fine silver; 14k gold,
pearl, shell. 5 × 2 × 2 in.

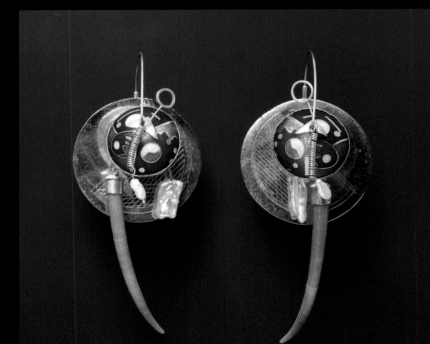

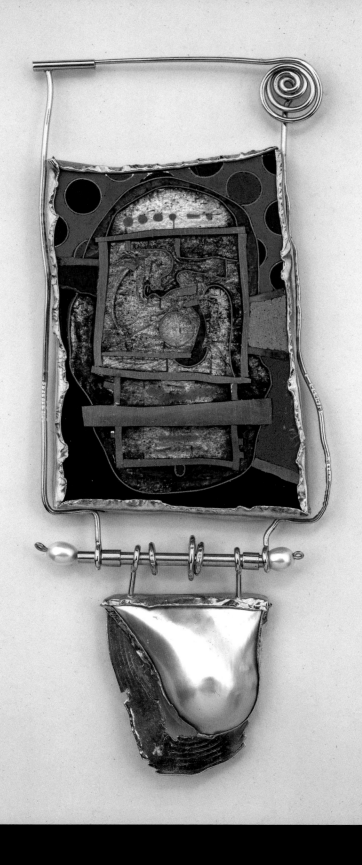

ENCLOSED TATTOO, 1979

Gold cloisonné enamel on copper, gold, and silver;
14k gold, sterling silver, pearl. 6 × 2.25 in.

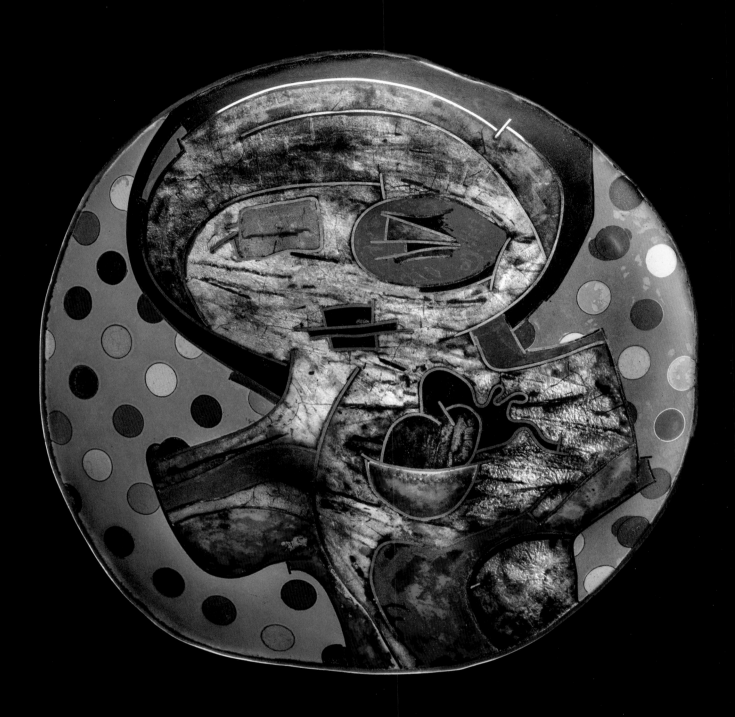

SELF PORTRAIT OF THE ARTIST
AS A TROLL, 1981

Silver cloisonné enamel on copper. 10.5 × 10 × 2 in.

BARBARIAN BRACELET I, 1980

Silver and gold cloisonné enamel on copper;
24k gold, sterling silver, fire gilding. 4.75 × 4.75 × 0.75 in.
Los Angeles County Museum of Art, Gift of Lois and
Bob Boardman (m.2015.252.9)

SAINT AGATHA, 1982

Gold and silver cloisonné enamel on copper and
fine silver; 14k gold, sterling silver, ivory, ebony,
shell, tourmaline. 7.25 × 2.75 in.

SAINTS, MARTYRS, AND SAVAGES

WILLIAM HARPER

These pieces are about religion. They are not intended to be religious jewelry, nor are they anti-religious. The initial impetus for the group resulted from similarities I noted in the iconographic images of two diverse and distinct religious cultural groups: the Songye tribes of the Congolese groups and medieval Catholicism. In the first group, a potent and imposing image results from a carved wooden male figure which is stuck with nails, razor blades, glass shards, and other lacerating forms to produce a power figure of intense emotional impact. I contrasted this with the St. Sebastian image of European Catholicism, a male figure shot with arrows yet usually contrasting a certain passive eroticism with the savagery of the act. In many respects, these two figure groups could not be more dissimilar, but I chose to fuse them through metamorphosis to create my own variation on their images, for I realized that the similarity existed not only in the passive/active aspects of their physical form but also in the cultural stimulants which led to their socio-religious significance. I soon found myself immersed in the labyrinth of the mythical elements of religion, both contemporary and of other times and other places—beautiful, elegantly imaginative, often violent tales of super beings, designed to touch the followers. I discovered figures like St. Agatha, St. Christopher, and St. Valentine, and I went on to merge these together, and to invent my own.

It seemed logical that they take the form of jewelry, since man throughout time has adorned himself with amulets and talismans designed to bring about him a good aura. But at what point does the hope for supernatural protection stop and the desire for individual adornment begin? Does the contemporary man who wears the large shiny cross or gold/turquoise mezuzah do so to demonstrate his religious beliefs or to add sex appeal, hence religious motifs as "disco jewelry"? He is probably doing both.

Is he dissimilar from the "savage" New Guinea tribesmen who lavishly paint their bodies and adorn them further with fresh flora and exotic feathers in order to participate in religious festivals? We might view this as barbarian, as savage. How might they view St. Sebastian?

It has been said that the artist-craftsman of the Middle Ages devoted his spiritual and physical creative energy in an act of intense, profound faith. Thus, his own culture and all the others that have followed have been richer for the art left through this devotional motivation. Ours is not an "Age of Faith." I choose to think that my motivation for these pieces resulted more from a certain cynicism about all of us and what we have learned, or not learned, from all the various cultural-political—religious—empires which have existed before us. What makes a saint, who is a savage? ◆

THE DARK ARCHANGEL, 1982

Gold and silver cloisonné enamel on copper,
fine silver, and fine gold; 14k and 24k gold, sterling
silver, bone, teeth, shell, pearl. 6.5 × 2.5 in.

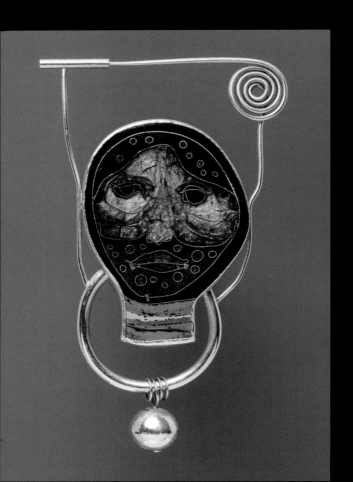

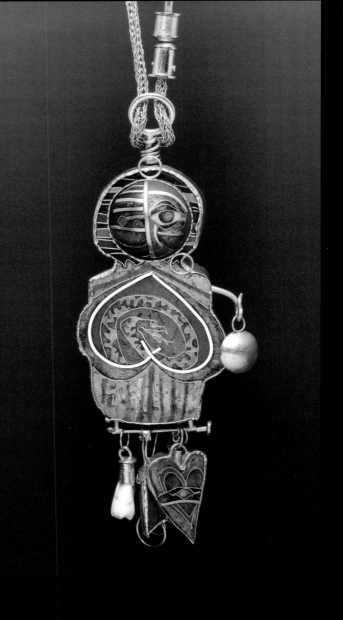

SAINT VALENTINE, 1981

Gold and silver cloisonné enamel on copper,
fine silver, and fine gold; 14k and 24k gold, sterling
silver, tourmaline, teeth, plastic. 6.5 × 2.5 in.

SAVAGE IV, 1982

Gold cloisonné enamel on fine silver; 14k gold, sterling silver, copper, pearl. 5.5 × 2.25 in.

SAVAGE II, 1982

Gold cloisonné enamel on fine silver; 14k gold, sterling silver, animal claw, copper. 4.75 × 2.25 in.

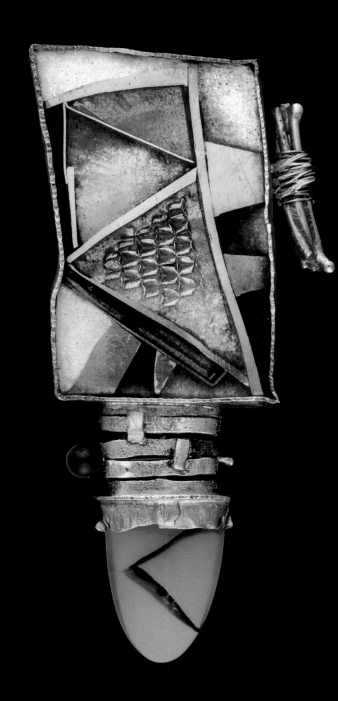

VARIATION ON A THEME
BY J.J. AND E.M., 1993

Gold cloisonné enamel on fine silver and fine
gold; 14k and 24k gold, sterling silver, agate,
pearl. 3 × 1.25 in.

BETWEEN THE BED AND THE BROOCH

ARTHUR C. DANTO

According to the myths ... the wearing of rings originated on the crags of Caucasus. It was of this rock that a fragment was for the first time enclosed in a rim of iron placed [by Prometheus] on a finger; and this, we are told, was the first ring, and this the first gemstone.

(Pliny the Elder, *Natural History*, Book 37.1)

The archetypical jewel is composed of two main elements: the gem, which is the bearer of light, and the setting, which serves the function of proclamation (the way trumpets herald the appearance of some luminary personage—a king or queen, say, or a pontiff). Gem and setting together form a union as intricate in its way as that of soul and body, and the analogy deepens when we reflect that the setting is not merely symbolic but practical as well; it not only celebrates but protects the gem. And it carries a meaning of its own through the way in which it gives the owner a means of attaching it to his or her person as ring, necklace, bracelet, brooch, or diadem, displaying the gem like a personal portable sun but also declaring his or her station in life through the placement of the jewel on the owner's body. The master jeweler has the option of countless variations in the relationship between the components, but it is essential to the meaning of the jewelry that it be worn, and that something be the bearer of light, whether gemstone or enamel, or be felt to possess an aura and hence a power.

We are, primordially and ineradicably, worshippers of light. Christ is depicted bearing a scroll with the text from the St. John Gospel—"I am the Light of the world"—and the Gospels were often, in the Middle Ages, densely covered with gemstones, the light of which was an instant metaphor for the Divine Light of the text. The book was by magic contagion as divine as its contents. Romeo has no resource for praising Juliet more highly than saying "Juliet is the sun," connecting together luminescence, the attribute of divinity and warmth, the attribute of love, thus making the jewel the only fitting gift with which to acknowledge the meshwork of interlaced meanings light carries in the intuitive symbolic language of adoration and erotic passion. It is altogether fitting that Prometheus, who stole fire from the gods for the benefit of humankind, should have been credited by the ancients as the first jewelry-maker.

I have always felt that a large part of what we respond to in the Old Masters is the light with which they infuse their paintings, irrespective of whether they also showed light. We are drawn to them by the same phototropism which draws us to the jewel. Light found its way into paintings in consequence of the fact that, with the dawn of our concept of art in late Gothic or early Renaissance times, small devotional images were treated as jewels and given settings worthy of the rarest gems. For a period around 1400, painting and jewelry were exact aesthetic peers, but paintings continued to be, in fact, bearers of light after they and jewelry went in different directions. The highlight on the enormous irregular pearl worn by Maddalena Doni in Raphael's portrait of her in the Palazzo Pitti defines the source of illumination in which that lady is bathed. It comes from the upper left (and is just possibly a metaphor for the splendor of her husband, Antonio, whose portrait hangs just next to her and who is *her* sun). But the light of the painting itself comes mysteriously from within and has neither source nor shadow. It is like the light *in* the pearl, as distinguished from the highlight *on* the pearl's iridescent surface. Or the light of a halo, which no more casts shadows than does the inner light of emeralds. (It would be a wicked joke to paint somebody reading by the light of someone's halo.)

Renaissance eyes doubtless saw some image in Maddalena's marvelous baroque pearl; indeed, it was for the sake of such natural resemblance and affinities that such gems were cherished far beyond the symmetrical spheres prized by the ancients. Possibly it is the image of a breast, which explains why it is worn just above Maddalena's gently arching bosom and is connected to the intricate trefoil, in gold and possibly red enamel, from which it dangles.

I thought of Maddalena's pearl the instant I first saw the jewelry of William Harper, who uses irregular and independent pearls in much the same way, attached to enameled pieces on which they comment and valued often for the formal resonances they may set up with the erotic geography of the body. Harper's jewelry is alive with erotic provocations, which fits with the fact that the very word "jewel" derives etymologically from *jouer*, "to play." Not only does the jewel have a role in the exchange of gifts, which solemnizes love, it belongs as well to the play of love. Think of the swaying jewels the passionate gods and goddesses of India wear in their strenuous copulations! But I also learned from Harper to think seriously about the jewelry in paintings and to take its appearance there as important to the understanding of the work (as I have always taken pictures within pictures to be).

Raphael, *Portrait of Maddalena Doni*, c. 1504–07, Uffizi Gallery

One suite of Harper's works in the present exhibition consists of homages to painting—to certain paintings of Jasper Johns and of Edvard Munch specifically—and it is not difficult for those familiar with the two artists to see how. From 1974 until 1982, Johns produced a sequence of what are called "cross-hatch" paintings and drawings, though in technical truth the pattern is not that of cross-hatching at all. They instead consist of irregularly shaped patches set at eccentric angles to one another, each covered with parallel lines in red or black or some other color, always the same within a given patch but differing from patch to patch. The lines do not cross but do form funny angles. The overall crisscross pattern of these surfaces, which Harper has not so much appropriated as interpreted in enamel, resemble a kind of crazy quilt. There is, indeed, a resemblance to the quilt which covers the bed in Edvard Munch's great self-portrait as an old man, *Between the Clock and the Bed*. Munch's painting was evidently not the inspiration for Johns's work of those years, but the resemblance must have been pointed out, and in fact he appropriated Munch's title for several outwardly abstract works in the striped-patch genre.

Harper celebrates both artists through executing a sort of patchwork pattern in cloisonné, though more Art Deco in feeling than either artist's relevant work. It consists of triangles with patterns picked out in dazzles of luminous dots and tiny curves. But in fact the tribute goes deeper than this,

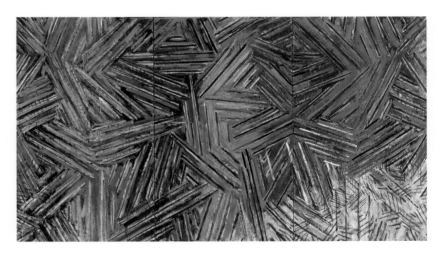

Jasper Johns, *Between the Clock and the Bed*, 1982–83. Encaustic on canvas, three panels. 73 × 126 in. The Museum of Modern Art, New York; Gift of Agnes Gund, 104.1982.a-c. © 2024 Jasper Johns/Licensed by VAGA at Artists Rights Society (ARS), NY

Edvard Munch, *Self-Portrait: Between the Clock and the Bed*, 1940–42. Oil on canvas. 58.75 × 47.5 in. Munchmuseet, Oslo, Norway; MM.M.00023

just because the works themselves have meanings deeper by far than similarities and differences in medium and in crazy quilt patterning. In Munch's painting, the artist stands between clock and bed, hence between time and death—and the crisscross quilt, for all the gaiety of its pattern, is the *memento mori* of that work. One of John's crisscross paintings is in two vertical panels, one the pale image of the other. This work is called *Corpse and Mirror*, which would certainly be an odd title if these works were mere abstractions, but in fact the crisscross paintings carry a very dense system of meanings, the interpretation of which has generated a kind of art historical industry.

Two paintings in particular are of great importance to Harper: *Dancers on a Plane* and *Cicada*, both from 1979. Both paintings make explicit reference to symbolism from Tantric art, which gets carried over into Harper's works. Tantric Buddhism, which evolved in Tibet, involves a particularly athletic form of sexual discipline; its devotional images often portray male and female deities in fierce embrace. Both deities have an extravagant number of arms, and the male presses the female to his body with several of them at once while she clamps her legs around his body. Locked into and onto one another's flesh, they execute a protracted dance of sustained intercourse. *Dancers on a Plane* distributes its crisscross patches in rough symmetry, and the matching zigs and zags are like the in and out, the up and down, the back and forth of a sexual rhythm which the bodies of the lovers are engaged in. Johns has placed emblems for the sexual organs at the top and bottom of the central axes of this painting and others. But inspired by the strings of skulls the Tantric lovers wear, he has also inserted the skull motif at various sites. Harper was struck by the fact that the painter appropriated the forms of jewelry into his art. That licensed Harper, he told me, to appropriate the forms of the paintings into his jewelry. So just as there is a line of descent of motifs back from jewel to painting to quilt, there is another genealogy from jewelry to tanka to painting to jewelry. These chains of reference connect both painting and jewelry to the themes of sex and death—and of the triumph over death that sex and art promise.

In Johns's *Cicada*, there is a row of icons beneath the crisscross which scholars like to characterize as a predella. If indeed a predella, the crisscross here becomes an altar piece which, in view of the cosmic character of the themes with which Johns is dealing (death and sex in art), is not altogether far-fetched. The icons are (among others) of male and female sexual parts, a skull, a schematized funeral pyre, and a cicada, which has whatever meaning it has for Johns. The images in the predella are independent of the main action but at the same time comment on it, and it is hardly surprising that Harper should have seized the opportunity to add similar "commentaries," typically sexual, to the main body of his pieces. (It is not uncommon, after all, to jocularly refer to the penis and testicles as "the family jewels.") Formally, these addenda have a life of their own, like Maddalena's seemingly engorged pearl. But they add immensely to the overall gorgeousness of the objects, which have the opulence of regalia for Tantric gods or priests and reflect and refract by means of their vitreous and metallic surface the light which is the reason, after all, for jewelry to exist.

The attachments—the transition into precious metals and jewels of Johns's icons, which are themselves translations into paint of real objects (skulls, penises) which have been given a certain ritual significance by Tantra—give Harper's jewels a certain barbaric extravagance and even a sense of magic, as if the attachments were vested with some power the wearer of the jewel commands. Sophisticated as the systems of reference are in the jewelry, the feeling they transmit is one of primordial beliefs and enactments. This is conspicuously true of the other main suite in the current [1992] exhibition, *Fabergé's Seeds*. Fabergé's name is inseparably connected with the lavish Easter eggs that the jeweler fabricated for Russian royalty as presents to one another, but the egg, like Easter itself, condenses the meanings of birth and rebirth, the return of light to the world and the return of the Light of the world. Easter was a Christian celebration grafted onto pagan celebrations, and nothing could be at once more spiritual and more earthly than the Fabergé egg with its complex program of gems and goldwork. The bodies of Harper's pieces seem like schematizations of the cross sections of the seed, the descriptive vocabulary for which, not surprisingly, is reproductive: endosperm, perisperm, ovule, embryo, etc. This makes it natural, but quite surprising, to add explicitly sexual attachments such as testes and phalluses. "Gem" and "germ" are not merely near rhymes—they are etymologically intertwined, and both have "bud" or "growth" as part of the evolution of their meaning.

More simply, the reference to Fabergé in the design and title of the pieces activates a composite Russian aesthetic. Just as the crisscross of Johns and Munch have been transformed into Art Deco triangles, the strata of the seed strike me as decoratively near of kin to the designs of Léon Bakst for the Ballets Russes. And the way the seed is surrounded by gemstones likewise strikes me as an echo of the way the icon was jeweled in acknowledgment of its tremendous power. But the icon, the ballet, and the Fabergé object together define the pinnacle of the Russian spirit in its artistic expression. It is something of a miracle for Harper to condense all this meaning into his extraordinary ornaments.

One final piece of iconography for the *J.J. & E.M.* suite: *Dancers on a Plane* is set into a painted bronze frame, embellished on its vertical sides by articles of ordinary tableware: knives, forks, spoons. The thematic connection between these altogether banal utensils and a shuddering dance of sex between a god and his consort has naturally given rise to questions of interpretation. While I am uncertain that I have anything to contribute to the so far indecisive conjectures of scholars, my sense is that the great sexual rhythms of the Tantric cosmos go on all the time in the midst of ordinary events of life—none more ordinary than the eating of meals. Whatever the case, *Jasper's Quilted Spoon* seems to me to condense spoon and crisscross quilt—picture and frame—into single object at once cosmic and mundane. But it would be absurd to seek a lexicon of point-for-point correspondences between the jewels and the paintings they celebrate. This suite is made up of variations on a theme of art and sexuality, as the Fabergé suite is made up of variations on the themes of birth and rebirth, and of the Russian spirit. No special key to individual works is required—simply an appreciation of the fertility of the artist's improvisational power and his virtuosity, and of the deep ingenuity with which he has fused into compelling luscious objects whole texts (religious, aesthetic, and even philosophical) which are to be worn like amulets and which, because of their dazzle and daring, must seduce all eyes. ◆

" WHAT MAKES A SAINT,
WHO IS ᴬ SAVAGE?

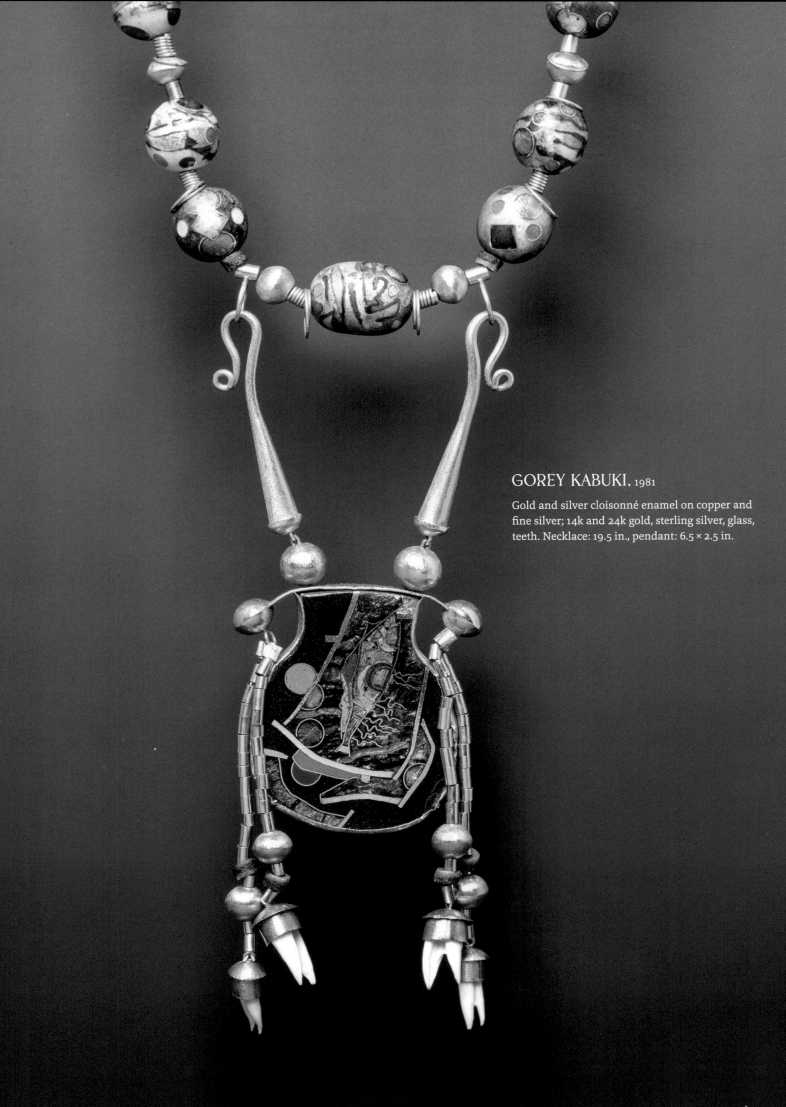

GOREY KABUKI, 1981

Gold and silver cloisonné enamel on copper and fine silver; 14k and 24k gold, sterling silver, glass, teeth. Necklace: 19.5 in., pendant: 6.5 × 2.5 in.

THE ROBE II, 1981

Gold cloisonné enamel on copper; 14k and 24k
gold, sterling silver, bronze, pearl. 5 × 3 in.

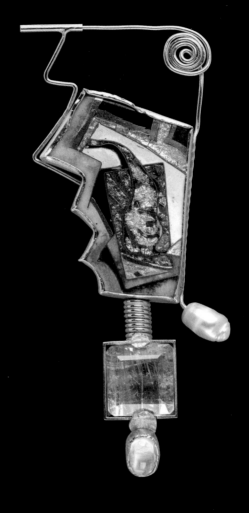

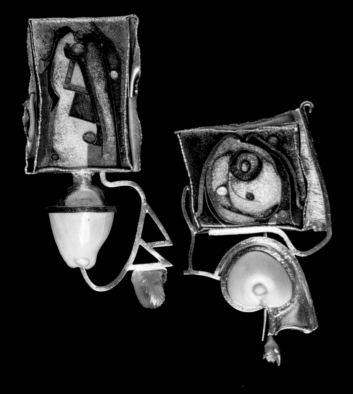

WHITE WITCH, 1984

Gold and silver cloisonné enamel on copper;
14k and 24k gold, sterling silver, rutilated quartz,
moonstone, pearl. 4 × 2 in.

NIGHT CREATURES BROOCHES, c. 1982

Gold cloisonné enamel on fine silver; 14k gold, shells,
pearl. 1 × 3 in. (left) and 1.5 × 1.5 in. (right)

LABYRINTH BROOCH, 1984

Gold and silver cloisonné enamel on copper;
fine silver and gold foil, 14k and 22k gold,
amethyst, tourmaline, pearl, snail shell.
3.75 × 1.25 in. The Enamel Arts Foundation,
Gift of the McLeod Family Foundation

THE SEDUCER (POETRY OF
THE PHYSICAL), c. 1985

Gold cloisonné enamel on fine silver; 14k gold,
fine silver. Length: 27 in.

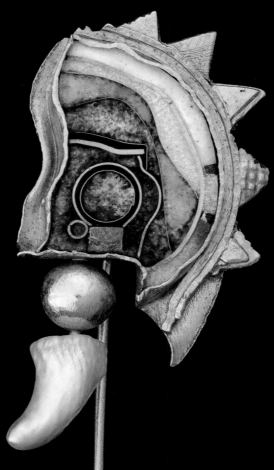

LA FLEUR DU MAL I, 1985

Gold cloisonné enamel on fine silver;
14k and 24k gold, pearl. 1.75 × 1 in.

LA FLEUR DU M

Gold cloisonné enamel
pearl. 3.5 × 1.5 in.

LA FLEUR DU MAL III, 1985

Cloisonné enamel on fine gold and fine silver;
14k gold, freshwater pearl. 2.75 × 1.25 in. Cooper

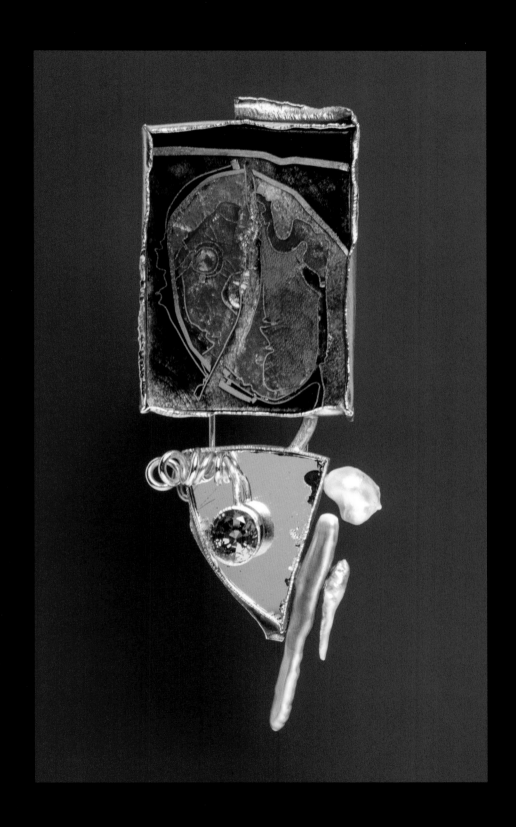

THE HEART OF THE SERPENT, 1986

Gold cloisonné enamel on fine silver and fine gold;
14k and 24k gold, sterling silver, peridot, pearl,
mirror. 5 × 1.75 in.

PENTIMENTI #11: THE COURTESAN, 1987

Gold cloisonné enamel on fine gold and fine silver;
14k and 24k gold, sterling silver, citrine, moonstone,
pearl, jade, glass, plastic. 5.5 × 2.75 in.

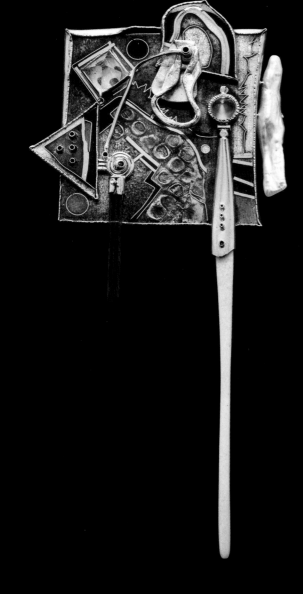

PENTIMENTI #8: HORROR VACUI, 1987

Gold cloisonné enamel on fine gold and fine silver;
14k and 24k gold, sterling silver, aluminum, tourmaline,
moonstone, quartz, pearl, ivory. 7 × 3 in. Hermitage
Museum, St. Petersburg, Russia, Gift of Joshua Harper
and Meredith Harper

PENTIMENTI #9: THE SECOND HORROR VACUI, 1987

Gold cloisonné enamel on fine silver; 14k and
24k gold, sterling silver, citrine, quartz, pearl,
pebble, shark tooth, 6 × 3 in.

PENTIMENTI #5: THE VEIL, 1987

Gold cloisonné enamel on fine gold and fine silver; 14k gold, sterling silver, pearl, plastic, mirror. 4 × 3.25 in.

JEALOUSY BROOCH FROM THE SEVEN DEADLY SINS, 1987

Gold cloisonné enamel on fine gold and fine silver; 18k, 22k, and 24k gold, pearl, glass. 6.75 × 1.5 in.

THE GRAND POTENTATE, c. 1987

Fine gold and silver on cloisonné enamel on fine silver; 14k, 18k, 22k, and 24k gold, plastic, blue topaz, steel, pearl

PENTIMENTI #12: THE EMPRESS, 1987

Gold cloisonné enamel on fine gold and fine silver;
14k and 24k gold, sterling silver, opals, moonstone,
jade, kyanite, ivory, plastic. 6.5 × 2.5 in. The Cleveland
Museum of Art, Gift of Riva Ross Harper (1993.173)

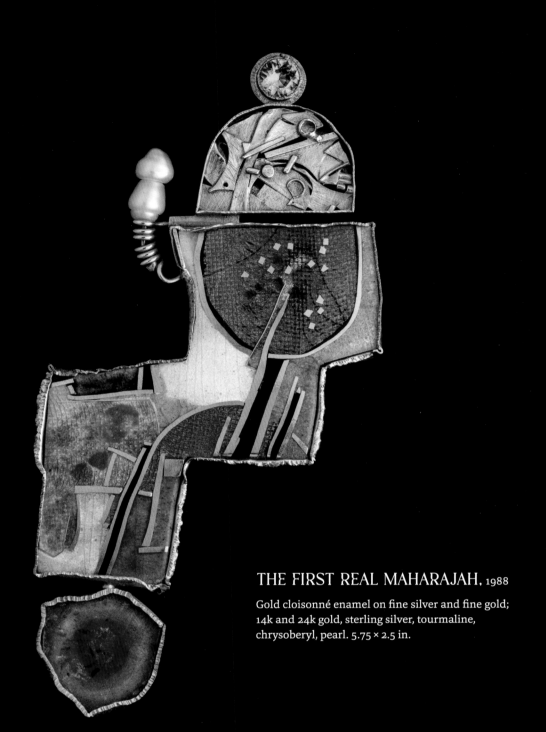

THE FIRST REAL MAHARAJAH, 1988

Gold cloisonné enamel on fine silver and fine gold;
14k and 24k gold, sterling silver, tourmaline,
chrysoberyl, pearl. 5.75 × 2.5 in.

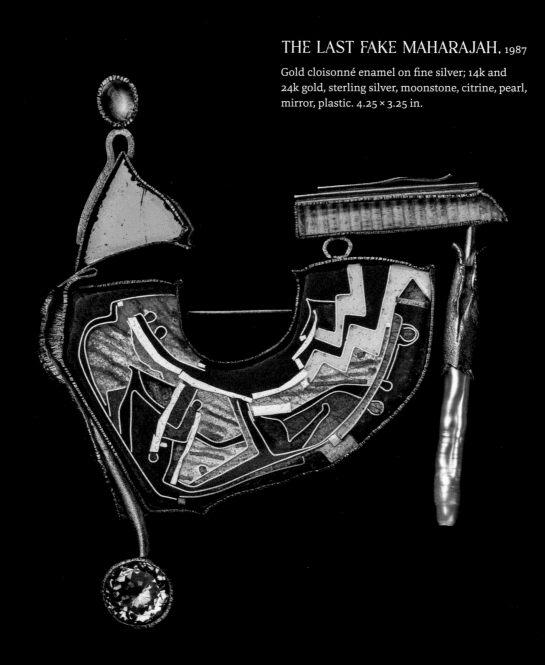

THE LAST FAKE MAHARAJAH, 1987

Gold cloisonné enamel on fine silver; 14k and
24k gold, sterling silver, moonstone, citrine, pearl,
mirror, plastic. 4.25 × 3.25 in.

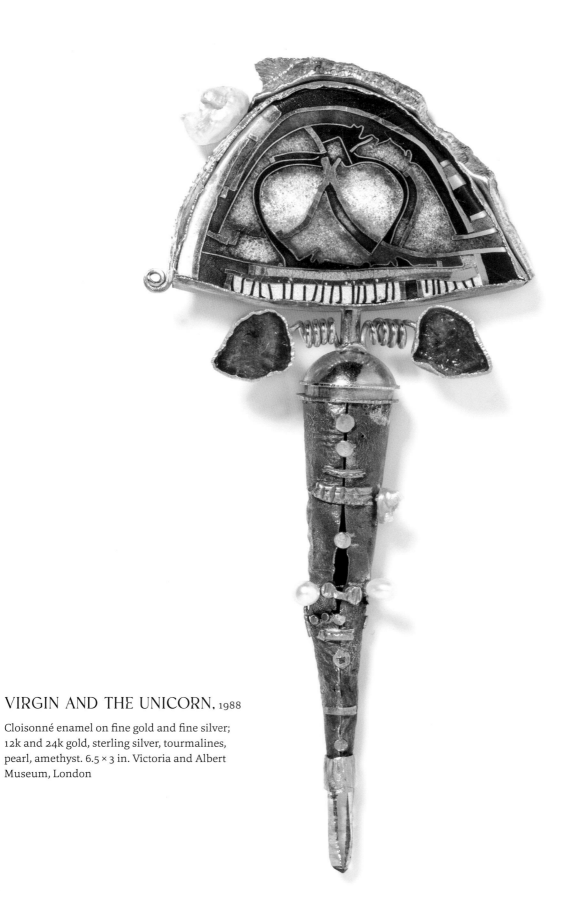

VIRGIN AND THE UNICORN, 1988

Cloisonné enamel on fine gold and fine silver;
12k and 24k gold, sterling silver, tourmalines,
pearl, amethyst. 6.5 × 3 in. Victoria and Albert
Museum, London

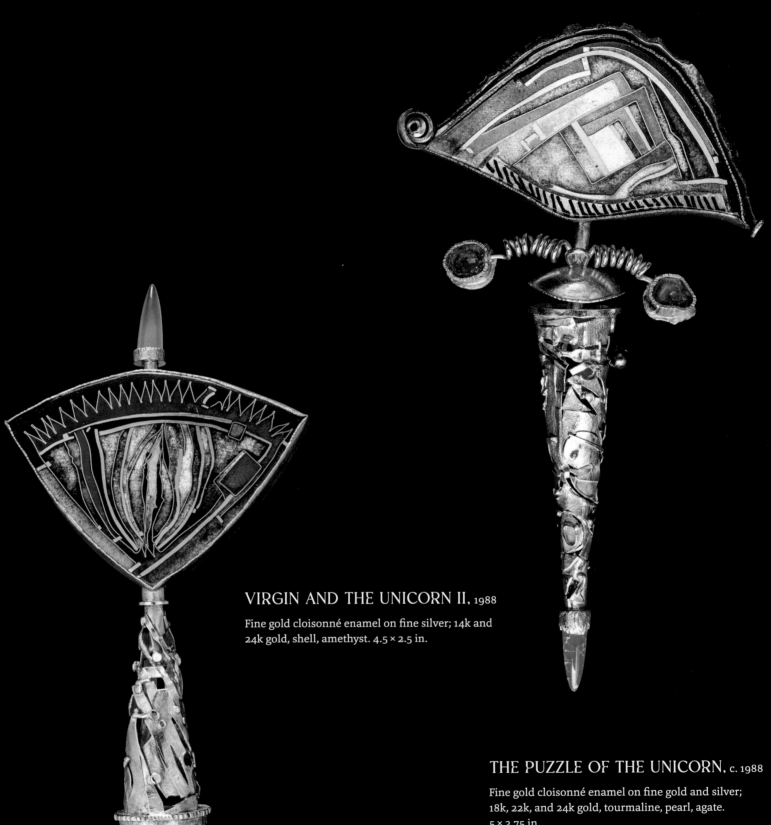

VIRGIN AND THE UNICORN II, 1988

Fine gold cloisonné enamel on fine silver; 14k and
24k gold, shell, amethyst. 4.5 × 2.5 in.

THE PUZZLE OF THE UNICORN, c. 1988

Fine gold cloisonné enamel on fine gold and silver;
18k, 22k, and 24k gold, tourmaline, pearl, agate.
5 × 2.75 in.

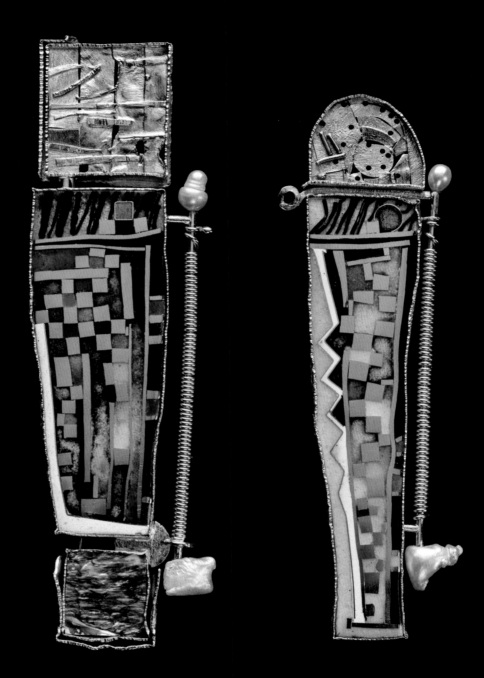

RAJA, 1989

Gold cloisonné enamel on fine gold and silver;
14k gold, fine silver, pearl, shell. 6 × 1.5 in.

RANI, 1989

Gold cloisonné enamel on fine gold and fine silver;
14k gold, fine silver, pearl. 5.25 × 1.5 in.

PENTIMENTI #4: GEMINI, 1987

Gold cloisonné enamel on fine gold and fine silver;
14k and 24k gold, sterling silver, opal, pebble,
glass, plastic, mirror. 4.75 × 3 in.

NEWS FROM ATLANTIS WILLIAM HARPER'S EXPANDED OEUVRE

JOHN PERREAULT

William Harper is now celebrated as the world's leading artist working in jewelry formats. His golden brooches are as much about empowerment as about adornment, revealing the inner meaning of the latter. They are flashes of rank but are also used to ward off encroachment and/or garner protection. Although his elaborate pins are informed by sub-Saharan tribal art, of which he is a serious collector, they do not look specifically African, but the use of found materials, the embrace of accumulation as a composition technique, and the suggestion of fetishistic content signal more than homage. His brooches—badges of fashion bravery, at the very least—can be seen as miniature, very portable paintings or sculptures that have as much impact as their larger brethren.

When does a brooch become a badge or a medal? When, as in the case of Harper's art, it takes both bravery and taste to pin it to your dress. In a world of diamonds, an outsized Harper pin is, to say the least, attention-getting. Women once jokingly referred to their make-up as war paint; I can imagine women referring to their Harper pins as shields, weapons, magnets.

Harper's use of cloisonné is revelatory; he eschews the traditional shiny surface, the better to reveal the layers of melted glass applied over reflective metal and to allow richer, more original colors. Not only has he written the book on cloisonné, he has accomplished the impossible: he has "de-Fabergéd" the technique. Furthermore his cloisonné "line" of demarcation between glass colors often moves out and carves the air. These spirals and other forms, along with various appendages, edge the brooch away from self-contained form toward assemblage, but assemblage that can be pinned to a lapel or a dress.

The news here, however, is that Harper's art has become even more complex. Many of the brooches (and so far two of the necklaces) now come with reliquary-like storage and display boxes, each heavily encrusted with materials: lead, nails, an insect or two, and sometimes jewels. They also come with and grow out of a narrative context.

Under the influence of 9/11—our artist saw the smoke clouds from his East Village roof and saw the uptown march of the dust-covered World Trade Center escapees—Harper began to create a "backstory" for his art that, if not an alternative world, is certainly an alternative ancient history. This "ancient history" explains the brooches and necklaces and the reliquaries Harper now uses to store and display his most recent brooches and necklaces. Stashing Harper jewelry in a drawer was always a waste. Now they can be displayed *and* protected when not being worn.

Here's the story: Harper transformed the WTC disaster and his own personal upheavals into the Atlantean apocalypse. Within this fiction, his jewelry (past, present, and future) is in the process of being "recovered" from around the world where it had been dispersed. The prequel has become the sequel.

Far be it for me to try to summarize the artist's dense narrative, written out here and there on collage works and in an actual book of drawings and texts. Until some lucky apprentice deciphers and types out all the details, we'll have to rely on the artist's more conversational version. Suffice to say, Harper's Atlantis existed around 20,000 BC and was ruled by a married pair of twins whom he calls Proteus and Psyche. From what I can understand (or project), their marriage may be a symbol of psychic wholeness, not unrelated to the Rosicrucian alchemical wedding or, let us say, the Masonic imagery in Mozart's *The Magic Flute.*

Then, as in Plato's Atlantis, something goes wrong and all hell breaks loose. The once powerful island culture is dispersed, explaining the similarities of art forms across the globe. It's the flood. It's the big bang theory of global culture.

Harper's brooches and necklaces and their boxes—and his non-wearable sculpture too—are meant to be examples of recovered Atlantean art. Influenced by cultures around the globe (including Appalachian folk forms in the US), Harper turns the influences inside out, making his jewelry the now newly acknowledged source of previously unexplained congruencies. The message or the hope, on one level, is that art can survive apocalypse. It did once before.

In the past, artists (and poets and composers) used culturally agreed-upon myths to inspire their work: personages in the form of gods and goddesses and narratives that embodied truths and revelations could be depicted and act as armatures for more personal emotions. We have no gods and goddesses now—at least outside of Hollywood. We have no Zeus, no Mercury, no Pluto; no stories of transformations and redemption. So it is not surprising that in a period of crisis and upheaval, some artists are beginning to make up their own myths.

Harper, of course, remains the master of enameling. But I would also say he may be the new master of the box. We have not seen anything as original as Harper's brooch and necklace reliquaries since the boxes of Joseph Cornell, and, best of all, they do not look like anything by that master (nor like the boxes of Lucas Samaras). By creating a world of his own, Harper is in a class of his own. Unlike other box art, Harper's reliquaries are beautiful *and* scary.

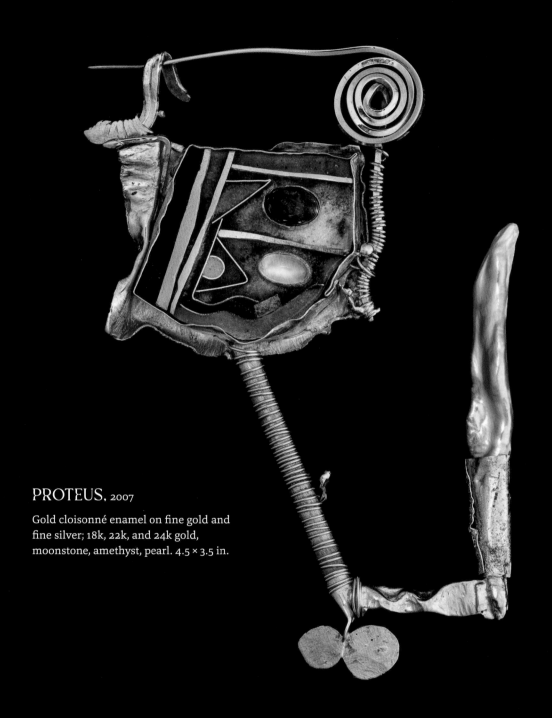

PROTEUS, 2007

Gold cloisonné enamel on fine gold and
fine silver; 18k, 22k, and 24k gold,
moonstone, amethyst, pearl. 4.5 × 3.5 in.

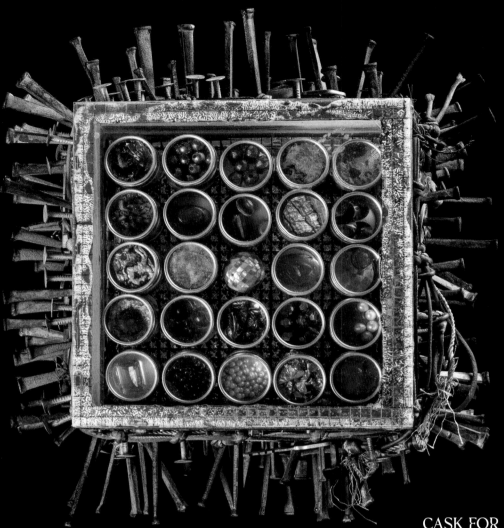

CASK FOR JOSEPH CORNELL
(cover), 2000

Mixed-media assemblage on snakeskin-covered
wooden box. 7 × 7 × 3.5 in.

JEWEL FOR JOSEPH, 2000

14k, 18k, 22k, and 24k gold, pearl. 4 × 3.5 in.

The jewelry, in any case, requires no justification. Harper's brooches which indeed have always looked spooky, transcultural, multicultural, and, most importantly, were made and continue to be made by a process of improvisation rather than by pre-set design, now come encased in ornate storage and display boxes.

The lavish use of gold in the jewelry signifies elegance but also sets up connections to cultic and ritualistic uses of gold in cultures from Egypt to Peru to Mexico and all the way to Byzantium and then on down to Rodeo Drive. The odd non-precious materials, however, link the works to folk magic: chicken legs from Appalachia, hair, teeth. The brooches are signs of power that, although gratifyingly elegant, sometimes look as if they might have been constructed by a hermit crab. The use of lead and iron on the outside of the reliquaries anchors the work in the real. Harper's art embodies the interstitial, a zone that allows the unification of painting and sculpture, sculpture and jewelry; male and female; gold and lead; the skillfully made and the found; abstract form and narrative. ◆

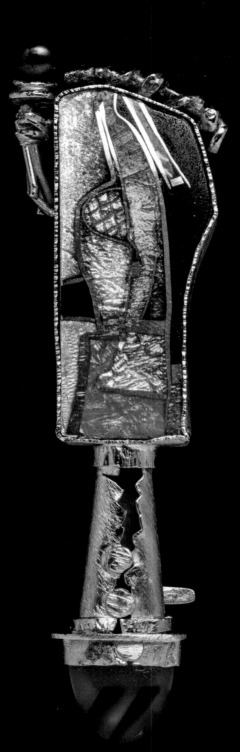

VARIATION #3 ON A THEME
BY J.J. AND E.M., 1993

Gold cloisonné enamel on fine silver and
fine gold; 14k and 24k gold, sterling silver,
agate, pearl. 4 × 1 in.

ON JASPER JOHNS

WILLIAM HARPER

I n 1980, I was fortunate to be able to be in Norway for the opening of my exhibition *Artist as Alchemist*, at the Museum in Trondheim. While in Oslo, I spent several hours at the Edvard Munch Museum, where I was particularly drawn to his self-portrait *Between the Clock and the Bed*. I knew that this painting was inspirational to Jasper Johns—a favorite of mine. In the Munch painting, the bed is covered with a quilt patterned with red and black cross-hatchings on a white background. This was motivational to Johns as a leitmotif for many works. I was very familiar with these and always found them to be rather mysterious as well as mesmerizing.

I have always believed that jewelry can be ABOUT something, have content, be more substantive than mere ornament. In other words, exist as Art, reflecting the zeitgeist of the period, and in doing so in such a way it is aesthetically and intellectually important as well as thought provoking: "Art about Art"—that is, Art that drew references from art of earlier periods. No artist did this as well as Jasper Johns.

Jasper's Variations consists of nine brooches and a major neckpiece. The initial group of six brooches is compositionally constructed with adjacent triangles, representing the three of us:

Munch, Johns, and myself, a presumptuous conceit, I must admit. These six brooches were titled *Variations on a Theme by J.J. and E.M.* Throughout his career Johns has borrowed bits of motifs from other paintings and then developed them into extremely personal visual manifestations of his own. Within his oeuvre exists an extensive series of paintings which are largely patterns of cross-hatchings. Although he was using this motif as early as 1972, a specific group stood out for me and served as reference points for my jewelry. This seems a fitting illustration of Art inspiring another form of Art. ◆

Jasper Johns, *Cicada*, 1979. Color screenprint on paper. 22×18 in. Whitney Museum of American Art, New York; Promised gift of Emily Fisher Landau, P.2010.147. © 2024 Jasper Johns/Licensed by VAGA at Artists Rights Society (ARS), NY

VARIATION #4 ON A THEME
BY J. J. AND E. M., 1993

Gold cloisonné enamel on fine silver and
fine gold; 14k and 24k gold, sterling silver,
agate, pearl. 4.5 × 2 in.

JASPER'S QUILTED SPOON, 1993

Gold cloisonné enamel on fine silver and fine gold;
14k and 24k gold, sterling silver, tourmaline, onyx.
5.25 × 1.5 in.

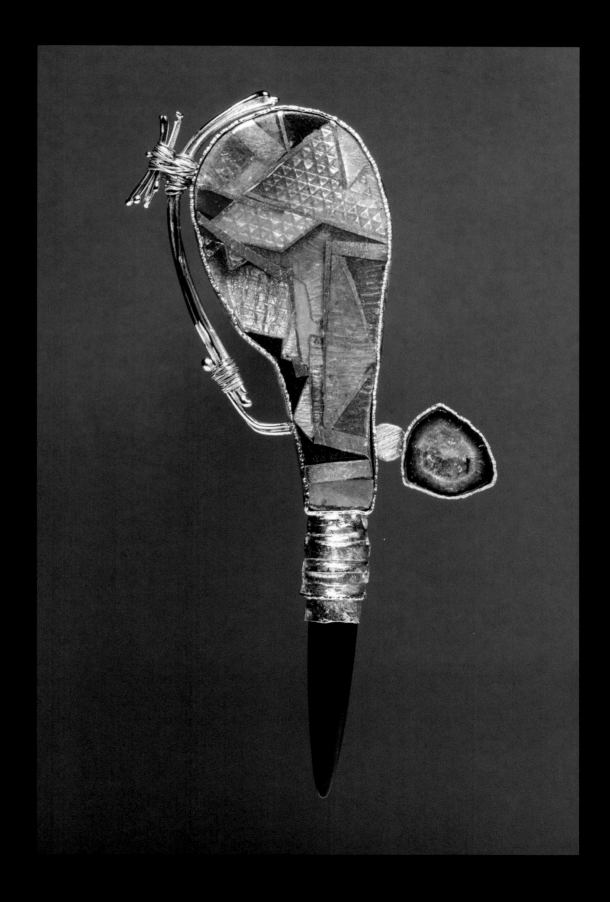

"

I HAVE ALWAYS BELIEVED
THAT JEWELRY CAN BE
ABOUT SOMETHING.

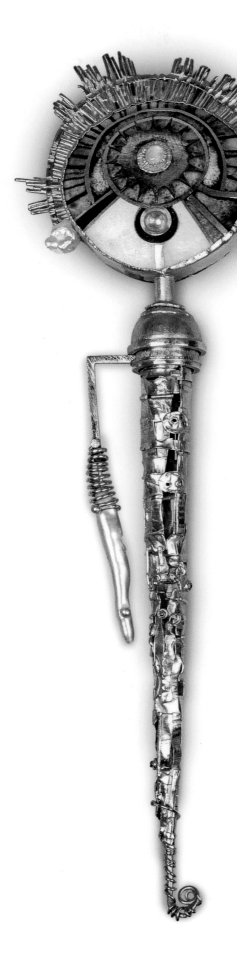

SELF-PORTRAIT OF THE ARTIST
AS AN ICON, 1990

Gold cloisonné enamel on fine silver; 24k and 14k gold,
sterling silver, steel, opal, pearl. 11.25 x 3.75 in. Detroit
Institute of Arts, Gift of Janis and William Wetsman
(2001.44)

SELF-PORTRAIT OF THE ARTIST WITH NOSE ENVY, 1990

Gold cloisonné enamel on fine silver; 14k and 24k gold, steel, pearl, plastic. 3.25 × 3.75 × 1.5 in.

GROTESQUE PORTRAIT OF THE ARTIST AS A MUTE ORACLE, 1990

Gold cloisonné enamel on fine silver; 14k and 24k gold, amethyst, plastic. 4.25 × 4.25 × 2.75 in. Spencer Museum of Art, The University of Kansas, Museum purchase: Friends of the Art Museum (1992.0038)

GROTESQUE SELF-PORTRAIT OF THE ARTIST AS AN ALCHEMIST, 1990

Gold cloisonné enamel on fine gold and fine silver; 14k and 24k gold, lead, blue topaz, quartz, rutilated quartz, plastic. 5 × 3.5 × 1.5 in.

GROTESQUE SELF-PORTRAIT OF THE ARTIST AS AN "ENFANT TERRIBLE", 1990

Gold cloisonné enamel on fine silver; 14k and 24k gold, aluminum, opal, moonstone, pearl. 3.25 × 3.75 × 2 in.

JANUARY FRAGMENT, 1991

Gold cloisonné enamel on fine gold and fine silver;
18k, 22k, and 24k gold, pearl, blue topaz. 4.5 × 3 in.

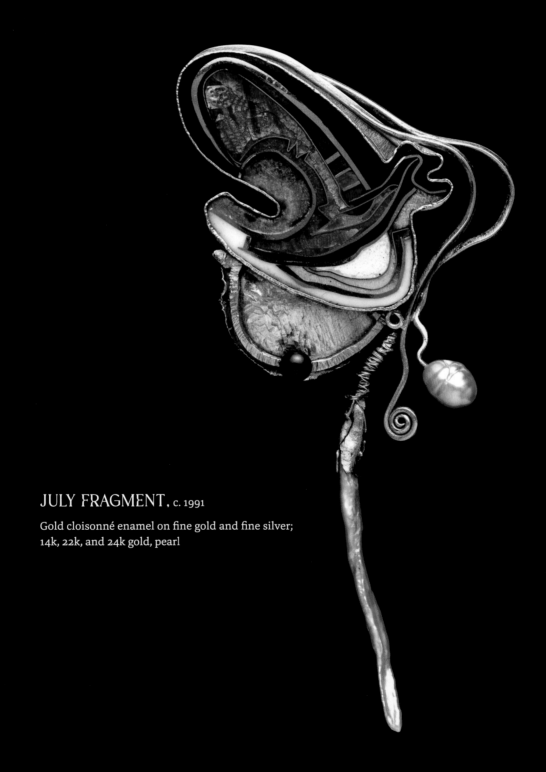

JULY FRAGMENT, c. 1991

Gold cloisonné enamel on fine gold and fine silver;
14k, 22k, and 24k gold, pearl

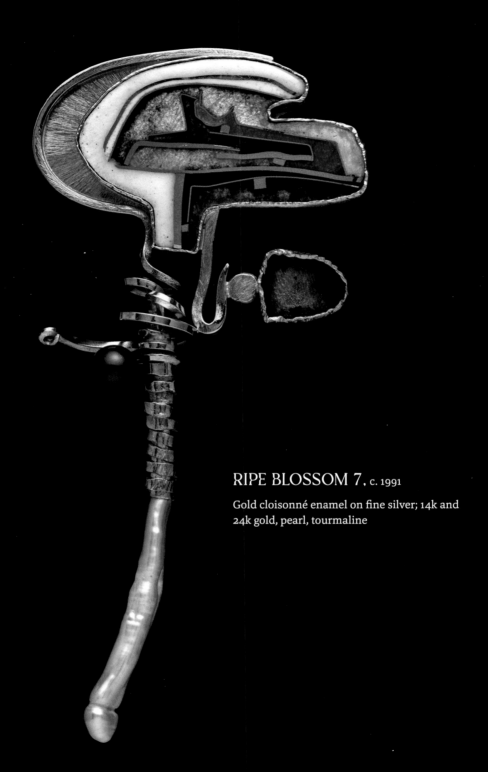

RIPE BLOSSOM 7, c. 1991

Gold cloisonné enamel on fine silver; 14k and
24k gold, pearl, tourmaline

RIPE BLOSSOM 11, c. 1991

Gold cloisonné enamel on fine gold and fine silver;
14k and 24k gold, pearl, tourmaline

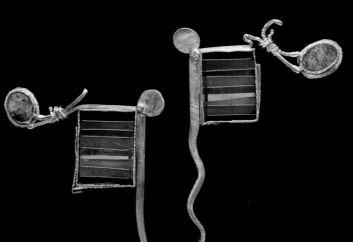

RIPE BLOSSOM EARRINGS, c. 1991

Gold cloisonné enamel on fine gold and fine silver;
14k and 22k gold, opals

FABERGÉ'S SEED #1, 1992

Gold cloisonné enamel on fine silver and fine gold;
14k and 24k gold, sterling silver, tourmaline, pearl.
4 × 2.25 in.

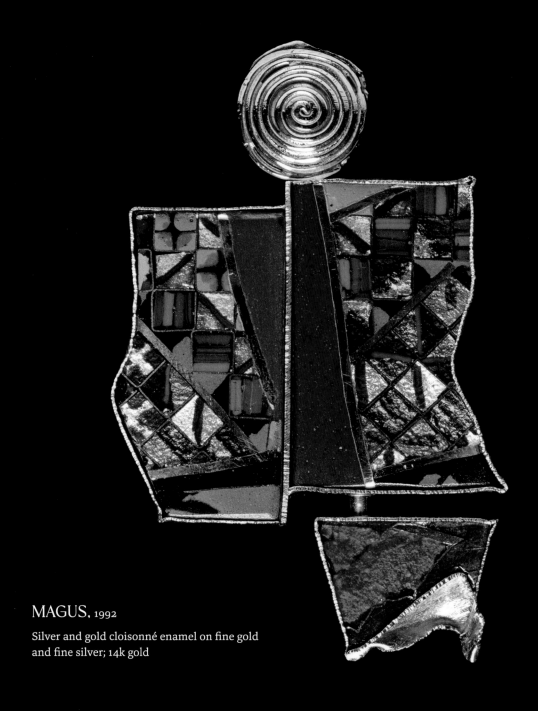

MAGUS, 1992

Silver and gold cloisonné enamel on fine gold
and fine silver; 14k gold

BABY BARBARIAN #1, 1998

Gold cloisonné enamel on fine gold and fine silver;
14k, 18k, 22k, and 24k gold, opal. 8 × 3.25 in.

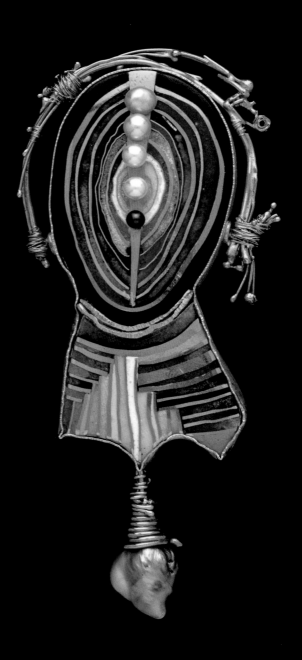

FABERGÉ'S SEED #9, 1993

Gold cloisonné enamel on fine silver and fine gold; 14k and 24k gold, sterling silver, pearl. 5.5 × 2.25 in.

FABERGÉ'S SEED #8, 1993

Gold cloisonné enamel on fine silver and fine gold; 14k and 24k gold, sterling silver, tourmaline, pearl. 6.5 × 2.25 in.

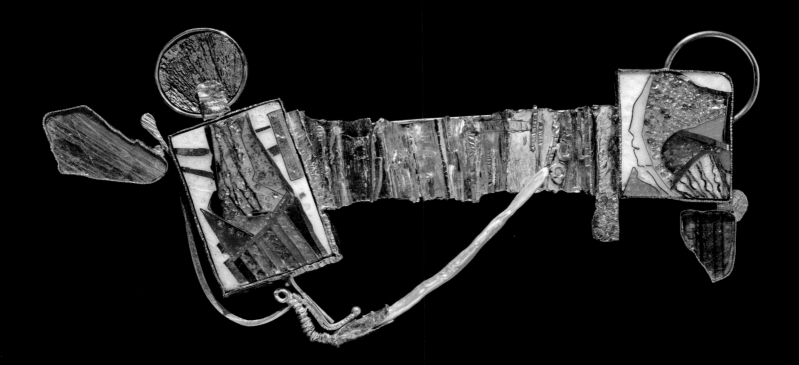

CY'S FIRST VARIATION
ON AN ANNUNCIATION, 1994

Gold cloisonné enamel on fine gold and fine silver;
18k, 22k, and 24k gold, pearl, tourmaline, hematite

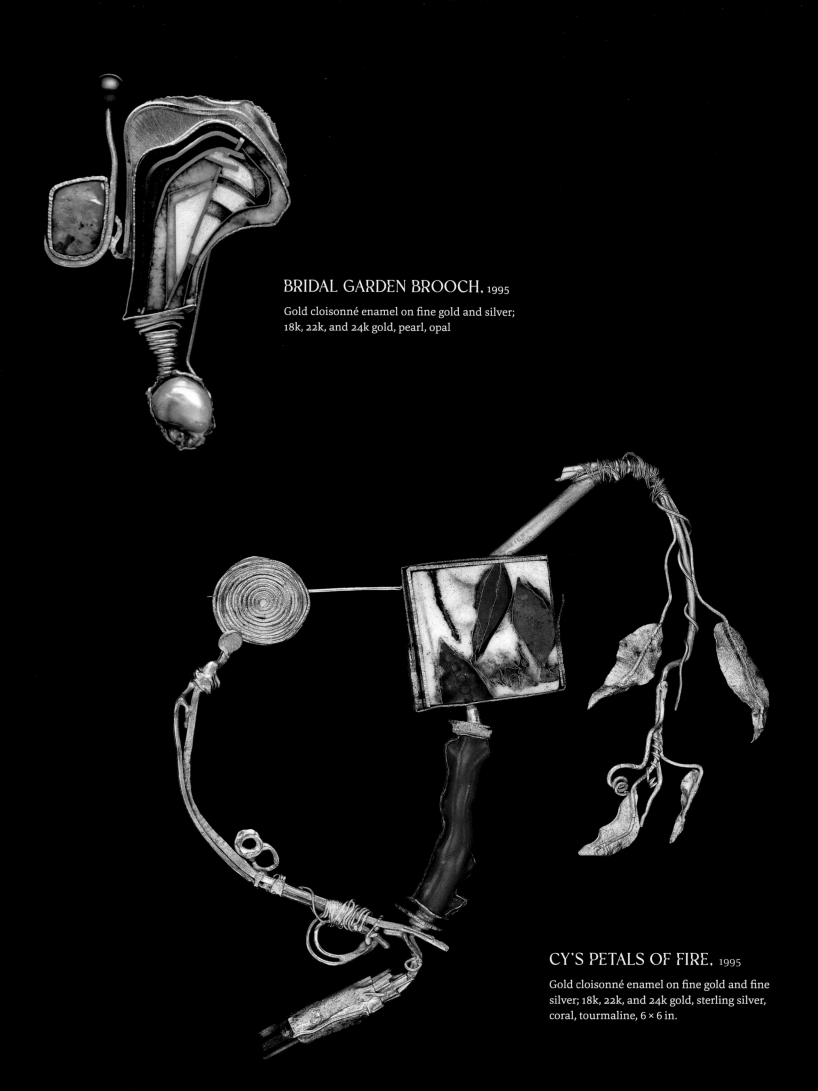

BRIDAL GARDEN BROOCH, 1995

Gold cloisonné enamel on fine gold and silver;
18k, 22k, and 24k gold, pearl, opal

CY'S PETALS OF FIRE, 1995

Gold cloisonné enamel on fine gold and fine
silver; 18k, 22k, and 24k gold, sterling silver,
coral, tourmaline, 6 × 6 in.

THE BEASTS AND DEMONS
OF A STRANGE AND SAVAGE
MIND: A GARDEN OF ART, 1995–96

Mixed media paint and collage on board; wood,
steel, silk, plastic. 240 × 36 × 32 in.

MUGHAL VARIATION II, 1998

Gold cloisonné enamel on fine silver; 18k, 22k,
and 24k gold, amethyst, glass

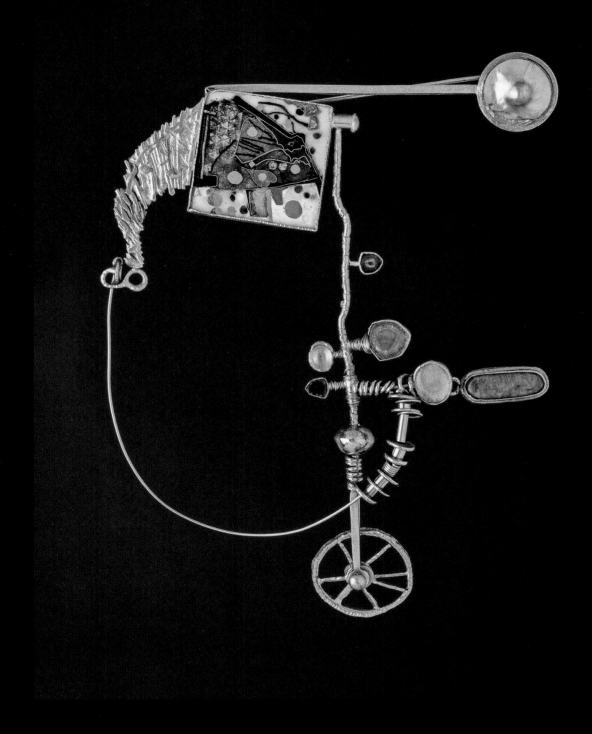

BARBARIAN'S BICYCLE II, 1998

Gold cloisonné enamel on fine gold and fine silver;
14k, 18k, 22k, and 24k gold, fine silver, tourmaline,
opal, moonstone, pearl

SELF-PORTRAIT OF THE ARTIST
AS A SPLIT PERSONALITY–GEMINI, 1992

Oil pastel, watercolor, charcoal, and gold glitter with graphite on
paper collage on paper. 46.5 × 45.5 in. Arkansas Museum of Fine
Arts Foundation Collection, Purchase, Tabriz Fund (1993.028)

SELF PORTRAIT OF THE ARTIST
WITH UNFULFILLED DREAMS, c. 2000

Gesso with water-based paint and oil stick on
heavy plywood with additional wooden pieces.
48 × 48 in.

THE JEWEL IS TOO BEAUTIFUL
NOT TO BE ART, 1999

18k, 22k, and 24k gold, pearl. 2 × 7 in.

HAND OF GOD, 2007

Gold cloisonné enamel on fine gold and fine silver;
sterling silver, 18k, 22k, and 24k gold. 2.5 × 1.5 in.

A PROFOUND AFFINITY
WILLIAM HARPER AND MEDIEVAL ART

CYNTHIA HAHN

I first saw Bill Harper's jewelry forty years ago, and I would have to say it took up definitive residence in my brain. Decades later, when I encountered a piece on display at the Renwick Gallery in DC, I instantly recognized it and got back in touch. Harper and I taught together briefly at Florida State University, and he occasionally came to my art history classes to explain the mysteries of the cloisonné technique.

For his part, Harper has always been a student of history, diving deep into the imagery and meanings of the past, interests that have persisted and grown in the *long durée* of his career and his personal collecting. In much of this, there is a profound affinity with things medieval.

As a historian of medieval art, my recent work centers on the interaction of the body with jewelry and an investigation of the processes it entails—artisanal, economic, and ritual. No matter how personal and "wildly imaginative" Harper's imagery is, at the same time it is also deeply situated in a centuries-long trajectory of powerful jewelry-making.

I would preface any further comments by saying that Harper's work is so beautiful, complete, and iconic that one readily enshrines it in a vitrine and contemplates it, isolated in bright light. It surely stands alone and sufficient. If, however, one wears such pieces—and indeed people do so, and with great pleasure—the jewelry reveals itself in a different way, lying upon the breast, over the heart. In this context of use, the pieces make a connection to the larger world—that is, through the body.

Practically speaking, the medieval brooch served as a pin, closing the cloak and protecting the chest. Harper often emphasizes the muscularity of that mechanism, strikingly recreating the tensions of, for example, a Celtic fibula.

Symbolically, the heart was a key locus for the positioning of jewels in the Middle Ages (and is to Harper as well). A thirteenth-century piece from Essex carries the inscription "I am the brooch to guard the breast."[1] As a centralized spot of precious material, the brooch or pendant could serve as a prayerful entrance into the body as well as a protective amulet. A pendant might contain a relic; a brooch might be inscribed with a prayer or a charm. Either was an artful working of precious as well as protective materials. The medieval artisan might include toadstone or unicorn horn, shell, rubies, sapphires, rock crystal, and/or gold. Harper, seemingly in contrast but in a similar spirit, might incorporate a broken bicycle reflector or the amuletic penis bone of a raccoon (powerful, at least for Southern gentlemen).

In Harper's *Self-Portrait as a Bocio*, the shining but mysteriously modulated central red gem has the depth and impression of the movement of a beating heart—the setting of the stone reads like a wound. It recalls images of the sacred heart of Jesus, a devotional motif from as early as the

---

1   John Cherry, ed., *Medieval Love Poetry* (Los Angeles: J. Paul Getty Museum, 2005), 9.

Brooch, c. 600 BCE, Celtic. Copper alloy. 6.5 × 2.75 in. The Metropolitan Museum of Art, Gift of J. Pierpont Morgan, 1917, 17.192.251a, b

BYZANTINE PIN. 1984

Gold and silver cloisonné enamel on copper;
14k and 24k gold, sterling silver, moonstones,
peridot. 4.25 × 2 in.

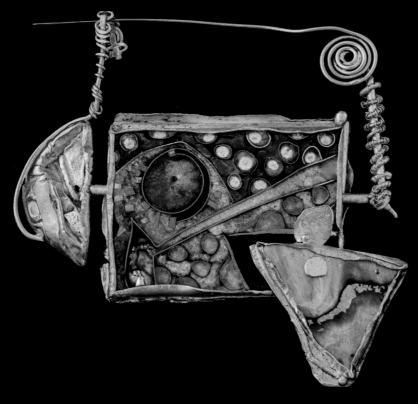

MOONTIDE. 2009

Gold cloisonné enamel on fine silver;
18k, 22k, and 24k gold, shell. 3.5 × 3.5 in.

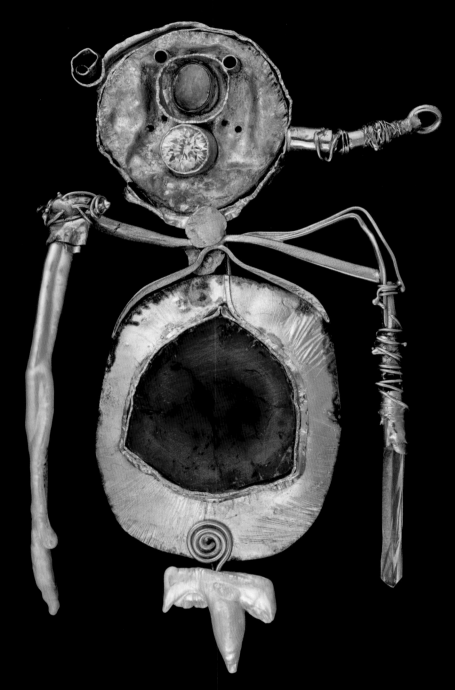

SELF-PORTRAIT OF THE ARTIST
AS A BOCIO, 1996

Aluminum, 14k, 18k, and 24k gold, tourmaline,
opal, pearl, aquamarine, glass. 5 × 3.25 in.

Mary Queen of Scots, Locket, late 16th century, Scottish and French. Gold, enamel, diamonds, ruby, onyx cameo. National Museum of Scotland

thirteenth century. The female mystic St. Gertrude of Helfta (1256–1302) experienced visions of the "blissful pulsations of the Sacred Heart." And a modern prayer attributed to her sums up her devotions: "I salute thee, O Sacred Heart of Jesus, living and vivifying source of eternal life, infinite treasure of the Divinity, ardent furnace of Divine love; Thou art the place of my repose and my refuge."[2] The nun desired that Christ's heart rule her, and also that her heart be joined to Christ's. She herself experienced in another vision the "wound of love" in which a ray of light "had a sharp point like and arrow and ... gently elicited my love."[3]

Jewelry is the perfect realization of this joining: the "sacred" heart bound to the heart of the wearer. This notion is not limited to Christian devotion, of course. It is used by lovers, and by politicians. A Renaissance pendant gem, perhaps given by Mary Queen of Scots to a supporter, features her portrait in cameo; it takes the center of a bejeweled and golden figurative heart, to be pinned over the wearer's real one—a gorgeous declaration of fidelity.

2   Gretchen Filz, "The History of the Sacred Heart of Jesus Devotion, Part One," *The Catholic Company Magazine* (June 13, 2012).

3   Madeleine Grace, "Images of the Heart as Seen in the Writings of Beatrice of Nazareth and Gertrude the Great," *Cistercian Studies Quarterly* 37, no. 3, 2002, 261–71, here 267.

Significantly, Harper adds to these medieval signs of fidelity and devotion a magical or amuletic charge. The Bocio, an African form that has also been made in the Caribbean, is one of his main references: it is the simulacrum of a body manufactured of wood, supplemented with rope and other bindings, padlocks, blood, and other libations—materials that both bind and disperse the power of the body.

Harper's brooch thus combines devotion to the beauty of the body with amuletic and protective features. The "face" is made of the aluminum end of a florescent light bulb. The eyes are mere apertures, but the nose is an opal and the mouth a piece of faceted pink glass. The arms are bound tightly with a "rope" of gold wire, and the genitals—a baroque pearl—are affixed with a tightly coiled spring of wire. Other mysterious protuberances are not to be explained.

All in all, the piece is much more than the sum of its parts. It produces that shock of dissonance that can be said to be the essence of magic—producing a collision of both materials and regimes of thought— a sudden and forced "encounter with the perceptual machinery we use to assemble reality."[4]

In these ways, consistently, Harper's jewelry and process of making shares its essence with the medieval. Both range across materials, taking what is beautiful, worthy, and useful and framing it with gold in often unexpected ways. Assemblage is not planned, but experiential. Harper's work arises from a deep knowledge of process, as does that of medieval artisans, but is always open to (divine?) inspiration. Often with the words of the title of a piece, Harper acknowledges his inspiration from the medieval past, citing icons, saints, pagans, reliquaries, barbarians.

All this is not to say that Harper's forms are directly referential to the medieval. Instead they are exquisitely suggestive of that era's concerns and references. For example, eyes, as in medieval examples, both lead into the body but may be blind. They look out, and also work to repel the alien gaze in the manner of the "evil eye."

Again, although not strictly medieval, a seventeenth-century Spanish saint referenced in one of Harper's series, similarly suggests issues of the body and its defense or openness. As above, like Gertrude's "wound of love" in which a ray of light "had a sharp point like and arrow," in these pieces a paradoxically aggressive baroque pearl penetrates the rectangle of the brooch. In the *Teresa* series, which expresses a more abstract concept of the body, there are intimations of softness: the red of the bicycle reflector in *Teresa I* suggests blood, while in *Teresa III*, under the gray arrow-like pearl, the pink striations of the shell at the bottom receives the blow. St. Teresa, we are told, "was filled with the radiance of his light." For her, this was the light of God; the beauty of Harper's pieces suggests that presence of the divine (as well as the carnal).

When worn, the very weight of these objects upon the chest makes the viewer continually aware of the power of Harper's pieces and their interaction with their own senses and self. But they do not remain small. As portals to the body they also open out into the world.

---

4   https://psyche.co/ideas/for-neuroscience-magic-opens-a-doorway-to-multiple-realities

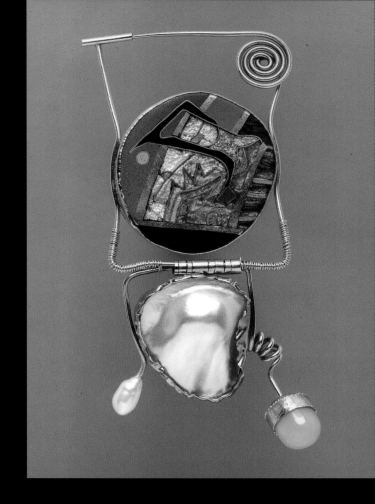

HARLEQUINADE, 1980

Gold cloisonné enamel on copper; 14k and 24k gold, sterling silver, bronze, pearl, moonstone. 4.25 × 2 in.

THE WIZARD, 1979

Gold cloisonné enamel on copper; 14k and 24k gold, sterling silver, shell, pearl. 2.75 × 1.5 in.

After *Mappa Mundi*, c. 1300, Hereford Cathedral, England

God Creating the Sun and the Moon, Guyart des Moulins,
Bible historiale, Vol. 1, c. 1420. British Library Archive

Tiny circles seem to reference *mappa mundi*, making a microcosm the
macrocosm, or even suggest the celestial spheres. Harper shares with the
medieval artist a diagrammatic, comprehensive impulse. Connected parts of
a brooch read like islands in a sea, linked by sailing routes as on a Portalan
map—the best chart for a navigator who is exploring the edges, the shores,
and ports of call. Harper also links the cosmic elements, the sun and the moon,
into a schematic juxtaposition. We might liken this dramatic opposition of
light and darkness to images of creation painted by medieval illuminators,
who used jewel-like colors instead of actual gems.

Above all, as in the pre-modern era, Harper's materials are defined not
by a gemologist's notion of the precious and rare but instead by the power

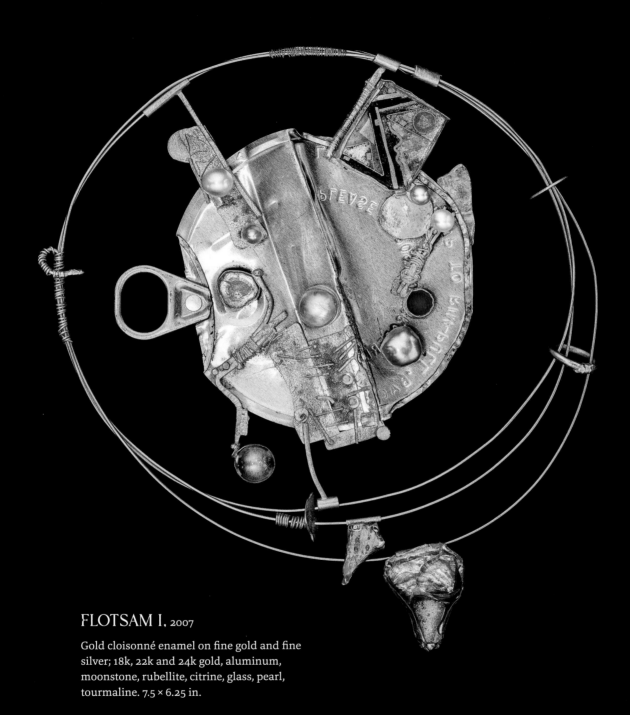

FLOTSAM I, 2007

Gold cloisonné enamel on fine gold and fine
silver; 18k, 22k and 24k gold, aluminum,
moonstone, rubellite, citrine, glass, pearl,
tourmaline. 7.5 × 6.25 in.

THE TEMPTATION OF ST. ANTHONY
AS THE ARTIST, 1986

Gold cloisonné enamel on fine silver; 14k gold, sterling
silver, aluminum, opal, quartz, pearl, tooth, shell, bone,
mirror. 7.5 × 2.25 in.

of individual stones. In the Middle Ages, certain gems even had names and were ascribed a particular force. The leading stone on the German Imperial Crown, for example, was dubbed the "Orphan," "a stone so peerless that it waives any mineralogical parentage."[5]

Baroque pearls and their suggestive shapes, so imaginatively used by Harper, are equally unique. Indeed, pearls in the Middle Ages were an apex embellishment, their mystical luminescence considered to be a perfect union of earth and heaven, created when dew was received into the open shells of the oysters. Bones and teeth could be ascribed tremendous elemental power as relics, and other stones such as coral were also considered amuletic.

Another clear medieval reference in Harper's work is his frequent use of saint imagery. A particular martyr favorite for the artist is the much-abused St. Sebastian, who was shot full of arrows. Harper's *Martyr I* might be a saint who has been beheaded but who defies his death by looking out at us through moody dark eyes set in his glowing enameled face. The golden balls that often adorn these figural works may signify the saints' victory over death and the mundane world.

For the visionary desert Father, St. Anthony—a hermit who lived in the desert and fought off demons and the temptation of lust—Harper elaborates in a different way. The distorted circle of an aluminum cap serves as a face. It is supplemented with gemstones, a bone, teeth, and a baroque pearl, which renders a halo in a quick slashed line. The saintly body is figured by a wondrous array of cloisonné color, a many-colored cloak laid over a corrugated *basse-taille* surface creating a glow and a pulse. The effect is reminiscent of Sutton Hoo pieces that used inset garnet pieces over worked gold surfaces.

St. Anthony is often depicted with a book. Perhaps we can understand the object that Harper's version of him "holds" as the holy scripture that defends him from demonic attacks. However, Harper has made the object out of a mirror and thereby incorporates us, the viewers, into the image—as threatening demons? Alternately we may be repulsed, pushed away, in a similar fashion to the working of the evil eye.

Anthony was associated in the Middle Ages with one of the most common amulets—the Anthony Tau sign (see his staff and pin in the book of hours). These would have been worn over the chest; similar to Harper's dangling pendant objects, such an object would have had two attached pearls on the wires, and a suspended bell at the bottom.[6] The images on the Tau are the Trinity and the Virgin, but the capsule may also have carried a herbal specific against "St. Anthony's fire" (a wonderful association to the enamel of this piece).

Harper titles another of his series with an epithet that vividly recalls the medieval—the *Barbarians*. The title is fitting as a reference to the "barbarian" tribes who were not given to monumental arts such as sculpture or architecture but instead made jewelry their premier art form. Metalworkers such as Wayland (in *Beowulf*) were legendary, and such artists held a high

Hours of Henry VIII, fol. 183v., c. 1500, Tours, France. The Morgan Library & Museum, Gift of the Heineman Foundation, 1977 (MS H.8)

---

5   Brigitte Buettner, *The Mineral and the Visual: Precious Stones in Medieval Secular Culture* (University Park: Penn State University Press, 2022), 32.
6   The Metropolitan Museum Collection: https://www.metmuseum.org/art/collection/search/469929

societal position. In Burgundian law, the murder of an enslaved goldsmith elicited a fine (*wergild*) equal to that of an upper-class free man. Throughout the pre-modern world, including in Asia and Africa, smiths were "recognized as masters of an extremely esoteric and supernaturally potent craft by which they completed the creative work of the gods."[7] Indeed Joseph, the foster father of Christ, is sometimes said to have been a metallurgist.

In the world of the "barbarian" migrations, between the ancient and the later medieval civilizations, brooches and clasps and belt buckles were hugely important signifiers of power and prestige. A leader might wear a magnificent pair of eagles in gold and garnet, their hooked raptor's beaks symbolizing martial power, their enlarged eyes referring to the sharpness of their vision, their *pendulia* (chains hanging with gems) signifying imperial pretentions. Such imagery could be broken down into semiotic bits and still carry its charge. In Harper's brooch, the bloody red enamel and the purple-red stones evoke garnets but are not garnets. The hooked beak might equally be seen as the end of an axe, the spots once again as watchful eyes. Rather than *pendulia*, however, we have horizontally jutting points that are simultaneously aggressive and precious.

Harper's reliquaries, which one might think would be his most obviously medieval objects, differ from Christian precedents—indeed he often calls them tombs or casks. In these, Harper works a reversal: most medieval reliquaries enclose and hide precious (if sometimes disgusting) body parts in a container of gold and gems. In Hunter's containers, the gold and gems are on the interior, nestled in a special, translucent, glowing plastic bed, while the exterior is studded with organic bits—bugs, here or there, a butterfly—and detritus of various sorts, including nails, cheap base-metal ornaments, and plastic beads. Sometimes chains hang from the surface in a purposefully sloppy and exuberant array.

In both "cases," the reliquary or these caskets, what lies within calls for our attention, but in Harper's tombs we are invited to open the box. Inside one such container is *Psyche's Brooch*, full of energy, juxtaposed to a textured gold surface studded with pearls. Pink, gray, black, and irregular, the pearls suggest a natural harvest, reflecting nature's bounty. But the revelation of natural diversity does not end there. Four varying golds (each with a different karat valuation) are incorporated into the piece, recalling passages in Theophilus Prespyter's *De Diversis artibus* (a twelfth-century technical compendium), which, following the Roman historian Pliny the Elder (*Natural History*, Book 33.23), praises the different colors and qualities of gold from different sources. A medieval viewer would have been able to identify the sources of these various materials (pearls from the East, red gold from Arabia) and appreciated the *varietas*, an important quality in medieval aesthetics.

In another example, *Tomb Reliquary*, we find a snakeskin and a snake's skull on the outside, a rather forbidding exterior despite other exuberant decoration. Inside in its plastic nest lies one of Harper's exquisite necklaces. Composed of cloisonné beads, ring and "coin" pendants, and a tiny ampulla-like glass bead reminiscent of an early Christian eulogia or pilgrim's blessing, it could almost be early medieval. A gold hand recalls an amulet against the

---

7   Stefan Esders, *Wergild, Compensation, and Penance* (Boston: Brill, 2021), pp. 5–6.

HAHN • A PROFOUND AFFINITY

THIRD BARBARIAN'S JEWEL, 1997

Gold polychrome cloisonné enamel on fine gold
and fine silver; 14k, 18k, 22k, and 24k gold,
tourmalines, opal, pearl. 3 × 3.25 in.

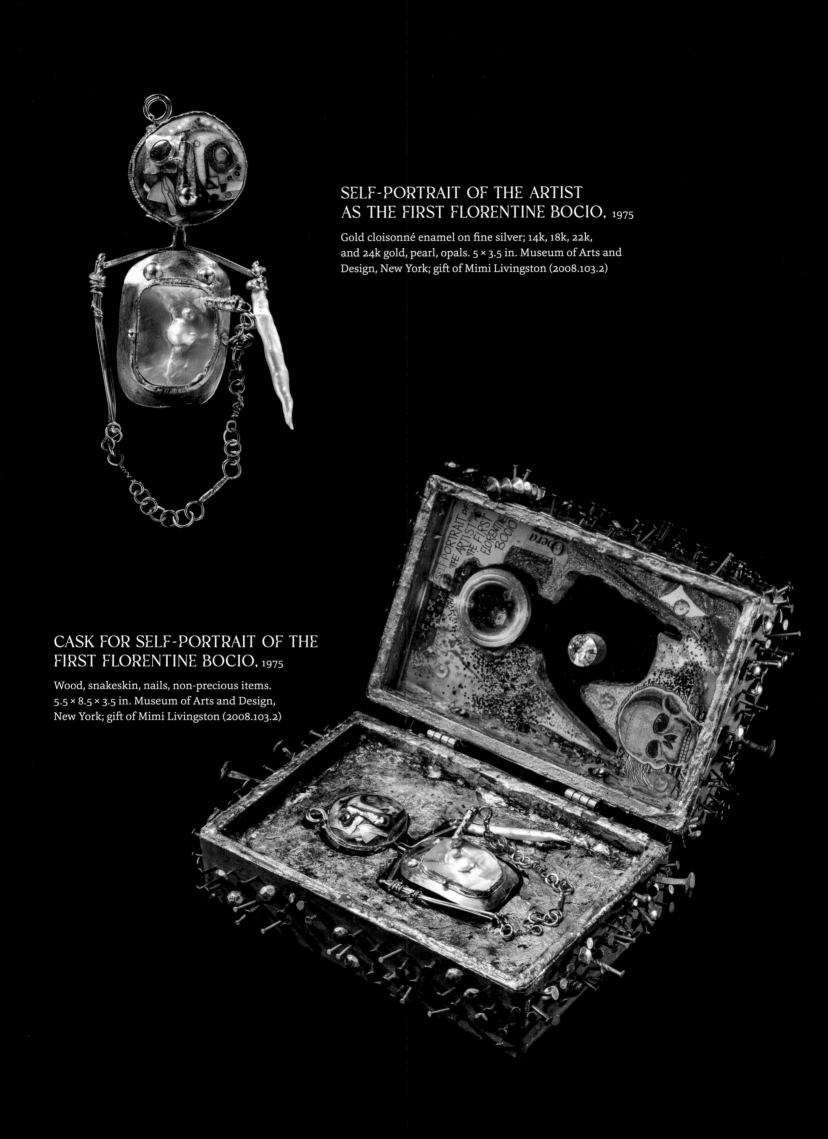

SELF-PORTRAIT OF THE ARTIST AS THE FIRST FLORENTINE BOCIO, 1975

Gold cloisonné enamel on fine silver; 14k, 18k, 22k, and 24k gold, pearl, opals. 5 × 3.5 in. Museum of Arts and Design, New York; gift of Mimi Livingston (2008.103.2)

CASK FOR SELF-PORTRAIT OF THE FIRST FLORENTINE BOCIO, 1975

Wood, snakeskin, nails, non-precious items. 5.5 × 8.5 × 3.5 in. Museum of Arts and Design, New York; gift of Mimi Livingston (2008.103.2)

CZARINA'S NECKLACE, 1992.

Gold cloisonné enamel on fine gold and fine silver;
18k, 22k, and 24k gold, mirror, tooth, pearl

Beaded Necklace, 500–600, Frankish. Glass, amber, shell, calcite. Length of string 15 in. The Metropolitan Museum of Art, Gift of J. Pierpont Morgan, 1917, 17.193.299

evil eye—here the Islamic "Hand of Fatima"—which would again make this object multi-faith and global in reference. The whole ensemble is quite literally a charm necklace.

Harper's work is indeed possessed of the variety and the exoticism of medieval art, in which the humble and the spectacular were often combined. The ceramic beads on a necklace now in The Metropolitan Museum of Art, recovered from a Merovingian grave, reflect a veritable global world of trade and wealth. Some of the beads would have been antiques already when the necklace was assembled, perhaps cherished for generations in families before being buried with a particularly powerful woman. Similarly, Harper's necklaces serve as markers of prestige and taste for those who own them and perhaps will become cherished heirlooms in their turn.

I end with just one of Harper's paintings, or rather a book of them, although many others could be discussed for their medieval affinities. It too is enclosed in a kind of reliquary (as important and sacred Irish books were, in what are called *cumdachs*), but this one is an abecedary of saints. The paintings unfold with hinges, revealing icons for each letter of the alphabet. In two volumes, the set of images are collages, reflecting the wonders and abilities of the saints, including Catherine and Lawrence, Bernadette and Cassian, Januarius and Felix. Harper's particular interest in each is revealed with an inscription along with notes of name, date, and place.

I am struck above all, in this series, by the image of St. Eligius, the patron saint of goldsmiths—and a powerful and miraculous worker of metals in his ownright. When asked by the Merovingian king, the saint took the gold allotted for a throne and made two! And of course, he was renowned for his bejeweled reliquaries. A portion of a large gold and gem-encrusted cross survives. Harper's image of Eligius may be yet another allegorical self-portrait, showing the golden face of the saint, richly textured in a gold-worked surface (although this is paint). The inscription concerning Eligius reads: "A master goldsmith … his art anticipates by 1300 years that of William Harper, the Craftsman." ◆

PAGES OF SAINTS VOL. I (detail), 1996–98

Mixed-media collage on board with wood, silk, plexiglass, steel, and mixed-media assemblage. 16 hinged panels, each 16 × 10.5 in., overall length: 170 in.

GOLDEN BIRTHDAY BEADS
FOR MARTHA, 2014

Gold cloisonné enamel on fine gold and
fine silver; 18k, 22k, and 24k gold. 8 × 8 in.

PAGES OF SAINTS VOL. II, 1996–98

Mixed-media collage on board with wood, silk,
plexiglass, steel, and mixed-media assemblage.
16 hinged panels, each 16 × 10.5 in., overall
length: 170 in.

SAINT
VERONICA...
WIPED AWAY
THE SWEAT
OF JESUS
WITH HER
VEIL AS
HE CARRIED
THE CROSS
HIS FACE
IMAGE
REMAIN
ON
THE
CLOTH

SCHÉHÉRAZADE, 1995

Gold cloisonné enamel on fine silver and fine gold;
14k and 24k gold, sterling silver, freshwater pearl, green
tourmaline, amethyst, glass. 4.5 ×5 in. Museum of Arts
and Design, New York, Gift of Barbara Tober, 2013

AN ORGY OF TONES
WILLIAM HARPER & THE BALLETS RUSSES

MARY E. DAVIS

"**A**stonish me!" This was Sergei Diaghilev's response to Jean Cocteau when the young poet asked the formidable impresario what he could do to secure a place in the artistic sphere of the Ballets Russes. The Russian troupe, an itinerant group established in Moscow and St. Petersburg under Diaghilev's aegis, earned its fame in Paris from the moment of its arrival in the French capital in 1909, wowing chic audiences for the two decades that followed with fresh interpretations of repertory standards and shockingly scandalous new ballets. Diaghilev's challenge, Cocteau claimed, moved him "to die and become born again."[1] Alas, while he would eventually astonish Diaghilev and the wider world, his first effort for the Ballets Russes, the 1912 one-act ballet *Le Dieu bleu*, was not the hoped-for ticket to success. Described unsparingly by the critic for the *Mercure de France* as "a failure in every sense of the word," it nonetheless stands among the early orientalizing works that vaulted the troupe to fame, thus occupying an important position in the Ballets Russes repertoire.[2]

---

1   Lynn Garafola, *Diaghilev's Ballets Russes* (New York: Oxford, 1989), 98.
2   Valery Svetlov, *Mercure de France*, 15 May 1912, quoted in Kevin Kopelson, *The Queer Afterlife of Vaslav Nijinsky* (Stanford: Stanford University Press, 1997), 151.

Michel Fokine and Vera Fokina as the Golden Slave
and Zobeïde in the 1910 Ballets Russes production
Schéhérazade

Léon Bakst, *Le Dieu bleu* set design, 1912

Created in the mold of the smash hit *Schéhérazade*, which had its pre-
miere two years earlier, *Le Dieu bleu* featured outré costumes and set designs
by Léon Bakst, star turns by dancer Vaslav Nijinsky, and a fantastical exotic
setting—"a warm night in fabulous India," as Cocteau put it, invoking Hindu
tradition.[3] The story—a tale of frustrated love and ultimate redemption
delivered by Krishna, the blue god of the title, in his guise as the god of
love—was utterly overshadowed by the production's arresting and densely
layered visual elements. Bakst's vividly colored set, depicting an ancient
temple in a strident Fauvist palette of green, blue, and orange, was described
by one contemporary critic as an "orgy of tones," and Nijinsky, in the title role,
wore a heavily decorated tunic and bejeweled tiara over his blue-painted
body.[4] Extravagant and dramatic, the production was a quintessential
expression of artistic maximalism.

Cocteau, Bakst, and their blue god provide a point of entry into William
Harper's *Diaghilev* series, suggesting not only a shared attraction to the

3   Jean Cocteau, "Argument du Dieu Bleu," *Comoedia illustré: Programme officiel des Ballets russes:
     Théâtre du Châtelet* (Paris, 1912), 223.
4   Louis Vauxcelles, in *Comoedia illustré*.
5   William Harper, "Diaghilev Series," in *William Harper: The Beautiful & the Grotesque* (Cleveland:
     Cleveland Institute of Art, 2019), 30.
6   Ibid.

deep pool of the exotic and erotic but a kinship rooted in the very notion of astonishment. Harper has written about his passion for ballet and his special enthusiasm for the Ballets Russes, whose "scenic and costume designs, made quite often by avant-garde artists and designers pushing the bounds of emotionally decorative design, have seldom been surpassed."[5] He has cited *Schéhérazade* as a work he knew from childhood that still holds "great sway" for him, and has singled out "the great Léon Bakst" as an artistic inspiration. While Harper cites no specific artists or works as direct influences for the *Diaghilev* series, the sensibility of maximalism so important to Bakst and so embedded in *Schéhérazade* shadows his work in palpable and persuasive ways.

Harper's stated "conceit" for the *Diaghilev* series, which includes fourteen exquisite brooches created between 2014 and 2017, is to envision his characters liberated from the stage and their balletic roles, instead roaming the city unfettered. He imagines the dancers, painters, and choreographers of the Ballets Russes cavorting until the break of dawn. The impresario, he explains, "summons his troops, spectacularly attired in provocative fancy-dress costumes, assuming new personalities to celebrate in an after-hours Parisian cabaret with all the decadence such a place might invite. These guests were outrageous denizens of the night—the club kids of their era."[6] Harper's scenario is not spun purely from fantasy; Diaghilev's artists and collaborators *were* celebrities in their time, especially during the troupe's pre-World War I heyday. Regulars in the city's cafés and cabarets, they were coveted invitees at the fancy-dress parties hosted by the *gratin* of Paris society, many of whom were key patrons of the troupe. Among these was couturier Paul Poiret; at his infamous *Schéhérazade*-inspired "One Thousand and Second Night" fête in 1911, to cite one example, harem-style attire was *de rigeur*. Poiret ruled as the Sultan, holding his wife, Denise, captive in a golden

Poiret Garden Party, Victoria and Albert Museum, London

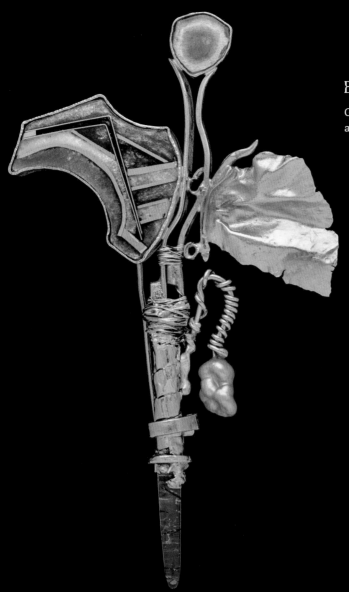

BLUEBIRD, 1995

Gold cloisonné enamel on fine silver; 18k, 22k, and 24k gold, aquamarine, pearl, tourmaline

THE FIREBIRD, 1995

Gold cloisonné enamel on fine gold and fine silver; 18k gold, pearl. 4.5 × 3.5 in.

cage for much of the evening. The swank Poiret garden was the nightclub of its day, and Diaghilev's artists were the louche event's A-list guests.

In a similar vein, the characters in Harper's *Diaghilev* series—he describes them as "ghosts" summoned "for inspiration"—are animated by imaginings of the East. As is Harper's convention, he has evocatively named each jewelry piece, folding untold mysteries into his brief titles, from the *Agnostic Caliph* and the *Flamboyant Sultana* to the *Hypocritical Tibetan Octoroon* and the *Toothless Courtesan*. Each of these quirky character sketches holds entwined stories and intrigues. Perfumes of oddity, eccentricity, and exoticism are pervasive: Afghan, Egyptian, Tibetan, Siberian; Aesthete, Dandy, Eunuch, Contessa, Courtesan, Czarina, Sultana; Albino, Octoroon. These are Harper's nocturnal creatures. By comparison, their historical Ballets Russes counterparts seem banal—a Golden Slave, a blue god, Cléopâtre. The dancers, of course, sprung to life on stage in compositions that included music and choreography as well as design. Harper's challenge is, in a sense, still higher: he animates his characters by insinuating sound, personality, and motion into essentially static artwork.

Decades before the *Diaghilev* series, Harper established a vocabulary and a practice perfectly suited to this task, a method one critic has described simply as "alchemy."[7] Color was from the start one of his prime tools; he has described his experiments with "color combinations and layering," referencing the hundreds of enamel powders he uses in his work.[8] By the 1970s, he had integrated the use of gold wire in his compositions to suggest movement and the tensions surrounding it, fashioning spring-like coils and stiff extensions to create a tension between stasis and activity in his designs. He used dangling bits of treasured collected objects—jewels, bones, shards of antique glass—to reinforce the sense of motion, sometimes with the felicitous effect of adding sound to the work. Harper has stated that his larger-scale ambition was to encompass an entire world into an intimate format, and this became one of his central preoccupations by the 1980s. This was his idiosyncratic conception of "preciousness," which he has described as the creation "of an object intimate in size, rich in detail, overwhelming in its delicate relationships of scale and proportion." He was, he has said, interested in the "invention of introspective objects—contemplative microcosms."[9]

A ballet, in its own way, is also a "contemplative microcosm," and this was particularly true of Bakst's orientalizing pageants, which conjured remote and mysterious worlds, both in their specific detail and in overall ambience. When considered through the lens of "preciousness," Bakst's art, which has been described by one critic as having been built on the "magnificence of color, tactility of form, and the ability to both vest and expose the primordial energy of the human body," resonates with Harper's work in striking and surprising ways.[10] Some more obvious connections between the two artists may be drawn in broad strokes: the saturated and luminous orange, green, yellow, and blue shades that inform Bakst's designs are also

7   Thomas A. Manhart, "William Harper: Artist as Alchemist," in *William Harper: Artist as Alchemist*, exh. cat., Orlando Museum of Art, 1989, 8.
8   Harper, quoted in ibid., 12.
9   Harper, quoted in *William Harper: The Beautiful & the Grotesque*, 19.
10   John Bowlt, "Léon Bakst, Natalia Goncharova, and Pablo Picasso," in Jane Pritchard, ed., *Diaghilev and the Golden Age of the Ballets Russes, 1909–1929* (London: V&A Publishing, 2010), 104.

Léon Bakst, Ballet Russes de Serge Diaghilev, M. Landoff, Marie Muelle, Costume for the Blue God, c. 1912. National Gallery of Australia, Kamberri/Canberra, purchased 1987

Léon Bakst, Costume design for the lead in *Le Dieu bleu*, 1911

foregrounded in Harper's *Diaghilev* series; both artists employ techniques of careful and plentiful layering and adornment; both incorporate abstract, geometrical design as an expressive formal language; both use decorative additions to suggest and exaggerate movement; both are drawn to excess and embellishment; both engage and celebrate sensuality and frank sexual display. One comparison of many that could be made, between Bakst's costume for the blue god and Harper's brooch titled *The Brothel's Favorite* (2016), simultaneously illuminates and complicates the understanding of possible links between these artists.

To fully comprehend Bakst's costume, it is helpful to study both iterations of its design: his color sketch for the costume, and the realized garment, which was created in the studio of one of the most famous costumiers of the day, Marcelle Muelle. The gap between the sketch and the completed costume is significant: Bakst's fanciful design was fabricated to ensure not only wearability and fit but also the sturdiness and pliancy required to meet the performance conditions and the physical requirements of the choreography. Bakst's sketch, depicting the blue god in a characteristically dynamic pose, conveys the artist's opulent intentions for his costume, which consists of a heavily jeweled tunic worn over embellished tights. A dizzying array of patterns populate the design—triangles, diamonds, half-circles, teardrops, and lotus flowers—and the sketch suggests that these be realized not simply in different-colored fabrics but through the addition of jewels and embroideries. Considerable detail and embellishment did indeed accrete to the costume by the time it was finished for Nijinsky; it was rendered in hand-painted silk and satin, decorated with velvet ribbon, braid, and embroidery thread and topped off with emerald-green sequins. As historian Sarah Woodcock has noted, like many of the costumes Bakst designed, it exhibits

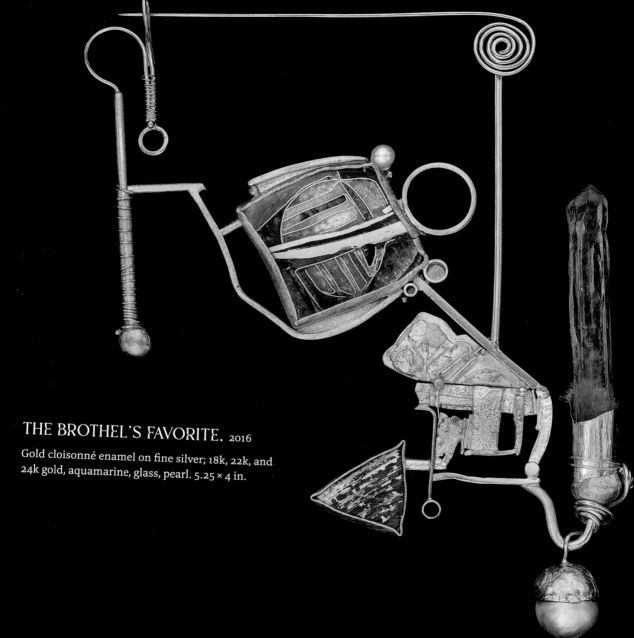

THE BROTHEL'S FAVORITE, 2016

Gold cloisonné enamel on fine silver; 18k, 22k, and 24k gold, aquamarine, glass, pearl. 5.25 × 4 in.

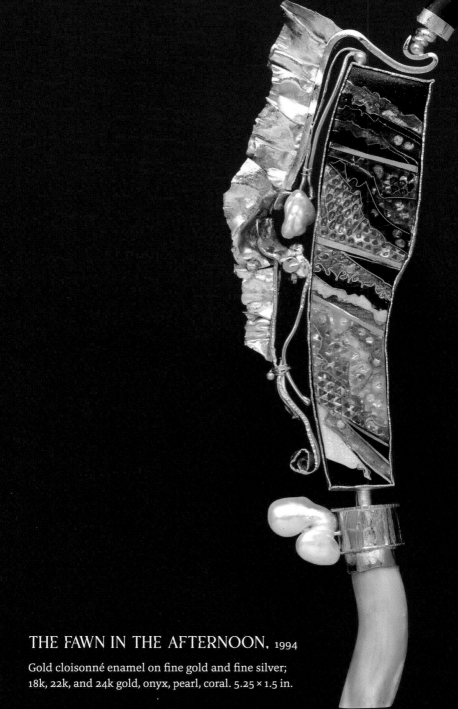

THE FAWN IN THE AFTERNOON, 1994

Gold cloisonné enamel on fine gold and fine silver;
18k, 22k, and 24k gold, onyx, pearl, coral. 5.25 × 1.5 in.

"an astonishing range of techniques, including applique, painting and dying, embroidery using flossing, flocking, beading, and metal studs."[11] The costume is an example of maximalism without obvious purpose, since these details would not have been seen by audiences; it is a collaborative work of art uniting Bakst, Muelle (and no doubt others in her workshop), and Nijinsky. While black-and-white publicity photos of the costumed Nijinsky attest to the stunning visual effects of this design, the tunic itself, now conserved in the collection of the National Gallery of Australia, is simply breathtaking.

While any one of the brooches in the *Diaghilev* series could be set in dialogue with Bakst's costumed blue god, *The Brothel's Favorite* offers an opportunity too irresistible to pass over. Most obviously, this brooch prominently features a blue jewel: a large aquamarine, which protrudes from the lower part of the composition in a gesture that Harper has described as "naughty."[12] This is not the only sexual element in the piece; the aquamarine is counterbalanced by, and connected to, other obvious phallic symbols, including a large, pointed arrow and a dangling gold orb, sheathed in a coil of gold wiring. Beyond the overt sexuality that links this piece to Bakst's god, Harper's imagined Diaghilev *confrère* shares other similarities with his predecessor. His outsize head, fashioned in gold cloisonné enamel, is the site of focused decoration, an intensely colorful mélange invoking the Bakst palette, heavy on yellow, orange, and blue tones. Although the features are abstract, the character is sharply drawn, appearing to have a toothy grin and a headdress ornamented with a pearl. Unlike some other characters in the series, he has a neutral, minimized trunk, which gives further emphasis to the drama of his appendages. Harper adds an additional dimension of theatricality through the implication of motion into the design; the character leans forward with what seems to be a sense of purpose, alert and poised for action, completely ready for the party that Harper has decided to throw for his Diaghilev "kids."

These two works, created over a century apart, are also separated by their media and their time. Yet the two artists worked to similar aesthetic codes. Maximalism and fantasy govern their expressive reach, in each case finding expression in refinement, meticulous detail, and exuberant adornment. In the end, Bakst's blue god and Harper's *Favorite* are both jewels sprung to life. In the end, both meet Diaghilev's challenge: to astonish us all. ◆

---

11   Sarah Woodcock, "Wardrobe," in ibid., 137.
12   William Harper, quoted in *William Harper: The Beautiful & the Grotesque*, 30.

"

I INVENTED
MY OWN RELIGION.
IT WAS FUN.

THE TONGUE OF KALI, c. 2001

Fine gold cloisonné enamel on fine gold and fine
silver; 18k and 22k gold, tourmaline, pearl.
5.5 × 2 in.

TREASURE CASK FOR TRICKSTER'S BEADS, 2002–18

Wood, leather, specimen insect, mixed-media
metals, pearl, glass, plastic. 15 × 20 × 7.5 in.

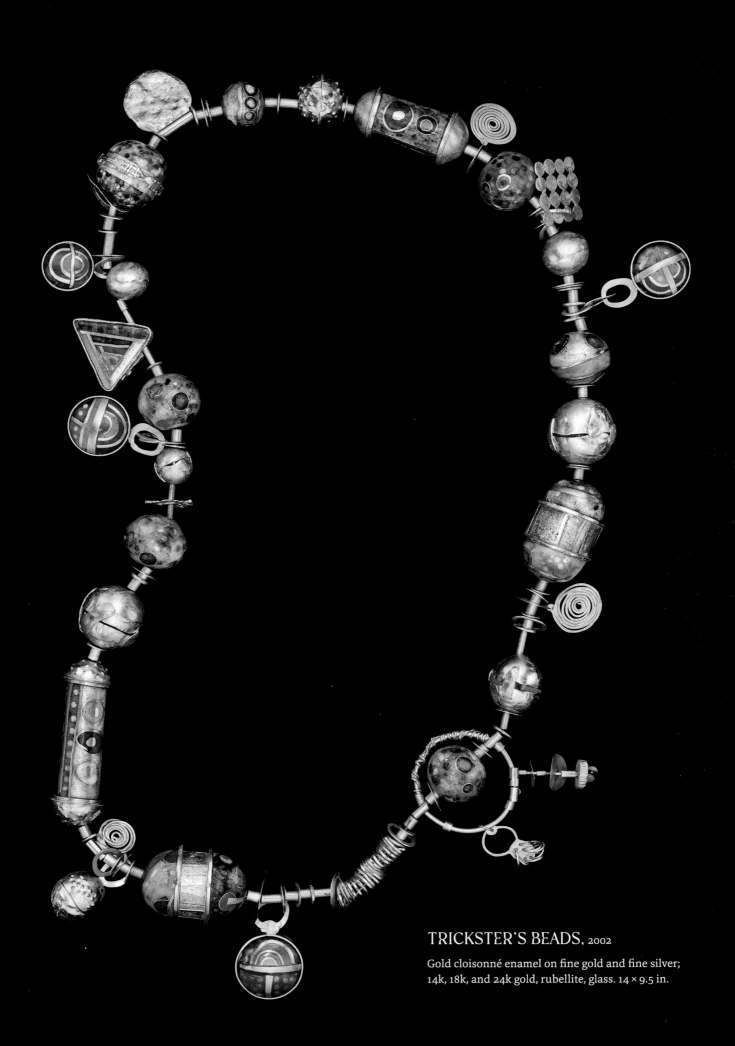

TRICKSTER'S BEADS, 2002

Gold cloisonné enamel on fine gold and fine silver;
14k, 18k, and 24k gold, rubellite, glass. 14 × 9.5 in.

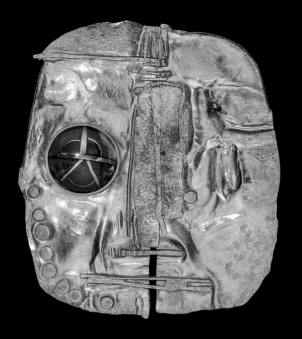

DEATH MASK #2, 2003

Gold cloisonné enamel on fine gold;
18k, 22k, and 24k gold, 3.3 × 2.9 in.

APPARITION BROOCH #2, 2004

Gold cloisonné enamel on fine silver; 18k and
24k gold, tourmaline, 3 × 1.5 in.

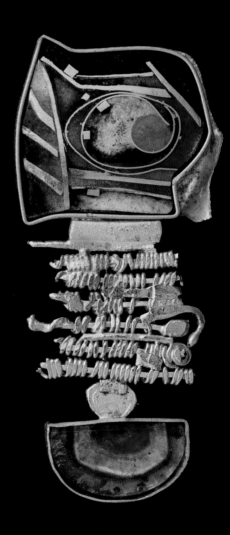

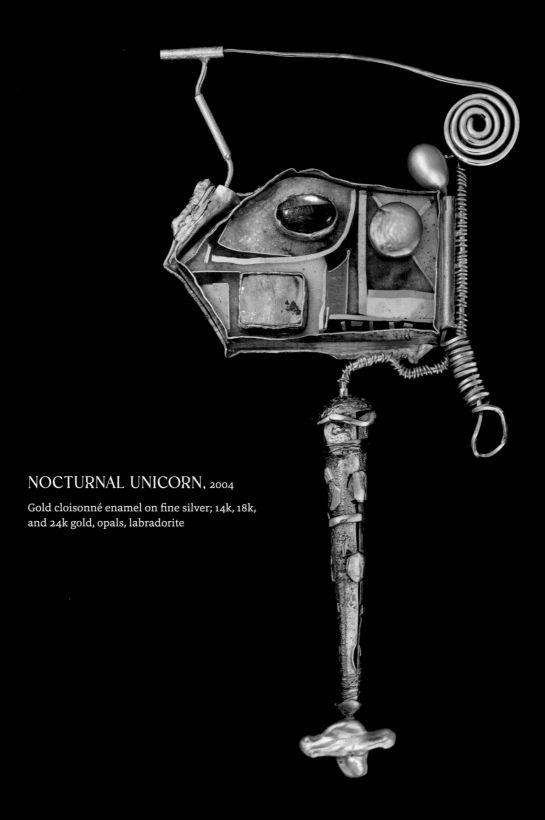

NOCTURNAL UNICORN, 2004

Gold cloisonné enamel on fine silver; 14k, 18k,
and 24k gold, opals, labradorite

TOMB RELIQUARY BEADS, c. 2004

Gold cloisonné enamel on fine silver; 18k, 22k, and
24k gold, antique Roman glass. Length: 26 in.

TOMB RELIQUARY, c. 2004

Wood box; miscellaneous beads, snakeskin,
brass mesh, animal skull. 10 × 20 × 7.5 in.

MIDSUMMER NIGHT BLOSSOM, 2007

Gold cloisonné enamel on fine silver; 18k, 22k,
and 24k gold, pearl. 3.25 × 1.5 in.

CASK FOR THE GRAND
BARBARIAN'S TRAPEZE. 1998

Cask in a wooden and plastic box with leather,
Tiffany glass fragment, paper collage, non-precious
metals. 12.8 × 5.5 × 5 in. The Newark Museum of Art

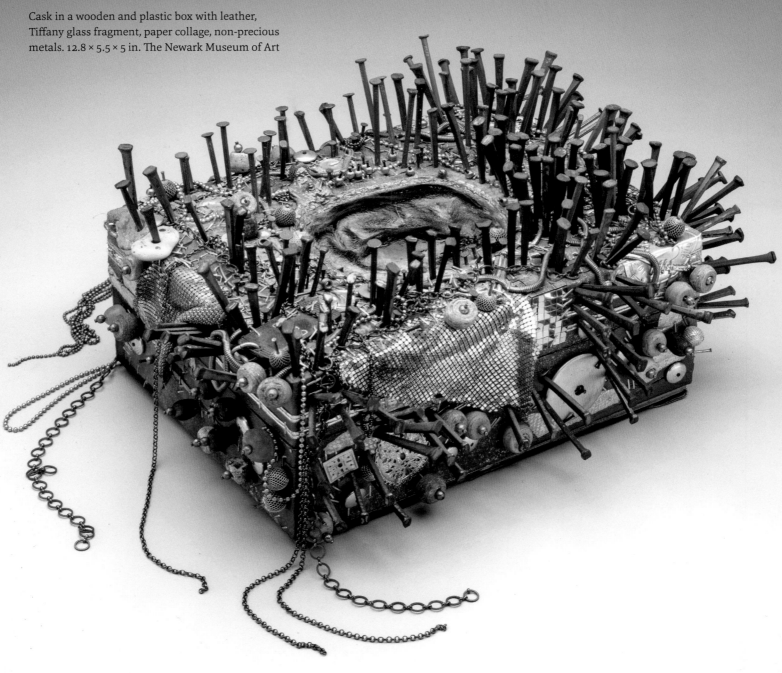

THE SPIRIT THAT MOVES

A CONVERSATION WITH UGOCHUKWU-SMOOTH NZEWI

GLENN ADAMSON   Before getting into Bill's collection of African art and its influence on his work, I wonder if you would first offer some context. As we know, European modernism took a great deal from African art, often through acts of appropriation. Those practices have rightly been critiqued, as have historic practices of collecting and display. How do you view the whole question of the collecting and presentation of African art today? Do you think it is possible to establish legitimate parameters for admiration and interpretation?

UGOCHUKWU-SMOOTH NZEWI   Perhaps it is useful to track back to European modernism's interest in African art, how it emerged, and the evolution of that relationship in terms of museological practices as well as critical responses over the past several decades.

Firstly, the invention of African art, both as a commodity and as a scholarly field, was first and foremost an act of colonial expropriation. The emergence of ethnological museums, starting in the latter half of the nineteenth century, was due in part to political and economic competition among European powers for access to a world market. At the same time, the Darwinian theory of evolution offered European colonial powers a warped viewpoint (or so it has been argued) with which to frame and sub-jugate peoples of their colonies. Thus, this initial interest in African art was shaped by commerce in the spirit of imperial expansion, but subsequent interest was scientific and soon expanded to include considerations of artistic merit.

William Harper's African art collection

This artistic interest resulted partly from a propagandistic campaign for the aesthetic recognition of "Negro" art by Carl Einstein, Vladimir Markov, and others. More importantly, however, ensuing exhibitions of primitive art in Western museums and world expositions shifted focus, from the documentation of non-Western art mainly as exotica to a recognition of aesthetics. Moreover, the increased availability of primitive art in Western museums provided an initial contact zone for the cultivation of a taste for primitive art among Western bourgeoisies. This was the context for the initial encounter of European avant-garde artists with African art. Imagined as *l'art primitif*, its process of aestheticization involved an epistemological assimilation of the other, and once European modernists caught on, a Barthesian reduction of content to form ensued. They sought the many qualities of African sculptures (the Fang mask being a prime example), such as the inherent expressive force, plasticity, reductive language, and what William Rubin referred to as "conceptual complexity and aesthetic subtlety."[1]

The African art field in terms of museology is going through a critical moment on several levels today. There have always been differing views about how to collect and present African art, but the situation has taken on a sharper focus especially since 2018 when the French president Emmanuel Macron commissioned a study on the restitution of African cultural heritage (the Felwine Sarr and Bénédicte Savoy report, 2018). The heightened debates about the repatriation of African objects in Western institutions since then, against the backdrop of the Diversity, Equity, Accessibility, and Inclusion (DEAI) impetus, have, in my view, escalated a fetish of identitarian representation that is long overdue, but there is an underlying problematic in the long term.

There have been fewer black curators with expertise in the field of African art, historically speaking. For a very long time, museum curators of African art were mainly white people and their gatekeeping practices reflected social codes of white society; the art historian Susan Vogel famously wrote about this in her 1991 essay "Always True to the Objects in Our Fashion."[2] It is equally instructive to read Vogel's "First Word" in the Spring 2023 issue of *African Arts Journal*.[3] To draw attention to fewer African art curatorial positions being filled, Vogel suggested that the field is "fading from view" due to the new wave of identitarian optics. In other words, museums are not hiring qualified white curators despite the shortage of African or black curators with expertise.

Without getting into the weeds of this argument, I do not believe that interpreting and representing African art should be reduced to identity politics. Some have suggested that the viability of African art in the long-term could be threatened by the exclusion of non-African or non-black curatorial expertise. My position is that any cultural field, be it white or black, should not be made exclusionary since civilization is universal. Conversely, one cannot help thinking that Vogel's doomsday scenario might be a little tone-deaf because it neither accounts for a history of gatekeeping that presented African art through social codes that conceived of its audience as white, nor addresses the legacy of extractive scholarship on which many have built their careers. What I mean is people going off to Africa to conduct research and producing scholarship that treats the knowledge mined from the so-called native informants as mere information gathering.

But to address your question of creating legitimate parameters for admiration and interpretation, I believe that new models are being conceived and tested that seek greater collaboration between African and Western institutions, such as the Benin Dialogue Group. Among recent attempts to rethink the mediation of African art are interventions by African artists such as Sammy Baloji at Mu.ZEE in Ostend (2016) and Emeka Ogboh at Museum für Völkerkunde, Dresden (2020–21) and the Humboldt Forum, Berlin (2021). The various projects by these artists nibble at the colonial histories of Western museums and, at the same time, offer a radical approach in addressing the fraught contexts that African art occupies in these institutions. For example, Baloji's ambitious *Hunting and Collecting* exhibition in the summer of 2014 engaged with the history of Belgian colonialism in Congo centered on an extractive economy and the collecting practice of Mu.ZEE during that period. Ogboh's *Vermisst in Benin* at Museum für Völkerkunde, Dresden (on view December 2020– January 2021) considered the question of restituting the Benin bronzes that were looted from the old Benin empire, now in present-day Nigeria, during the infamous British punitive expedition by British colonial forces in 1897. Through their interventions, the artists offer bold roadmaps for rethinking the interpretation and reception of African art in Western collections.

Sammy Baloji, *The Album*, 2015 (Pauwel's Album, p. 24 installation detail), Installation of 20 digital photographs on Hahnemühle PhotoRag, 16 × 22 in.

1   William Rubin, ed., *Primitivism in 20th Century Art* (New York: The Museum of Modern Art, 1984), 7.
2   Susan Vogel, "Always True to the Objects in Our Fashion," in Ivan Karp and S. D. Lavine, eds, *Exhibiting Cultures: The Poetics and Politics of Museum Display* (Washington, DC: Smithsonian Institution Press, 1991).
3   Susan Vogel, "The Long View: Leadership at a Critical Juncture for 'African Art' in America," *African Arts* 56, no. 1 (Spring 2023), 10–12.

Bill's collecting practices have always been eclectic, but in the case of African art he has focused especially on the Fon people of West Africa. Can you give some sense of what is noteworthy about this ethnic group and their art?

The Fon people are part of the larger Yoruba, one of the largest ethnic groups in Africa and one of the most influential on the West African coast. The Yoruba inhabit southwestern and parts of central Nigeria, while the Fon people occupy the southern part of the country of Benin (not to be mistaken for the historical Benin kingdom) and present-day Togo. The Fon are in fact the largest ethnic group in the modern country of Benin, and successor of the historical kingdom of Dahomey, which was the subject of the Netflix film *The Woman King*. Seventeenth-century Dahomey was famous for its all-female battle-tested warrior force, the Agooji. The warriors were known for their bravery, and their loyalty to the King of Dahomey—they were considered his wives. Most were former slaves who were captured in internecine wars.

Dahomey was a major player during the transatlantic slave trade, and the Agooji were very much involved in raiding villages and settlements for people who were sold to European slave traders. Dahomey's military dominance waned in the second half of the nineteenth *century*, however, with the rise of European colonialism and the demise of trade in human commodities. One tragedy of French colonization was its impact on women's rights in Dahomey. Women were barred from political leadership, and, of course, the woman warrior class disappeared.

Like most traditional African societies, the Fon have a rich culture and a complex social structure. Their physical and spiritual worlds are interwoven and shape how Fon people imagine the communal self and the world around them. This is articulated in their art objects, which have ritual as well as secular functions. There are two main categories of Fon art. First are bronze and forged iron objects, of which the "Asen" altar staffs are emblematic. These feature a forged iron rod surmounted by figures cut out of metal sheets or cast in bronze, placed on a metal disk in the shape of an umbrella. The scepters are kept in family altar houses to represent and commemorate ancestors and serve as a link between the living and the dead.

The second category is the enigmatic Bocio power bundles that represent the deceased or ancestors. These are wooden figures administered by Fa diviners. With a tapering peg that is typically driven into the ground, Bocio objects are covered with dried encrustation comprising substances such as animal fat, blood, palm oil, soil, plant matter, and minerals that ritually charge or enliven these objects used in religious ceremonies wherein help is sought from supernatural forces and/or to tame deviant spirits. They act as safeguards against misfortune, death, and sorcery. Some Bocio objects are bound with fiber strings, which scholars have interpreted as a poignant reference to the bygone period of the transatlantic slave trade when state-induced violence held sway. *Over centuries,* this became part of the visual lexicon of the Fon peoples. Given this history, they are not particularly pretty objects. It does raise the question why they hold such fascination for Bill who has quite a collection of these objects and has drawn inspiration from them for his art.

African sculptures from William Harper's collection.
Top: both Fon tribe. Bottom: Adja tribe, Yoruba tribe

African art has been a significant influence in Harper's work, not necessarily in the form of direct borrowing of forms or motifs, but definitely in regard to the embodiment of potency in a physical artifact. How do you see this aspect of his work?

Bill has a bifurcated interest in African objects as a collector and as a maker. His collection of art serves as a reference for his artistic creation. You could say that his interest as a maker does not stem from the idea of resolving formal questions, although in some of his works you do see semblances with African objects. His *Archaic Self-Portrait of the Artist* (1988), a work in the collection of art patron and philanthropist Aggie Gund, for example, reminds one of Akuaba, the fertility doll of the Akan peoples of Ghana. It is an interesting proposition to consider given that he takes on this visual image of a feminine object to refer to himself. Yet, as we know with African objects such as in the case of the Yoruba Gelede masks or the Igbo Agbogho muo masquerades, for example, they are worn or performed by male masqueraders. Bill has also represented himself as a Bocio, a testament to the enduring inspiration of the Fon power bundle figures in his art.

I like to think of Bill's relationship with African art (West African art specifically) as having been inspired by the same origin story: the Western fascination with the "magic" of these objects. But he has forged his own solitary path, immersing himself in the moving spirit of African objects but not necessarily learning how or what evokes that spirit that has so mesmerized him. His interest in African art was ignited as an art student at the Cleveland Institute of Art. He took art history classes at Case Western Reserve and viewed objects at the Cleveland Museum of Art in the late 1960s, at a time when the Cleveland collector Katherine White had donated many African objects, mostly from West Africa. Another catalyst for Bill was the slew of exhibitions that Susan Vogel organized at the defunct Museum for African Art in Soho in the 1980s.

Bill's interest in African art is not like that of the modernist avant-garde, who saw it as providing clues as to the representation of abstract reality in plastic form. Instead, it is a quest for spiritual essence, that vital force that is inherent in the objects. He claims that he is interested in their "messiness," which suggests why he is drawn to objects with accretions such as the Bocio, as well as Bamana Boli and Warakun from Mali, and Senufo from Côte d'Ivoire and Burkina Faso. He does not copy the forms of these objects; instead, they serve as a conceptual basis for his experiments. Here I am calling to mind works such as the *Grand Barbarian's Trapeze with Cask* (1998) and *Tomb Box #4* (1999), which borrow from Kongo Nkisi Nkondi power figures that have nails and metal spikes as surface embellishments.

I was intrigued by something Bill mentioned to me when I last interviewed him—that he saw a parallel between the Christian myth of St. Sebastian, who was martyred by being shot with arrows, and the well-known Nkisi Nkondi figures from the Kongo. What do you make of his instinct to seek out comparisons across such a diverse cultural gap?

I would not necessarily characterize the Christian myth of St. Sebastian as holding a similar cultural resonance as the Nkisi Nkondi for the Kongo and the surrounding cultures. Perhaps where we can draw a parallel is that St. Sebastian was revered as a protector from the bubonic plague, and a patron saint of plague victims during the Middle Passage. The fierce-looking power figure was used historically as a protective totem to ward off malevolent spirits, prevent or cure illness. It is also used offensively to hunt down people with the intention to cause harm. Where the two cultural objects depart from each other is in the story of their becoming. The myth of St. Sebastian is built around the idea that he was pierced by arrows and left for dead. On the other hand, for the Nkisi Nkondi objects, the number of metal spikes or nails demonstrate the many times the object has been ritually activated to act as a buffer against perceived danger or to administer retributive justice.

Bill is not the only artist who has sought to connect the two cultural ideas visually and conceptually. I remember seeing *Beyond Compare*, an exhibition at the Bode Museum, Berlin, in 2018 and being impressed and inspired by the many juxtapositions of African and European objects based on history and formal qualities. In the section "Feeling Protected," the curators placed several power figures from the Loango coast of the Kongo in dialogue with reliquary busts of St. Sebastian and St. James the Greater, from circa 1500.

> Are there other artists working today who seem to have a similarly informed response to African art? Anyone you would compare to Bill, or whose approach you would contrast with his?

Brussels-based South African artist Kendell Geers has extensively explored historical African objects in conjunction with his interest in Christian icons to reconcile his European-Calvinist heritage within the Dutch Reformed Church and his roots as an Afrikaner (a descendant of Dutch settlers in South Africa). Between 2002 and 2008, Geers created the *Twilight of the Idols* series, inspired by Friedrich Nietzsche's iconoclastic text from 1888, which called for war against religious icons and relics, which he framed as eternal idols. Geers has deployed Nietzsche's exhortation as a conceptual trope in several of his works, but especially in *Twilight of the Idols*. In the ten works that comprise the series, the artist appropriated various power figures that were no longer in use which he found in flea markets in Brussels.

Geers refers to such decommissioned or inactive figures as lost objects. He considered them as no longer possessing efficacy or power and disconnected from their cultural origins. He wrapped them with red-and-white Chevron tape—the South African equivalent to the yellow-and-black caution tape utilized in the United States to demarcate the scene of a crime. The gesture simultaneously signals danger and acts as a shield. The layers of meaning in this complex sculpture prompts the viewer to reconsider the contemporary presentation and understanding of historical African art; Geers's use of the term "fetish" in his titles deliberately evokes colonial prejudices—notably primitivism—associated with African art. He inverts the conventional understanding of "the fetish" by highlighting the desirability of African art to Western collectors who fetishize it.

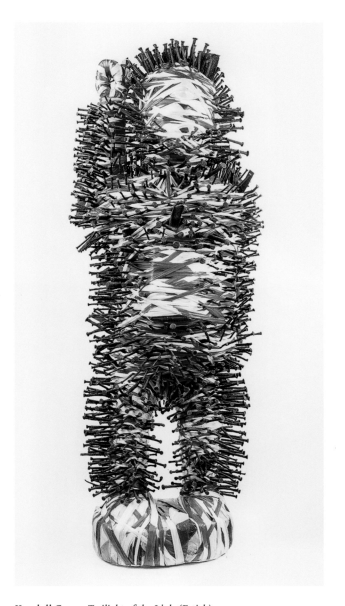

Kendell Geers, *Twilight of the Idols (Fetish) 3*, 2005. Wood, plastic tape (polyethylene, polypropylene, nylon, or vinyl), iron. 55 × 17 × 15.5 in.

Geers is one of many contemporary artists that explore African art forms. But I think there is something in his approach that invites comparison to Bill's, although their strategies are obviously different. Both are drawn to the "spirit" that culturally moves African objects.

> Is there a particular example of Bill's work that captures your own imagination? If so, what does it say to you?

I find the delectable quality of the *Grand Barbarian's Trapeze* incredibly appealing, although the title quite troubling because of the word "barbarian" and its baggage in respect of certain cultural groups and races, Africa most especially. I am particularly drawn to the casket or container which is as important as or even more important than the jewelry work it carries. In other words, *Grand Barbarian's Trapeze* is a work that features this complex case and the jewelry inside. The container borrows its iconography from the Central Africa power figures such as Nkisi Nkondi. That is precisely why I am drawn to the work as well as *Tomb Box #4* (and its associated *Armored Tomb Jewel*, 1999) and the more subtle *Treasure Cask for Trickster's Beads* (2002–18). What Bill does with the Nkisi Nkondo iconography is remarkable because he takes it in a new exciting and distinctive direction. He is not the only contemporary artist who has explored that form either conceptually or more directly. When Bill says that he is not interested in copying the form of African objects, in this set of works he makes that argument convincingly and with clarity. Yet his reference is recognizable. I also think that these works effectively embody the imbrication of art and craft that lies at the heart of Bill's practice. The containers that bear the exquisite jewelry pieces are wonderfully made, irresistible. They push at the boundaries of formal inquiry and innovation. The jewelry objects that that lie in the inside of the cases in these works are well-crafted, yet simultaneously they capture the "messiness," albeit in a distilled way, of the old forms of Africa that so enthrall him. ◆

William Harper: The Beautiful and the Grotesque exhibition at Cleveland Institute of Art, Reinberger Gallery, 2019. Foreground: *Treasure Cask for Trickster's Beads*, 2002–18

FABERGÉ'S ASHANTI BEADS, 1994

Gold cloisonné enamel on fine gold and fine silver;
14k, 18k, 22k, and 24k gold, pearl, glass. Circum-
ference: 33 in.

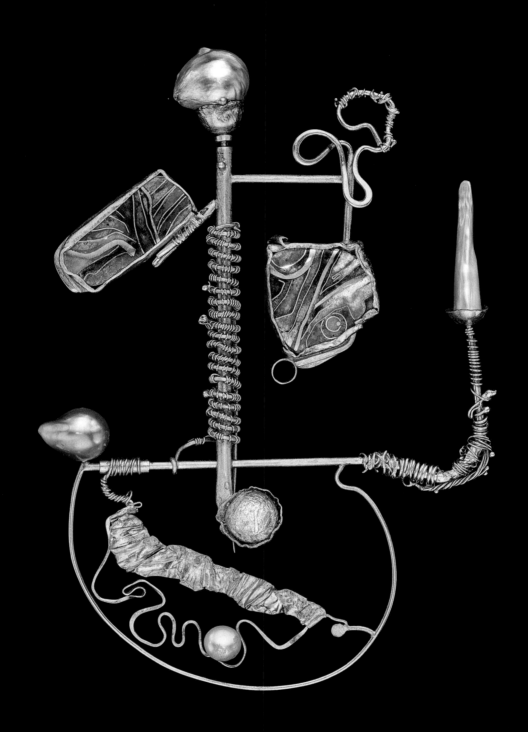

THE TAINTED FRUIT OF THE
POISON TREE, 2020

Gold and silver cloisonné enamel on fine gold
and fine silver; 18k, 22k, and 24k gold, pearl.
5.75 × 4 in.

LORD LOVE A DUCK
WILLIAM HARPER'S QUARANTINE SERIES

TONI GREENBAUM

The ten brooches that comprise William Harper's most recent series, *Quarantine*, were prompted by the harrowing social, emotional, and political climate generated by Covid-19. He made them during a period of isolation caused not only by the pandemic but by surgeries on his right shoulder and back, as well as a bout with Guillain-Barré, a rare auto-immune disease. Although mindful of the totemic images, myths, legends, and folkloric spirits that guided his earlier series, these works respond specifically to current events and were developed in keeping with his politically liberal views. The brooches' rugged appearance was directly inspired by two ancient gold death masks that had been buried for centuries, resulting in surfaces which had become so severely altered that portions appeared crushed and rough-looking. Gold, in fact, eclipses all other materials in the *Quarantine* series. Formed from the inordinate amount of gold tubing and wire necessary to obtain such coarse and irregular affects, they are more structurally complex than anything Harper has attempted in the past, though with their reliance on outline rather than mass, they are somewhat reminiscent of earlier series, such as *Alchemical Pieces* (1997) and *The Barbarian's Trapeze* (1998), as well as the more recent *Dubu* (2018).

The first brooch in the *Quarantine* series is *The Tainted Fruit of the Poison Tree*, which Harper began when he first started grappling with the question of how to approach works tangentially aligned with the explosive political situation engendered by both the pandemic and our nation's ongoing divide. The bottom third of the brooch, representing the tree's root system—as in, the foundation of our government at the time—is composed of gold and pearls,

Mask of Agamemnon, 1550–1500 BC. Archaeological Museum of Athens

while the two rectangular enamels placed above signify the fruit, dictums emanating from a perverse rule of order. On the right, an attenuated, finger-like pearl points upward, admonishing viewers not to eat the fruit (meaning, not to "drink the Kool-Aid"), because by embracing such dangerous directives one aids a malevolent system. The second brooch, *Escape from the Palace* (originally titled *The Palace Is Empty*), was inspired by *The Palace at 4 a.m.*, a 1932 Surrealist sculpture by Alberto Giacometti in the collection of the Museum of Modern Art. The two enamel components in *Escape from the Palace*—repurposed from a three-year-old unused enamel element—face one another in the upper left quadrant of the brooch, denoting persons on the run. The brooch also contains a Byzantine coin, a historical relic that can be interpreted as representing monarchies, or even dictatorships. Harper thus stages a critical assault on the "palace," that vexing seat of government, filled with autocrats who gaze down cavalierly at those trying to find a more humane set of circumstances.

Although pithy titles frequently reveal Harper's mindset at the time the works were conceived, the symbolism of his own special blend of materials and imagery may indicate something different to each viewer and, in this case, is honed further by current affairs. In fact, though the titles help to illuminate and contextualize Harper's narratives, they sometimes precede the actual piece. Conversely, as with *Escape from the Palace*, Harper may change the initial title after the work is completed. *A Duck Caught in a Thicket* was originally called *Sitting Duck*, but ultimately Harper felt that nomenclature wasn't "heavy" enough. The naturalistic depiction of this easily recognizable waterbird is most unusual for Harper. Nevertheless, the duck's cuteness is deceptive. The "thicket" represents the distressing environmental, social, and political conditions in which the populace has become entrenched. The message is that these problems have been exacerbated because half the nation has either protested the judicious directives emanating from well-informed governmental agencies, or simply turned a blind eye, justifying selfishness and lack of communal responsibility with battle cries for personal freedom.

The Parasite is the smallest work in the series. Suggested by television news programs, it speaks of an exploitative system in which the "little guy," represented by a small figure made from gold and shell, attempts to evade the political apparatus, which, ironically, appears to be a larger version of himself. Humorously grotesque, *The Pompous Charlatan*—signifying Donald Trump—confronts the viewer in all his overbearing albeit fatuous glory. Golden "horns" grace the top of his head like a crown, while his ample but empty torso—fashioned from a 1950s blue glass Evening in Paris perfume bottle, purchased on Etsy—flaunts applied gold testicles and what appears to be a shriveled erection that has been fashioned from a baroque pearl. The figure is kinetic. When tilted, he rocks back and forth—a narcissistic, imperious potentate who opts to be surrounded by "glitz" rather than execute the public-spirited acts needed to address the calamitous international and domestic crises that whirl chaotically around him. *Golem* (at nine and a half inches one of the longest brooches in the series) is also meant to symbolize America's erstwhile president. According to Jewish legend, the Golem—a humanoid figure—was formed from dust and earth and then brought to life to aid the community. Over time, however, the character has taken on evil characteristics as well and is sometimes regarded as a monster. Harper adopted the latter set of associations for his Golem: an entity intent on destroying everything with which it comes into contact. Another brooch that channels malice is *The Banished One*. Suggested to Harper by a documentary series, *The Rise of the Nazis*, this equivocal work lends itself to dual interpretations. The brooch clearly portrays deportation, as a "tyrant" with a torpedo-like head who appears to banish a tiny solitary being—perhaps a member of a disdained minority—represented by a silver scrap overfired with clear enamel. Conversely, the large figure, comprised of richly colored enamels, pearls, and glass, might be looked upon as a crowd of dissidents, intent on deposing a despot.

The last three works in the *Quarantine* series are less political and more typical of Harper's work in their erotic allusions coupled with an implication of hope. *A Bloom for the Ignorant* grows out of a prior series based on *Les Fleurs du mal*, a collection of poems by Charles Baudelaire, published in 1857. By adapting Baudelaire's customary themes of eroticism, decadence, and decline, Harper addresses the inevitable loss of potency—physical, sexual, creative, and intellectual—due to aging and, ultimately, death. When discussing *A Bloom for the Ignorant*, Harper readily acknowledges these concerns, stating, "We reach our peak and then it's all downhill," along with the equally unfortunate truth that "a thing of great beauty can often be misunderstood by lazy-minded people." A downward-pointing, phallus-shaped pearl seems

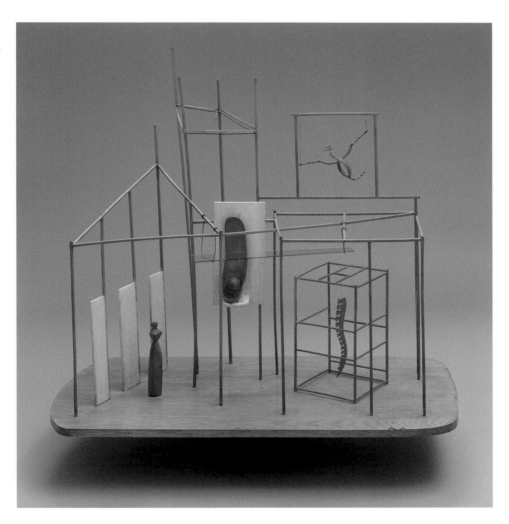

Alberto Giacometti, *The Palace at 4 a.m.*, 1932. Wood, glass, wire, and string. 25 × 28.25 × 15.75 in. The Museum of Modern Art, New York. © 2024 Alberto Giacometti/Licensed by VAGA at Artists Rights Society (ARS), NY

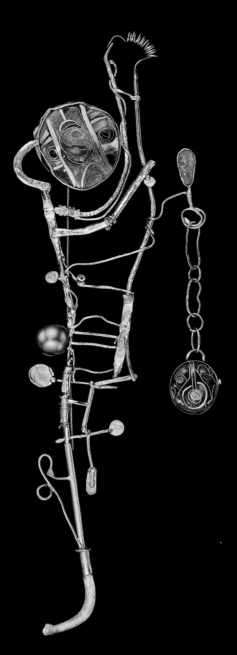

A GATHERER OF SOULS, 2020

Gold cloisonné enamel on fine silver and fine gold;
18k, 22k, and 24k gold, sterling silver, opal, pearl,
marsupial penis bone. 9 × 2.5 in.

THE PARASITE, 2020

Gold cloisonné enamel on fine gold and fine silver;
18k, 22k, and 24k gold, shell. 3 × 4.25 in.

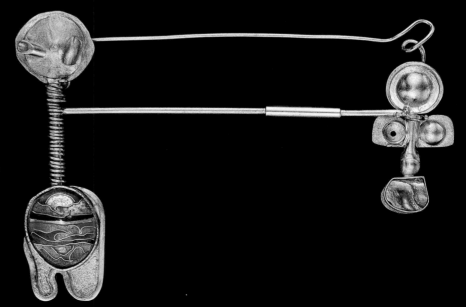

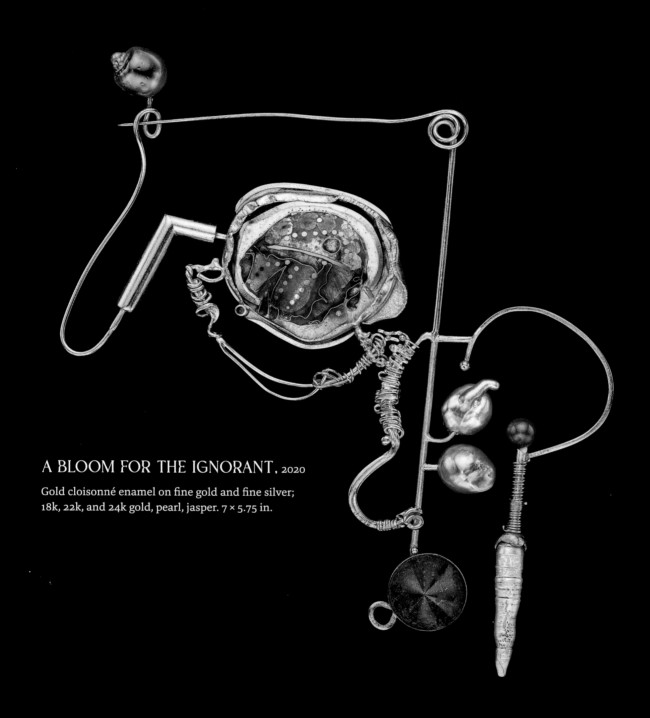

A BLOOM FOR THE IGNORANT, 2020

Gold cloisonné enamel on fine gold and fine silver;
18k, 22k, and 24k gold, pearl, jasper. 7 × 5.75 in.

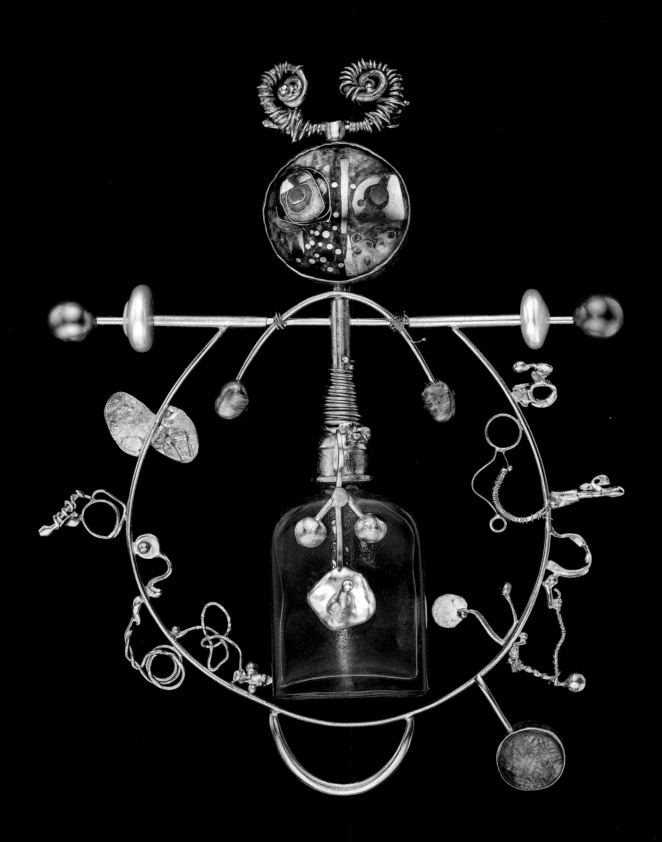

THE POMPOUS CHARLATAN, 2020

Gold cloisonné enamel on fine gold and fine silver;
18k, 22k, and 24k gold, sterling silver, glass
perfume bottle, glass, pearl. 6 × 4.75 in.

to embody these disappointments; he has, nonetheless, nicknamed the brooch *La Fleur du Mal Redux*, thereby leaving space for a positive message even though the inevitability of decay and indifference is beyond dispute.

The Annunciation, replete with both male and female sexual iconography, represents the moment—subject of myriad paintings—when the angel Gabriel announces to Mary that she will bear the Christian Messiah through a virgin birth. Harper's treatment of the theme positions an "angel," formed intricately from gold in the shape of a halo signifying his otherworldliness, opposite female genitalia rendered in cloisonné enamel, while a wire-wrapped, rigid gold shaft terminating in a pearl "penis" descends between the two elements, implying the mystical nature of this particular act of coitus. *The Annunciation* emits a decidedly generative vibe, as does *A Gatherer of Souls*, Harper's favorite piece in the series (and not only because it contains a marsupial's penis bone). Constructed like a ladder, *A Gatherer of Souls* is intended to channel a feeling of optimism; the "gatherer" is a beneficent being, set on rescuing the spiritual lifeblood of others.

Harper is unabashed by his own passions and consistently engages people with his idiosyncrasies. I own one of his works, *Ecstasy of St. Teresa I … and she knew confusion* (1985), purchased during a period of intense personal turmoil. The brooch exudes a strong amuletic power, which I sorely needed at the time, and although the upheaval that led to its acquisition has long since dissipated, and its psychic impact might be somewhat lessened, this extraordinarily beautiful jewel still offers me much satisfaction, as its visual splendor remains undiminished. Harper's body of work can be appreciated on many levels. Each piece is multilayered, with some references fairly obvious, others more coded. His opulent, technically complex works investigate historical aesthetics while questioning the present.

Harper states that preparing the *Quarantine* series helped him maintain his sanity during the turbulence of these last two years, although he doesn't believe the works radiate his usual sense of humor or *joie de vivre*. On March 22, 2021, Harper had finished the ten brooches which comprise the *Quarantine* series, and was in the midst of an eleventh. He awoke about ten days later, paralyzed from the neck down. Diagnosed with Guillain-Barré Syndrome, he spent a total of eleven weeks either in the hospital or a rehabilitation facility, or bedridden at home with a visiting healthcare aid. He slowly regained his ability to walk and use his arms and hands. It took weeks for him to be able to sign his name, let alone deploy the fine motor skills required to make jewelry. For a time, he was creating collage-drawings, until he eventually regained the precision essential for metalwork and enamel. As luck would have it, the *Quarantine* pieces were not Harper's last body of work in jewelry, yet they are among his strongest and have the quality of a consummating statement, not only aesthetically but by virtue of the controversial topics they tackle. Whatever Harper makes next, it will follow from a supreme high point, sparked by the *Quarantine* series. ◆

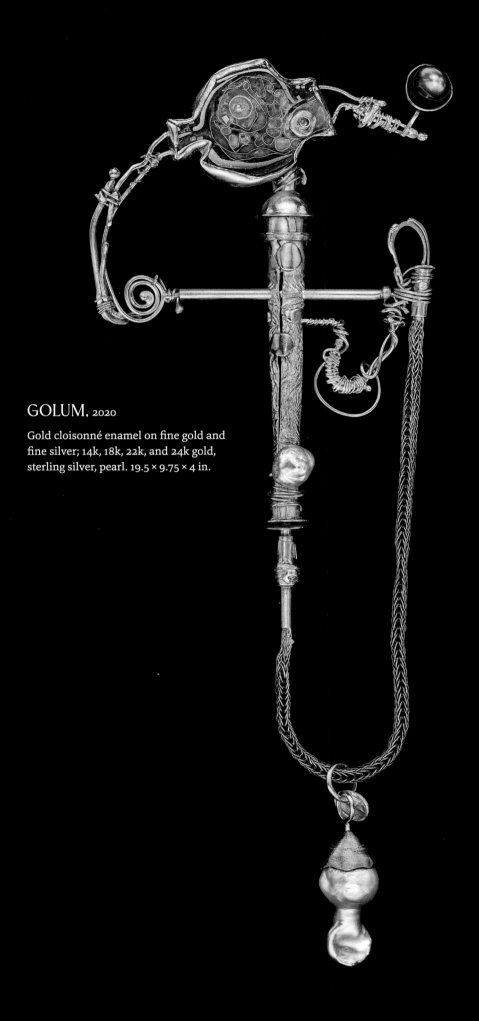

GOLUM, 2020

Gold cloisonné enamel on fine gold and
fine silver; 14k, 18k, 22k, and 24k gold,
sterling silver, pearl. 19.5 × 9.75 × 4 in.

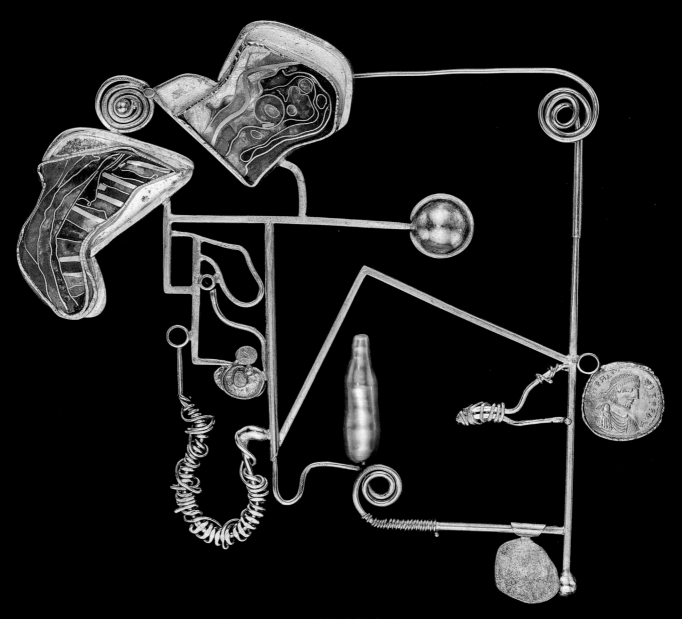

ESCAPE FROM THE PALACE, 2020

Gold and silver cloisonné enamel on fine gold and
fine silver; 18k, 22k, and 24k gold, antique
Byzantine coin, pearl. 4.5 × 5 in.

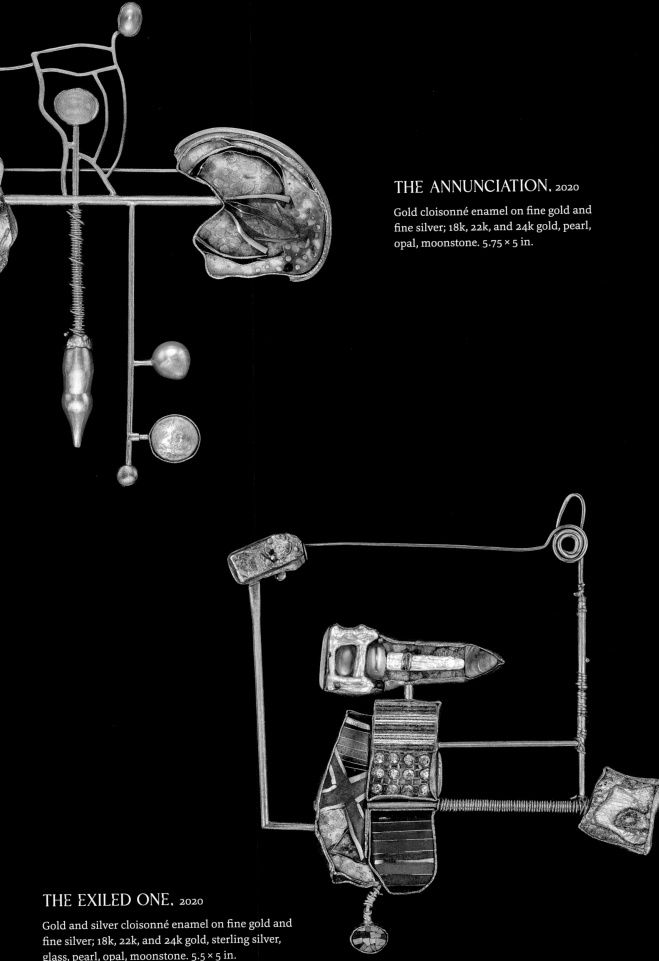

THE ANNUNCIATION, 2020

Gold cloisonné enamel on fine gold and fine silver; 18k, 22k, and 24k gold, pearl, opal, moonstone. 5.75 × 5 in.

THE EXILED ONE, 2020

Gold and silver cloisonné enamel on fine gold and fine silver; 18k, 22k, and 24k gold, sterling silver, glass, pearl, opal, moonstone. 5.5 × 5 in.

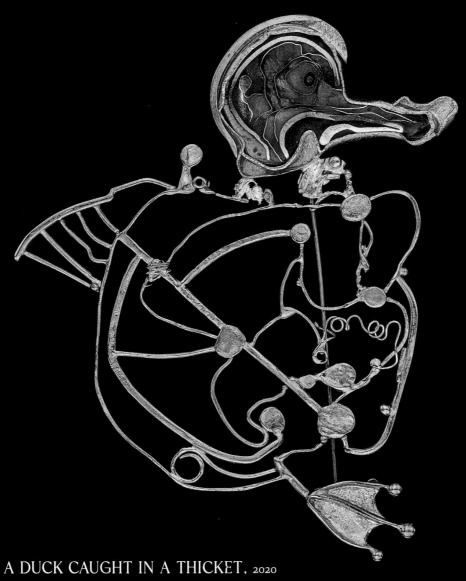

A DUCK CAUGHT IN A THICKET, 2020

Gold cloisonné enamel on fine gold and fine silver;
18k, 22k, and 24k gold. 4.5 × 3.75 in.

"

I HAVE ALWAYS BEEN
CONCERNED WITH
THE POWER OF ART
TO TRANSCEND TIME, AND
BECOME IMMORTAL.

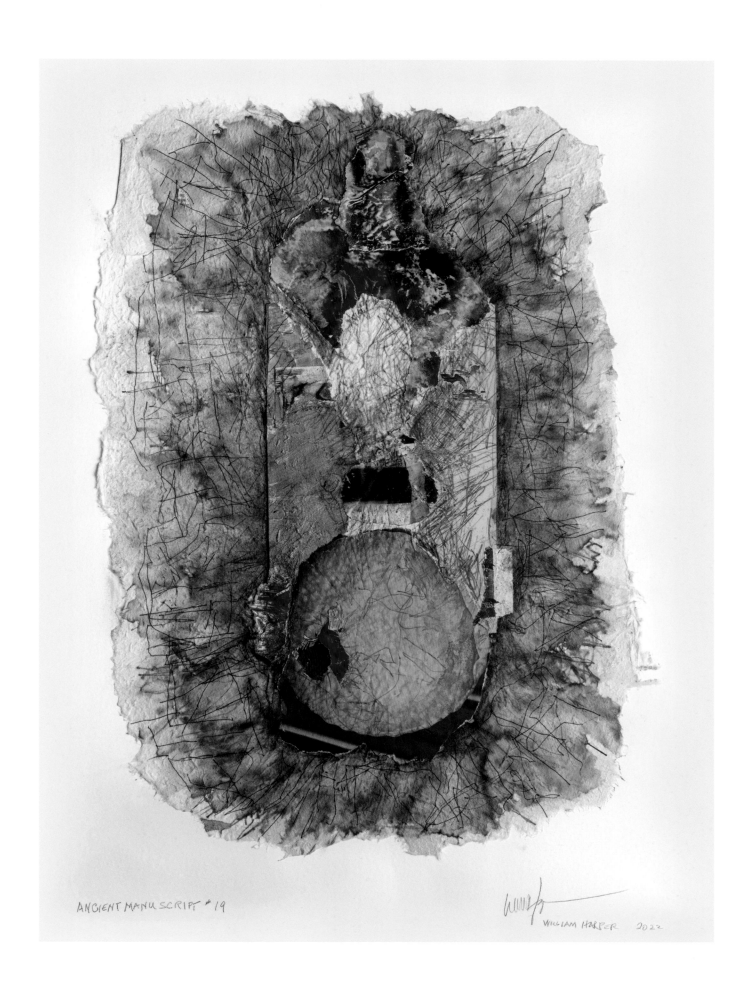

ANCIENT MANUSCRIPT #19

WILLIAM HARPER 2022

ANCIENT MANUSCRIPT #19, 2022

Water-based paint on collage paper. 24 × 18 in.

SNAILTAIL I and SNAILTAIL II, 2023

Gold cloisonné enamel on fine gold and fine silver; 18k, 22k, and 24k gold, pearl. 5 × 1.25 in. and 6 × 1.5 in.

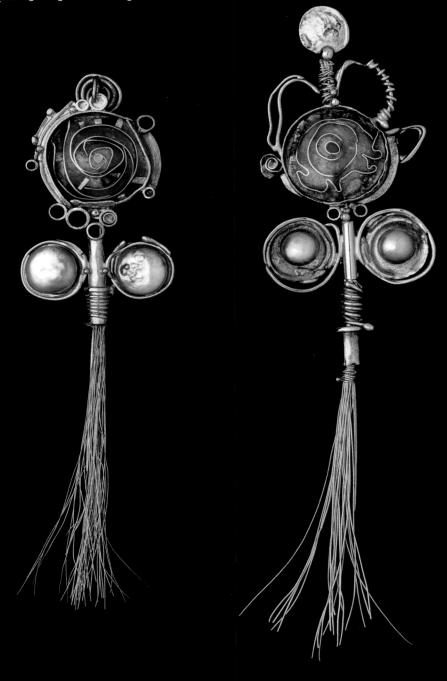

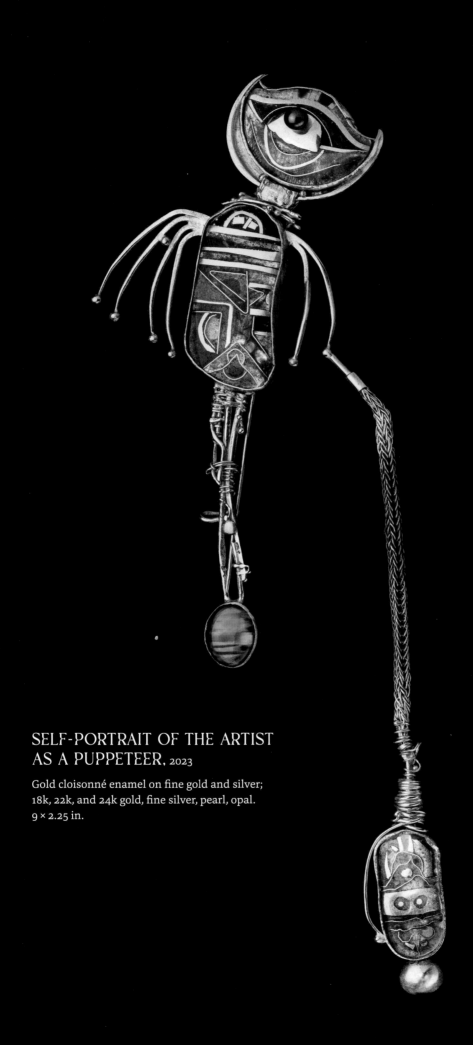

SELF-PORTRAIT OF THE ARTIST
AS A PUPPETEER, 2023

Gold cloisonné enamel on fine gold and silver;
18k, 22k, and 24k gold, fine silver, pearl, opal.
9 × 2.25 in.

VENUS'S NAVEL, 2023

Fine gold cloisonné enamel on fine gold and silver;
18k, 22k, and 24k gold, shell, glass, plastic, opal,
pearl, topaz. 3 × 1.5 in.

CHRONOLOGY
1944-2023

1944
William Harper is born on June 17 in Bucyrus, Ohio, to Margaret
  Annibel and William C. Harper, Sr.

1948
Harper's brother Michael is born.

1955-1960
Harper creates a marionette theater, for which his father makes a
  collapsible stage and Bill designs and makes the various characters.
  He writes scripts, and he and his three classmates put on many
  performances at church, school, and social clubs.

1956
Harper's brother Jonathan is born.

1957
At age thirteen, Harper begins taking private art lessons with a local
  amateur artist, Alice Tupps. At the same time, he volunteers to make
  objects, including costumesfor local theater productions and floats
  for parades.

1962-1979
The Cleveland Museum of Art receives over a hundred objects of
  African Art from Cleveland native and collector Katherine Coryton
  Reswick White.

1962
Harper begins his studies in Art Education at Western Reserve University
  (now Case Western Reserve University) and the Cleveland Institute of
  Art. In this joint program, he takes liberal arts and art history courses
  through the University and studio art courses at the Institute.
Harper meets Charles Mayer, a senior art education major, who introduces
  Harper to the techniques of vitreous enamel.

1963
During an introductory design course at the Cleveland Institute of Art,
  master enamelist and professor Kenneth Bates takes Harper under
  his wing. He encourages Harper to pursue enameling and ultimately
  becomes an important mentor to Harper.

1965
As part of his studies, Harper takes a design course with jeweler
  John Paul Miller.
Harper takes his first enameling course. His teacher, Mary Ellen
  McDermott, gives him and his classmates the opportunity to
  experiment.

1966
Harper travels to New York City for the first time. He visits The Museum
  of Modern Art and the Craft Museum (now called the Museum of Arts
  and Design), where he sees exhibitions of June Schwarcz's enamels
  and fiber assemblages by Dominic Di Mare.
Harper receives a Bachelor of Science from Western Reserve University
  in Cleveland, Ohio.
Award: Special Juror's Mention, The Cleveland Museum of Art May Show.

1967
Harper completes his five-year course of study Case Western Reserve
  University, receiving a Master of Science in art education and a
  certificate in teaching training from the Cleveland Institute of Art.
  Begins teaching enameling as an adjunct there.
Harper presents his first one-man exhibition of enamels, drawings,
  and prints at the Massillon Museum in Massillon, Ohio.
Harper marries Riva Ross.
Harper receives a wedding gift of Senufo African sculpture from his wife.
  This is his first acquisition of African sculpture: a mother and child
  fertility figure, from Ross Widen Gallery in Cleveland.
Harper begins teaching art at Parma High School in Parma, Ohio.
  He remains there for three years.
Harper begins teaching enameling at the Cleveland Institute of Art.
  He continues teaching there until 1969.

1968
Solo exhibition presented at Canton Art Institute, Canton, Ohio.

1969
Harper begins teaching enameling in the summer at Penland School
  of Crafts in North Carolina, meeting jeweler Thomas Gentille, weaver
  Bernard Kester, furniture maker Sam Maloof, and jeweler Mary
  Ann Scherr. He continues teaching at Penland for the following
  seven summers.
Creates *Freudian Toy* series.
Solo exhibition presented at the Philadelphia Art Alliance, Philadelphia,
  Pennsylvania.

EARLY 1970S

Harper begins using the electroforming technique.

1970

Harper moves to Kent, Ohio, where he accepts a position at Kent State University as a visiting artist.

Harper becomes an adjunct instructor of enameling and design at Case Western Reserve University, teaching until 1972.

Harper's daughter, Meredith Jennifer, is born.

Solo exhibition presented at the Massillon Museum, Massillon, Ohio.

Solo exhibition presented at the Asheville Museum of Art, Asheville, North Carolina.

Award: First prize, Sidney S. Cohen Award, Enamels '70, Saint Louis Craft Alliance.

Award: Purchase Award, Butler Institute of American Art: Sculpture and Ceramic Exhibition.

Award: First prize, "The Boundless-Limitations," Fort Wayne, Indiana, Designer-Craftsmen Guild

1971

Solo exhibition presented at Asheville Museum of Art, Asheville, North Carolina.

Solo exhibition presented at the Craft Alliance Gallery, St. Louis, Missouri.

1972

During the summer, Harper teaches at Arrowmont School in Gatlinburg, Tennessee.

In December, Harper meets Mary Ann Scherr, Brent Kington, and Bob Ebendorf at a two-week-long cross-media workshop hosted by the Penland School of Crafts in North Carolina.

Begins *Mirror/Rattle* series.

Solo exhibition presented at Southern Illinois University, Edwardsville, Illinois.

Award: First Prize in Enamel, Decorative Arts Exhibition, Wichita Art Association, Wichita, Kansas.

Award: Award for Outstanding Body of Work, Massillon Museum, Ohio, Artists-Craftsmen Show.

Awards: Purchase Award for Permanent Collection; Best in Enamel; *Designer-Craftsmen '72*, Columbus Gallery of Fine Arts, Columbus, Ohio.

Award: The Horace E. Potter Award for Excellence in Craftsmanship, The Cleveland Museum of Art May Show.

1973

Whilst teaching at the Penland School of Crafts, Harper visits a small folk art museum in the area, where he discovers a collection of birds' feet cast in precious metals. These objects are part of a tradition from Northern Europe, whereby the birds' feet are used as amulets for warding off evil. The feet become an impetus for a new series of five works. Featuring three-dimensional structures, found objects, sound-generating devices, and an overall emphasis on magic, this series is a notable departure from earlier works.

William Milliken, longtime director of the Cleveland Museum of Art, purchases Harper's *Rattle for Medusa*, which he gifts to the museum. It is the first William Harper work to enter the permanent collection of the Cleveland Museum of Art.

Harper's son Joshua Marc is born.

Harper's book *Step-by-Step Enameling* is published by the Western Publishing Company; 100,000 copies are sold worldwide, in four languages.

Harper leaves teaching for seven months and moves with his family to Lindenwold, New Jersey.

Harper moves to Tallahassee, Florida, to accept a teaching position in jewelry and enameling at Florida State University.

Award: Juror's Award, the Marietta Crafts Regional, Marietta College, Ohio.

Award: $1,000 for Best in Crafts, The Cleveland Museum of Art May Show.

Awards: Best in Show; Best in Enamel; Purchase Award; *Designer-Craftsmen '73*, Columbus Gallery of Fine Arts, Columbus, Ohio.

Award: First Prize, *Toys and Games*, Birmingham Bloomfield Art Center, Birmingham, Michigan.

1974

Harper is granted the Craftsman's Research Fellowship by the National Endowment for the Arts. He is given $3,000 to travel to Europe and study the *en resille* enamel technique. Harper travels abroad for the first time to London and Paris to study the collections at the British Museum, the Victoria and Albert Museum, and the Musée de Arts Décoratifs.

Delivers a lecture on his work at the World Craft Conference in Toronto, Canada.

Award: Purchase Award; Merit Award; *The Goldsmith*, The Renwick Gallery of the Smithsonian and Minnesota Museum of Art

1975

Harper begins to make jewelry with strings of fabricated metal and enamel beads. In addition, he begins to combine found objects with precious materials.

Travels to Japan.

Solo exhibition presented at the University of North Dakota Art Gallery, Grand Forks, North Dakota.

Award: Médaille de la Ville de Limoges; Biennale Internationale L'Art de L'Émail, Limoges, France.

Award: Honorable Mention; Crafts of the Americas, Colorado State University, Fort Collins.

Award: Best in Show; Crafts of Florida, Stephen Foster Memorial, White Springs.

Award: Best in Show; 25th Florida Crafts Exhibition, Florida State University.

1976

Executes *Fetish Pin* series incorporating shells and animal bones.

Executes *Mystery* series.

Harper receives an invitation from Stanley Lechtzin of the Tyler School of Art, Temple University, in Philadelphia, Pennsylvania, to participate in a two-week seminar, where he is offered innovative equipment to experiment with new techniques.

Harper meets Helen Drutt, who becomes his representative through 1980.

Solo exhibition at the Arkansas Art Center, Little Rock, Arkansas.

Award: Second Prize; International Festival of Enamels, Laguna Beach Museum, California.

1977

Harper presents a one-man exhibition at the Renwick Gallery of the National Museum of American Art, Smithsonian Institution, Washington, DC.

Harper executes his *Pagan Babies* series (1977–78), elevating found objects, including animal hair and teeth, snake rattles, and shells, to the status of precious.

Award: Purchase Award; *Profiles in Jewelry, 1977*, Texas Tech University, Lubbock, Texas.

1978

Harper is granted a second Craftsman's Research Fellowship and $5,000 by the National Endowment for the Arts.

Solo exhibition *William Harper: Contemporary Jewelry* is presented at Helen Drutt Gallery, Philadelphia, Pennsylvania.

Solo exhibition *William Harper: Fetish Jewels* is presented at Florida State University Fine Arts Gallery and Museum, Tallahassee, Florida.

Presents at Goldsmith's Hall in London as part of the *Rings and Rattlesnakes: Four Americans* exhibition.

Travels to London, Spain, and Morocco.

Solo exhibition *William Harper Mysteries* is presented at Yaw Gallery, Birmingham, Michigan.

Exhibits his work at the Vatican Museum, Vatican City, Italy.

1979

Harper is awarded the Master Craftsman Apprentice Grant by the National Endowment for the Arts.

Travels with his family to Mexico and Guadeloupe.

Solo exhibition *William Harper* is presented at Electrum Gallery, London, England.

Harper spends a year commuting to New York to teach at Parsons School of Design.

1980

Harper meets Lawrence Fleischman of Kennedy Galleries in New York City. Fleischman became Harper's exclusive dealer for three years.

Exhibits Torah pointer, purchased by American Friends of the Vatican, at the Vatican Museums.

Completes *Nine Sketches* series.

Harper is awarded a one-year sabbatical from Florida State University.

Travels to Guadeloupe again.

Solo exhibition *William Harper* is organized by Florida State University Fine Arts Gallery and Museum, Tallahassee, Florida, and travels to Helen Drutt Gallery, Philadelphia, Pennsylvania.

Harper is granted both an Individual Artist Fellowship by the Florida Arts Council and the Master Craftsman Apprentice Grant by the National Endowment for the Arts.

1981

Harper begins to explore religious symbolism with his series *Saints, Martyrs and Savages*, executed in 1981 and 1982.

Solo exhibition *William Harper* is presented at the Chautauqua Art Association, New York City, New York.

Solo exhibition *The Art of William Harper* is presented at Kennedy Galleries, New York City, New York.

1982

Harper is commissioned to create the Yale collar and Yale jewel for the Office of President, Yale University, New Haven, Connecticut.

Solo exhibition *Saints, Martyrs and Savages: Enameled Jewelry by William Harper* is presented at Kennedy Galleries, New York City, New York.

Solo exhibition *William Harper* is presented at the Phoenix Art Museum, Phoenix, Arizona.

Solo exhibition *William Harper* is presented at the Southeastern Center for Contemporary Art, Salem, North Carolina.

1983

Travels with family to England, the Netherlands, Belgium, and France.

1984

Commutes to Cleveland, Ohio, as a visiting professor at the Cleveland Institute of Art.

Solo exhibition presented at Esther Saks Gallery, Chicago, Illinois.

1985

Harper completes the *La Fleur du mal* series.

Spends three weeks in the summer as master artist in residence at the Atlantic Center for the Arts, New Smyrna Beach, Florida.

Travels with family in the summer to Germany and Austria.

Completes *The Ecstasy of Saint Teresa* series. *Ecstasy II* is purchased by Schmuckmuseum, Pforzheim, Germany.

Harper is granted a second Individual Artist Fellowship by the Florida Arts Council.

Albertson-Peterson Gallery becomes Harper's representative in Winter Park, Florida.

Solo exhibition presented at Yaw Gallery, Birmingham, Michigan.

Solo exhibition presented at Albertson-Peterson Gallery, Winter Park, Florida.

1986

Harper completes his first self-portrait in jewelry: *The Temptation of Saint Anthony as the Artist*.

Begins the series titled *The Fake Maharajahs, the White Hermaphrodite, and Other Baroque Grotesqueries*.

1987

Lectures at Orlando Museum, Florida, where he meets William and Norma Canelas Roth of Winter Haven, Florida, major collectors of all aspects of fine and decorative arts, including ethnological material. Over a thirty-five year friendship, they acquire more than fifty pieces of Harper jewelry, as well as paintings, drawings, and sculptural objects by Harper.

Executes the *Pentimenti* series.

Serves as one of four advisors to evaluate the role of craft art at the Renwick Gallery and the Smithsonian Institution.

Resumes works on paper, focusing his subject matter on completed jewelry pieces.

Exhibits in *Eloquent Object*, a major touring exhibition by the Philbrook Museum of Art, Philbrook Museum, Tulsa, Oklahoma.

Solo exhibition *William Harper: Assemblages and Drawings* is presented at Ruth Siegel Ltd., New York City, New York, and Susan Cummins Gallery, Mill Valley, California.

1988

Awarded a one-year sabbatical from Florida State University.

Delivers lecture at Biennale Internationale L'Art de L'Émail, in Limoges, France.

In October, Harper became the visiting artist at Cranbrook Academy of Art in Bloomfield Hills, Michigan.

Award: Outstanding Undergraduate Under 25 Years of Age by Case Western Reserve University.

Begins *Self-Portrait of the Artist with a Migraine* series.

Solo exhibition *William Harper: Goldsmith* is presented at Yaw Gallery, Birmingham, Michigan.

1989

Travels to India and Nepal in February and March.

The Orlando Museum of Art hosts a major retrospective entitled *William Harper: Artist as Alchemist*. The exhibition travels globally, to Nordenfjeldske Kunstindustrimuseum, Trondheim, Norway; Kunstverein, Coburg, Germany; Deutsches Goldschmiedehaus, Hanau, Germany; L'Art de L'Émail, Limoges, France; American Craft Museum, New York City, New York; Cummer Gallery of Art, Jacksonville, Florida; Arkansas Art Center, Little Rock, Arkansas; Cleveland Institute of Art, Cleveland, Ohio.

Franklin Parrasch becomes Harper's dealer in New York.

Solo exhibition *Rajasthan Series* is presented at Albertson-Peterson Gallery, Winter Park, Florida.

Harper is the visiting lecturer at the Royal College of Art.

1990

Franklin Parrasch Gallery hosts the solo exhibition *William Harper: Self Portraits of the Artist, Sacred and Profane*.

Both of Harper's retinas detach. Following seven surgeries and laser treatments, he is left with no vision in his left eye and limited peripheral vision in his right. At this moment, he returns to painting, creating self-portraits that speak to his loss of sight.

1991

Harper is granted the Craftsman's Fellowship from the National Endowment for the Arts, an award worth $25,000.

Harper travels to Barcelona, Spain, to see the architecture of Antoni Gaudí, and to Lisbon, Portugal, to see the works by René Lalique at the Museu Calouste Gulbenkian.

Harper is named Distinguished Research Professor at Florida State University.

Harper resigns from Florida State University in order to pursue studio work.

Solo exhibition *William Harper: Selected Works, 1978–1991* is presented at Franklin Parrasch Gallery, New York City, New York.

Solo exhibition *William Harper: Talismans for Our Time* is presented at Art Space, Atlanta, Georgia.

Solo exhibition *William Harper: Baroque Fragments—A Cycle* is presented by Franklin Parrasch Gallery at Chicago International New Art Forms Exposition, Chicago, Illinois.

1992

Solo exhibition *William Harper: Alchemical Jewels* is presented at ProArt, St. Louis, Missouri.

1993

Solo exhibition *William Harper: Mythmaker and Shaman* is presented at Images Friedman Gallery, Louisville, Kentucky.

1994

Solo exhibition *William Harper: Jasper's Variations and Fabergé's Seeds* is presented at Peter Joseph Gallery, New York City, New York.

1995

After visiting *Pages of Perfection*, an exhibition of Islamic manuscripts hosted by The Metropolitan Museum of Art, Harper begins creating artist books.

Harper moves to New York City.

Solo exhibition *William Harper: Ear Follies* is presented at Peter Joseph Gallery, New York City, New York.

Solo exhibition *William Harper: The Dark Self* is presented at Marsha Orr Contemporary Fine Art, Tallahassee, Florida.

Solo exhibition *William Harper: Homage to the Ballets Russes* is presented at Peter Joseph Gallery, New York City, New York.

1998

Harper is elected Fellow of the American Craft Council.

Harper travels to Greece, Turkey, and Israel.

Solo exhibition *William Harper: The Barbarian's Trapeze and Other Jewels* is presented at Primavera Gallery, New York City, New York.

Solo exhibition *William Harper: Volumes of Souls* is presented at Kennedy Galleries, New York City, New York.

1999

Harper travels to Venice, Ravenna, and Florence, Italy.

2002

Harper divorces Riva Ross Harper.

Harper travels to Greece to see the Museum of Cycladic Art and the National Archeological Museum in Athens.

He travels to Erfurt, Germany, as the sole American invited to participate in "Die Erfurter Schmucksymposium."

2004

Solo exhibition *Treasured Jewelry from the Collection of Norma Canelas and William Roth* is presented at the Orlando Museum of Art, Florida.

2008

Harper is featured in the exhibition *Painting with Fire: American Enamels, 1930–1980*, presented by the Long Beach Museum of Art, California.

2016

Harper marries William Benjamin.

2017

Harper travels to London, England, and to the Loire Valley, France.

On the occasion of the Renwick Gallery of Art's exhibition of June Schwarcz's enamels, Harper delivers the lecture "June, John Paul and Me."

2018

Harper travels to Spain again, where he visits the Prado Museum, Madrid; the Picasso Museum, Barcelona; the interior of Sagrada Família in Barcelona; and Toledo.

2019

On April 4, *William Harper: The Beautiful & the Grotesque*, a comprehensive solo exhibition of Harper's work, opened at the Cleveland Institute of Art's Reinberger Gallery as part of the "Think Craft" program. Closes in June.

2020

Executes the *Quarantine* series.

2021

Harper is afflicted with Guillain-Barré Syndrome, an auto-immune disease that severely affects bodily muscle movement. He is hospitalized for thirteen weeks, and in physical therapy for six months.

2021–2022

Lacking the manual skills necessary to continue jewelry, works in his studio creating drawings, paintings, and collages on the metaphorical theme of self-portraiture.

2023

Creates ten new jewelry works, revisiting themes from earlier series.

Portrait of William Harper and William Benjamin-Harper, 2023

EXHIBITION HISTORY

SOLO EXHIBITIONS

2019
William Harper: The Beautiful & the Grotesque, Cleveland Institute of Art, Cleveland, Ohio.

1998
William Harper: The Barbarian's Trapeze and Other Jewels, Primavera Gallery, New York City, New York.
William Harper: Volumes of Souls, Kennedy Galleries, New York City, New York.

1995-1996
William Harper: Ear Follies, Peter Joseph Gallery, New York City, New York.

1995
William Harper: The Dark Self, Marsha Orr Contemporary Fine Art, Tallahassee, Florida.
William Harper: Homage to the Ballets Russes, Peter Joseph Gallery, New York City, New York.

1994
William Harper: Jasper's Variations and Fabergé's Seeds, Peter Joseph Gallery, New York, New York.

1993
William Harper: Mythmaker and Shaman, Images Friedman Gallery, Louisville, Kentucky.

1992
William Harper: Alchemical Jewels, ProArt, St. Louis, Missouri.

1991
William Harper: Selected Works, 1978–1991, Franklin Parrasch Gallery, New York City, New York.
William Harper: Talismans for Our Time, Art Space, Atlanta, Georgia.
William Harper: Baroque Fragments—A Cycle, Franklin Parrasch Gallery at Chicago International New Art Forms Exposition, Chicago, Illinois.

1990
William Harper: Self-Portraits of the Artist, Sacred & Profane, Franklin Parrasch Gallery, New York City, New York.

1989-1991
William Harper: Artist as Alchemist, organized by the Orlando Museum of Art, Orlando, Florida; Nordenfjeldske Kunstindustrimuseum, Trondheim, Norway; Kunstverein, Coburg, Germany; Deutsches Goldschmiedehaus, Hanau, Germany; L'Art de L'Émail, Limoges, France; American Craft Museum, New York City, New York; Cummer Gallery of Art, Jacksonville, Florida; Arkansas Art Center, Little Rock, Arkansas; Cleveland Institute of Art, Cleveland, Ohio.

1989
Rajasthan Series, Albertson-Peterson Gallery, Winter Park, Florida.

1988
William Harper: Goldsmith, Yaw Gallery, Birmingham, Michigan.

1987-1988
William Harper: Assemblages and Drawings, Ruth Siegel Ltd., New York City, New York; Susan Cummins Gallery, Mill Valley, California.

1985
Albertson-Peterson Gallery, Winter Park, Florida.
Yaw Gallery, Birmingham, Michigan.

1984
Esther Saks Gallery, Chicago, Illinois.

1982
Saints, Martyrs and Savages: Enameled Jewelry by William Harper, Kennedy Galleries, New York City, New York.
William Harper, Phoenix Art Museum, Phoenix, Arizona.
William Harper, Southeastern Center for Contemporary Art, Salem, North Carolina.

1981
William Harper, Chautauqua Art Association, New York City, New York.
The Art of William Harper, Kennedy Galleries, New York City, New York.

1980-1981
William Harper, organized by Florida State University Fine Arts Gallery and Museum, Tallahassee, Florida; Helen Drutt Gallery, Philadelphia, Pennsylvania.

1979
William Harper, Electrum Gallery, London, England.

1978
William Harper: Contemporary Jewelry, Helen Drutt Gallery, Philadelphia,
Pennsylvania.
William Harper: Fetish Jewels, Florida State University Fine Arts Gallery
and Museum, Tallahassee, Florida.
Yaw Gallery, Birmingham, Michigan.

1977–1978
William Harper: Recent Works in Enamel, Renwick Gallery, Smithsonian
American Art Museum, Washington, DC.

1976
Arkansas Art Center, Little Rock, Arkansas.

1975
University of North Dakota Art Gallery, Grand Forks, North Dakota.

1972
Southern Illinois University, Edwardsville, Illinois.

1971
Asheville Museum of Art, Asheville, North Carolina.
Craft Alliance Gallery, St. Louis, Missouri.

1970
Massillon Museum, Massillon, Ohio.
Asheville Museum of Art, Asheville, North Carolina.

1969
Philadelphia Art Alliance, Philadelphia, Pennsylvania.

1968
Canton Institute of Art, Canton, Ohio.

1967
Massillon Museum, Massillon, Ohio.

GROUP EXHIBITIONS

2020
45 Stories in Jewelry: 1947–Now, Museum of Arts and Design,
New York City, New York.

2018–2019
Jewelry: The Body Transformed, The Metropolitan Museum of Art,
New York City, New York.
Iridescence, Cooper-Hewitt, Smithsonian Design Museum,
New York City, New York.

2015
Ralph Pucci: Mannequins and Display by Isabel and Ruben Toledo,
Museum of Arts and Design, New York City, New York.

2014
Unique by Design: Contemporary Jewelry in the Donna Schneier Collection,
The Metropolitan Museum of Art, New York City, New York.

2008
Masterpieces of Modern Design: Selections from the Collection, The
Metropolitan Museum of Art, New York City, New York.

2007
*Ornament as Art: Avant-Garde Jewelry from the Helen Williams Drutt
Collection*, The Museum of Fine Arts, Houston, Texas.

2006
One of a Kind: The Studio Craft Movement, The Metropolitan Museum
of Art, New York City, New York.

2004
Treasured Jewelry from the Collection of Norma Canelas and William Roth,
Orlando Museum of Art, Florida.

2000
Silver and Gold, Baldwin Gallery, Aspen, Colorado.
Collector's Choice: Contemporary Art from Central Florida Collections,
Orlando Museum of Art, Orlando, Florida.

1995
Body Language: Jewelry and Accessories at the National Design Museum,
Cooper-Hewitt, Smithsonian Design Museum, New York City,
New York.
Jewelry from the Permanent Collection, American Craft Museum,
New York City, New York.
The White House Collection of American Crafts, Smithsonian American
Art Museum, Washington, DC.
Internationale Schmuckschau, Internationale Handwerksmesse,
Munich, Germany.

1993
Facet 1: International Jewelry Biennial, Kunsthal Rotterdam, Rotterdam,
the Netherlands.

1990
Collecting for the Future, Victoria and Albert Museum, London, England.

1989

Albertson-Peterson Gallery, Winter Park, Florida.

Helen Drutt Gallery, Fifteen Years 1974–89, Helen Drutt Gallery,
    New York City, New York.

Infinite Riches: Jewelry through the Centuries, Museum of Fine Arts,
    St. Petersburg, Florida.

Two Modern Masters: Jun Kaneko and William Harper, Society for Art
    in Crafts, Pittsburgh, Pennsylvania.

1988–1990

Alice (and Look Who Else) through the Looking Glass, Bernice Steinbaum
    Gallery, New York City, New York.

1988

Extraordinarily Fashionable, Columbia Museum of Art, Columbia,
    South Carolina.

Bijoux d'Émail 1988, Limoges Musée Municipal de L'évêché, Limoges,
    France.

'88 Jewels, San Francisco Craft and Folk Art Museum, San Francisco,
    California.

Korean/American Metal Exhibition, Walker Hill Art Center Museum,
    Seoul, South Korea.

1987–1989

The Eloquent Object, organized by Philbrook Museum of Art, Tulsa,
    Oklahoma; Oakland Museum, Oakland, California; Museum of Fine
    Arts, Boston, Massachusetts; Chicago Public Library Cultural Center,
    Chicago, Illinois; Orlando Museum of Art, Orlando, Florida; Virginia
    Museum of Fine Arts, Richmond, Virginia; Museum of Contemporary
    Art, Kyoto, Japan; Museum of Contemporary Art, Tokyo, Japan.

1986

Poetry of the Physical, American Craft Museum, New York City, New York.

Contemporary Arts: An Expanding View, Monmouth Museum, Lincroft,
    New Jersey; The Squibb Gallery, Princeton, New Jersey.

1985–1986

Modern Jewelry 1864–1986: The Helen Williams Drutt Collection, Château
    Dufresne, Montreal Museum of Decorative Arts, Montreal, Canada;
    Honolulu Museum of Art, Honolulu, Hawaii; Cleveland Institute of Art,
    Cleveland, Ohio; Philadelphia Museum of Art, Philadelphia,
    Pennsylvania.

1985

New Visions, Traditional Materials: Contemporary American Jewelry,
    Carnegie Museum of Art, Pittsburgh, Pennsylvania.

Masterpieces of Contemporary American Jewelry, Victoria and Albert
    Museum, London, England.

1984

Jewelry: USA, American Craft Museum II, New York City, New York.

5 Artists, Massachusetts College of Art, Boston, Massachusetts.

Multiplicity in Clay, Metal, Fiber, Skidmore College Art Center, Saratoga
    Springs, New York.

Precious Objects, Worcester Center for Crafts, Worcester, Massachusetts.

1983

*Remains to be Seen: The Use of Bone, Antler, Horn and Ivory Throughout
    History and in Contemporary American Art*, John Michael Kohler Arts
    Center, Sheboygan, Wisconsin.

1982

The Cleveland Institute of Art: 100 Years, Cleveland Institute of Art,
    Cleveland, Ohio.

Enamelists: Ronnen-Wall, Schwarcz, Harper, Craft and Folk Art Museum,
    Los Angeles, California.

Schmuck 82—Tendenzen, Schmuckmuseum, Pforzheim, Germany.

1981–1982

Enamel, Brisbane Civic Art Gallery and Museum, Brisbane, Australia;
    Tasmanian Museum and Art Gallery, Tasmania, Australia; National
    Gallery of Victoria, Victoria, Australia; Art Gallery of South Australia,
    Adelaide, Australia; Art Gallery of Western Australia, Perth, Australia;
    Newcastle Region Art Gallery, Newcastle, Australia; Museum of
    Applied Arts and Sciences, Sydney, Australia.

Art of America/Selected Painting and Sculpture: 1770–1981, Kennedy
    Galleries, New York City, New York.

1980

Email: Schmuck und Gerät in Geschichte und Gegenwart, Schmuckmuseum,
    Pforzheim, Germany; Deutsches Goldschmiedehaus, Hanau,
    Germany; Galerie am Graben, Vienna, Austria.

Opening Exhibition, Greenwood Gallery, Washington, DC.

Southeastern Contemporary Metalsmiths, organized by Mint Museum of
    Art, Charlotte, North Carolina; Appalachian Center for the Crafts,
    Cookeville, Tennessee; North Carolina AT&T University, Greensboro,
    North Carolina; Birmingham Museum of Art, Birmingham, Alabama;
    LeMoyne Art Foundation, Inc., Tallahassee, Florida; Pensacola
    Museum of Art, Pensacola, Florida; East Carolina University, Gray
    Gallery, Greenville.

Robert L. Pfannebecker Collection, Moore College of Art, Philadelphia,
    Pennsylvania.

Copper 2: The Second Copper Brass and Bronze Exhibition, University of
    Arizona Museum of Art, Tucson, Arizona.

1979–1981

American Goldsmiths, organized by the Society of North American
    Goldsmiths; Schmuckmuseum, Pforzheim, Germany; Deutsches
    Goldschmiedehaus, Hanau, Germany; Städtisches Museum,
    Schwäbisch Gmünd, Germany; Het Sterckshof, Provinciaal Museum
    Voor Kunstambachten, Antwerp, Belgium; Amersfoortse Culturele
    Raad, Amersfoort, the Netherlands; Kunstindustriemuseet, Oslo,
    Norway; Suomen Taideteollisuusyhdistys Konstflitföreningen,
    Helsinki, Finland; Goldsmith's Hall, London, England; Museum
    Bellerive, Zurich, Switzerland.

Clay, Fiber, Metal, Southeastern Massachusetts University, North
    Dartmouth, Massachusetts.

1978

Rings and Rattlesnakes: Four Americans, Goldsmith's Hall, London, England.

New Work: Old Friends, University of North Dakota, Grand Forks, North Dakota.

Landscape: New Views, Herbert F. Johnson Museum of Art, Cornell University, Ithaca, New York.

International Shippo Exhibition, Tokyo, Japan.

Five Craftsmen, North Texas State University Art Gallery, Denton, Texas.

Florida Crafts Exhibition, Cummer Gallery, Jacksonville, Florida.

Southeast Crafts '78, Berea College Art Gallery, Berea, Kentucky.

Craft, Art and Religion, Vatican Museum, Vatican City, Italy.

1977

Heirs to Cellini, Humboldt State University, Arcata, California.

American Crafts, Philadelphia Museum of Art, Philadelphia, Pennsylvania.

Seven Man Invitational, Skidmore College, Saratoga Springs, New York.

Profiles in Jewelry, 1977, Texas Tech University, Lubbock, Texas.

Focus on Crafts: An Exhibition, University of Minnesota Goldstein Galleries, St. Paul, Minnesota.

1976

International Festival of Enamels, Laguna Beach Museum, Laguna Beach, California.

Arts of Craft: The American View 1976, Illinois State University, Normal, Illinois.

Enamelists and their Students, Case Western Reserve University, Cleveland, Ohio.

Beyond Fabergé: Contemporary Enamel, Huntsville Museum of Art, Huntsville, Alabama.

National Metal Invitational, Montana State University, Bozeman, Montana.

American Crafts '76, Museum of Contemporary Art, Chicago, Illinois.

American Crafts Council S.E. Regional Exhibition, Metro Museum, Miami, Florida.

Clay + Metal Works, Fine Arts Gallery, State University College of New York at Oneonta, Oneonta, New York.

1975

Biennale Internationale L'Art de L'Émail, Limoges, France, 1975.

Fourth National Invitational Craft Exhibition, Hathorn Gallery, Skidmore College, Saratoga Springs, New York.

25th Florida Crafts Exhibition, Florida State University, Tallahassee, Florida.

Crafts of the Americas, Colorado State University, Fort Collins, Colorado.

International Festival of Enamels, Laguna Beach Museum, Laguna Beach, California.

Looking Forward: Outstanding College Art Teachers and Their Students, Fairtree Gallery, New York City, New York.

Master Craftsmen, John Michael Kohler Art Center, Sheboygan, Wisconsin.

The Uncommon Metalsmith, Eastern Michigan University, Ypsilanti, Michigan.

National Enamel Invitational, Craft Center, Worcester, Massachusetts.

200 Years of American Gold and Silversmithing, Lowe Art Gallery, Coral Gables, Florida.

Metals Invitational 1975, State University of New York at New Paltz, New York; Indiana State University, Terre Haute, Indiana; Virginia Commonwealth University, Richmond, Virginia.

Crafts of Florida, Stephen Foster Memorial, White Springs, Florida.

1974

The Goldsmith, Humber College, Toronto, Ontario, Canada.

The Goldsmith, Renwick Gallery of the National Collection of Fine Arts, Smithsonian Institution, Washington, DC; Minnesota Museum of Art, Saint Paul, Minnesota.

Second Invitational Contemporary Crafts Show, Skidmore College Art Center, Saratoga Springs, New York.

Baroque '74, American Craft Museum, New York City, New York.

Distinguished Alumni Exhibition, Cleveland Institute of Art, Cleveland, Ohio.

Piedmont Craft Exhibition, Mint Museum, Charlotte, North Carolina.

The Art of Enamels, Birmingham Bloomfield Art Center, Birmingham, Michigan.

The Uncommon Smith, John Michael Kohler Art Center, Sheboygan, Wisconsin.

Craft Art II, Langman Gallery, Jenkintown, Pennsylvania.

Metal + 1974, State University of New York, Brockport, New York.

24th Florida Crafts Exhibition, Pensacola Junior College, Pensacola, Florida.

1973

May Show, The Cleveland Museum of Art, Cleveland, Ohio.

Art of Enamels, State University of New York, New Paltz, New York.

Toys and Games, Birmingham Bloomfield Art Center, Birmingham, Michigan.

Designer-Craftsmen '73, Columbus Gallery of Fine Arts, Columbus, Ohio.

Beaux-Arts Designer-Craftsmen Exhibition, Columbus Gallery of Fine Arts, Columbus, Ohio.

Arts/Objects: USA, Lee Nordness Gallery, New York City, New York.

National Craft Invitational, University of Wisconsin.

Piedmont Craft Exhibition, Mint Museum, Charlotte, North Carolina.

1972

National Enamel Invitational, Academy of Art, Memphis, Tennessee.

Group Invitational, State University College of New York, New Paltz, New York.

Contemporary American Silversmith and Goldsmith, Fairtree Gallery, New York.

May Show, The Cleveland Museum of Art, Cleveland, Ohio.

The Art of Enameling, Lowe Art Museum, Coral Gables, Florida.

The Decorative Arts Exhibition, Wichita Art Association, Wichita, Kansas.

Designer-Craftsmen '72, Columbus Gallery of Fine Arts, Columbus, Ohio.

Ohio Artists-Craftsmen Show, Massillon Museum, Massillon, Ohio.

Beaux-Arts Designer-Craftsmen Exhibition, Columbus Gallery of Fine Arts, Columbus, Ohio.

Lake Superior Craft Exhibition, Tweed Gallery, University of Minnesota, Duluth, Minnesota.

Marietta College Crafts Regional, Marietta, Ohio.

North Carolina Designer-Craftsmen Exhibitions, North Carolina Museum, Raleigh, North Carolina.

1971

May Show, The Cleveland Museum of Art, Cleveland, Ohio.

Forms: Fiber, Clay, Metal, State University College of New York, Oneonta, New York.

Ohio Artists-Craftsmen Show, Massillon Museum, Massillon, Ohio.

Second Invitational Contemporary Crafts Show, Skidmore College Art Center, Saratoga Springs, New York.

Four Man Show, Kent State University, Kent, Ohio.

Ohio Craft Invitational Show, Mansfield Fine Arts Guild, Mansfield, Ohio.

1970

Sculpture & Ceramic Exhibition, Butler Institute of American Art, Youngstown, Ohio.

Enamels '70, William Rockhill Nelson Gallery and the Nelson-Atkins Museum of Fine Arts, Kansas City, Missouri.

Craftsmen of the Southern Highlands, Birmingham, Alabama Museum, Birmingham, Alabama.

The Boundless Limitations, Fort Wayne Designer Craftsmen Guild, Fort Wayne, Texas.

Ohio Artists-Craftsmen Show, Massillon Museum, Massillon, Ohio.

Artists-Craftsmen Exhibition, Canton Institute of Art, Canton, Ohio.

1969

Sculpture & Ceramic Exhibition, Butler Institute of American Art, Youngstown, Ohio.

Craftsmen of Penland, Clemson University, Clemson, South Carolina.

1968

25th Ceramic National, Everson Museum of Art, Syracuse, New York.

Ohio Artists-Craftsmen Show, Massillon Museum, Massillon, Ohio.

Beaux-Arts Designer-Craftsmen Exhibition, Columbus Gallery of Fine Arts, Columbus, Ohio.

Ohio Religious Art Exhibition, Schumacher Gallery, Capital University, Columbus, Ohio.

1967

Sculpture & Ceramic Exhibition, Butler Institute of American Art, Youngstown, Ohio.

49th May Show: Annual Exhibition of Artists and Craftsmen of the Western Reserve, The Cleveland Museum of Art, Cleveland, Ohio.

Ohio Artists-Craftsmen Show, Massillon Museum, Massillon, Ohio.

1966

Sculpture & Ceramic Exhibition, Butler Institute of American Art, Youngstown, Ohio.

May Show, The Cleveland Museum of Art, Cleveland, Ohio.

Ohio Artists-Craftsmen Show, Massillon Museum, Massillon, Ohio.

1965

Ohio Artists-Craftsmen Show, Massillon Museum, Massillon, Ohio.

BIBLIOGRAPHY

EXHIBITION CATALOGUES

Allen, Jane Addams. *William Harper: Self Portraits of the Artist, Sacred & Profane*. New York: Franklin Parrasch Gallery, 1990.

American Craft Museum II. *Jewelry: USA*. New York: American Craft Council and International Paper Company, 1984.

Art of America/Selected Painting and Sculpture: 1770–1981. New York: Kennedy Galleries, 1981.

Baratte, John J., Peter Bohan, Bob Ebendorf, and Henry P. Raleigh. *200 Years of American Gold- and Silversmithing*. Coral Gables, Florida: The Lowe Art Gallery, 1975.

Bernice Steinbaum Gallery. *Alice (and Look Who Else) through the Looking Glass*. New York, 1988.

Biennale Internationale L'Art de L'Émail. Limoges, France: Limoges Musée Municipal, 1975.

Bijoux d'Émail 1988. Limoges, France: Limoges Musée Municipal de L'évêché, 1988.

Brisbane Civic Art Gallery and Museum. *Enamel*. Brisbane, Australia, 1981.

Cardinale, Robert L., and Lita S. Bratt. *Copper 2: The Second Copper Brass and Bronze Exhibition*. Tucson, Arizona: University of Arizona Museum of Art, 1980.

Cleveland Institute of Art. *William Harper: The Beautiful & the Grotesque*. Cleveland, Ohio, 2019.

The Cleveland Museum of Art. Lee, Sherman E. "48th May Show: Annual Exhibition of Artists and Craftsmen of the Western Reserve." *Bulletin of the Cleveland Museum of Art* 53, no. 5, 1966.

The Cleveland Museum of Art. Lee, Sherman E. "49th May Show: Annual Exhibition of Artists and Craftsmen of the Western Reserve." *Bulletin of the Cleveland Museum of Art* 54, no. 5, 1967.

The Cleveland Museum of Art. Lee, Sherman E. "52nd May Show: Annual Exhibition of Artists and Craftsmen of the Western Reserve." *Bulletin of the Cleveland Museum of Art* 58, no. 5, 1971.

The Cleveland Museum of Art. Lee, Sherman E. "53rd May Show: Annual Exhibition of Artists and Craftsmen of the Western Reserve." *Bulletin of the Cleveland Museum of Art* 59, no. 5, 1972.

The Cleveland Museum of Art. Lee, Sherman E. "54th May Show: Annual Exhibition of Artists and Craftsmen of the Western Reserve." *Bulletin of the Cleveland Museum of Art* 60, no. 5, 1973.

Columbus Gallery of Fine Arts. *Designer/Craftsman '72*. Columbus, Ohio, 1972.

Columbus Gallery of Fine Arts. *Seventh Biennial/Beaux Arts Designer/Craftsman Exhibition*. Columbus, Ohio, 1973.

Committee of Religion and Art of America. *Craft, Art and Religion: Second International Seminar*. New York, 1978.

Corporal Identity—Body Language: 9th Triennial for Form and Content. Offenbach, Germany: Klingspor Museum, and New York: Museum of Arts and Design, 2003.

Craft and Folk Art Museum. *Enamelists: Vera Ronnen-Wall, June Schwarcz, William Harper*. Los Angeles, California, 1982.

Duval, Cynthia. *Infinite Riches: Jewelry through the Centuries*. St. Petersburg, Florida: Museum of Fine Arts, 1989.

English, Helen W. Drutt. *Contemporary Arts: An Expanding View*. Princeton, New Jersey: The Squibb Gallery, 1986.

Falk, Fritz. *Schmuck 82—Tendenzen*. Pforzheim, Germany: Schmuckmuseum, 1982.

Florida Craftsmen, *25th Annual Florida Craftsmen Exhibition*. Florida State University, Tallahassee, Florida, 1975.

Galerie am Graben. *Email: Schmuck und Gerät in Geschichte und Gegenwart*. Vienna, Austria, 1980.

Greenwood Gallery. *Opening Exhibition*. Washington, DC, 1980.

Helen Drutt Gallery. *William Harper/Contemporary Jewelry*. Philadelphia, Pennsylvania, 1978.

Hughes, Graham. *Rings and Rattlesnakes (Four Americans)*. London: Goldsmith's Hall, 1978.

Illinois State University Center for the Visual Arts Gallery. *Arts of Craft: The American View 1976*. Normal, Illinois, 1976.

International Festival of Enamels. Laguna Beach, California: Laguna Beach Museum, 1976.

Jazzar, Bernard N., and Harold B. Nelson. *Painting with Fire: Masters of Enameling in America, 1930–1980*. Long Beach, California: Long Beach Museum of Art, 2006.

Kennedy Galleries. *The Art of William Harper: Enameled Jewelry and Objects*. New York, 1981.

Kennedy Galleries. *Saints, Martyrs and Savages: Enameled Jewelry by William Harper*. New York, 1982.

Kennedy Galleries. *William Harper: Volumes of Souls*. New York, 1998.

Landscape: New Views. Ithaca, New York: Cornell University, 1978.

Lang, Brian J. *Glass Fantasies: Enamels by Thom Hall*. Little Rock, Arkansas: Arkansas Arts Center, 2016.

Manhart, Marcia, and Tom Manhart, eds. *The Eloquent Object*. Tulsa, Oklahoma: The Philbrook Museum of Art, 1987.

Monroe, Michael W. *William Harper: Recent Works in Enamel*. Washington, DC: Renwick Gallery of the National Museum of American Art, Smithsonian Institution, 1977.

Moore College of Art. *Robert L. Pfannebecker Collection*. Philadelphia, 1980.

Museum of Contemporary Art. *American Crafts '76: An Aesthetic View.* Chicago, 1976.

Museum of Contemporary Crafts. *Baroque '74.* New York, 1974.

National Association of Handscraftsmen. *Focus on Crafts: An Exhibition.* St. Paul, Minnesota: University of Minnesota Goldstein Galleries, 1977.

North Texas State University Gallery. *Exhibition/5 Artists.* Denton, Texas, 1978.

Ohio Artists-Craftsmen Exhibition. Canton, Ohio: Canton Institute of Art, 1970.

Orlando Museum of Art. *William Harper: Artist as Alchemist.* Jacksonville, Florida, 1989.

Peter Joseph Gallery. *William Harper: Jasper's Variations and Fabergé's Seeds.* New York, 1994.

Primavera Gallery. *William Harper: The Barbarian's Trapeze and Other Jewels.* New York, 1998.

Rago Wright Auctions. *Structure & Ornament: Studio Jewelry 1900 to the Present.* Curated by Mark McDonald. Lambertville, New Jersey, and Chicago, 2020.

Ramljak, Suzanne. *Unique by Design: Contemporary Jewelry in the Donna Schneier Collection.* New York: The Metropolitan Museum of Art, 2014.

Saint Louis Craft Alliance. *Enamels '70.* Kansas City, Missouri: The Nelson-Atkins Museum of Art, 1970.

Schmuck Unserer Zeit, 1964–1993: Sammlung Helen Williams Drutt, USA. Zurich: Museum Bellerive, 1994.

Schmuckmuseum Pforzheim. *Society of North American Goldsmiths.* Pforzheim, Germany, 1979.

Skidmore College Art Center. *Multiplicity in Clay, Metal, Fiber.* Saratoga Springs, New York, 1984.

Skidmore College Art Center. *Second Invitational Contemporary Crafts Show.* Saratoga Springs, New York: Saratoga Print Co., 1971.

Smith, Paul, and Edward Lucie-Smith. *Craft Today: Poetry of the Physical.* New York: Weidenfeld & Nicholson, 1986.

Society for Art in Crafts. *Two Modern Masters: Jun Kaneko and William Harper.* Pittsburgh, Pennsylvania, 1989.

Southeastern Contemporary Metalsmiths. Preface by Jane Kessler. Charlotte, North Carolina: Mint Museum of Art, 1980.

Southeastern Massachusetts University. *Clay, Fiber, Metal.* North Dartmouth, Massachusetts: Gallery of the College of Visual and Performing Arts, 1979.

State Hermitage Museum. *Gifts from America: 1948–2013: Modern and Contemporary Applied Arts from the Hermitage Museum Foundation.* St. Petersburg: State Hermitage Publishers, 2014.

State University College of New York at Brockport. *Metal '74.* Brockport, New York: Fine Arts Gallery, 1973.

State University College of New York at New Paltz. *The Art of Enamels.* New Paltz, New York: College Art Gallery, 1973.

Stewart, Albert, and Elayne H. Varian. *William Harper.* Tallahassee, Florida: Florida State University Fine Arts Gallery and Museum, 1980.

Strauss, Cindy. *Ornament as Art: Avant-Garde Jewelry from the Helen Williams Drutt Collection,* Houston, Texas: Museum of Fine Arts, 2007.

Taylor, Joshua C., and Malcolm E. Lein. *The Goldsmith.* Saint Paul, Minnesota: Minnesota Museum of Art, 1974.

Texas Technological University Museum. *Profile of U.S. Jewelry 1977.* Lubbock, Texas, 1977.

University of Wisconsin. *A Comment on Contemporary Crafts.* Milwaukee, Wisconsin, 1973.

Victoria and Albert Museum. *Masterpieces of American Jewelry: Sources and Concepts.* London, England, 1985.

Wichita Art Association. *The 22nd Wichita Competitive Decorative Arts and Ceramics Exhibition.* Wichita, Kansas, 1972.

Worcester Center for Craft. *Precious Objects.* Worcester, Massachusetts, 1984.

BOOKS

Bates, Kenneth F. *The Enamelist.* New York and Cleveland: World Publishing Co., 1967.

Berea College Galleries, *Southeast Crafts '78.* Berea, Kentucky, 1978.

Cartlidge, Barbara. *Twentieth-Century Jewelry.* New York: Harry N. Abrams, 1985.

Chadour-Sampson, Beatriz, and Janice Hosegood. *Barbara Cartlidge and Electrum Gallery: A Passion for Jewelry.* Stuttgart, Germany: Arnoldsche Art Publishers, 2016.

Chambers Mills, Rosie, and Bobbye Tigerman. *Beyond Bling: Contemporary Jewelry from the Lois Boardman Collection.* New York: Prestel, 2016.

Darty, Linda. *The Art of Enameling: Techniques, Projects, Inspiration.* New York: Lark Books, 2004.

Dormer, Peter, and Ralph Turner. *The New Jewelry: Trends and Traditions.* London: Thames & Hudson, 1985.

Dubin, Lois Sherr. *History of Beads.* New York: Harry N. Abrams, 2009.

English, Helen W. Drutt, and Peter Dormer. *Jewelry of Our Time: Art, Ornament and Obsession.* London: Thames & Hudson, 1995.

Esteve-Coll, Elizabeth. *The Victoria and Albert Museum.* London: Scala Books, 1991.

Experiment Schmuck: Das Erfurter Schmucksymposium 1984–2002. Erfurt, Germany: Angermuseum, 2002.

Getty, Nilda C. Fernandez. *Contemporary Crafts of the Americas: 1975.* Fort Collins, Colorado: H. Regnery Co., 1975.

Grant Lewin, Susan. *One of a Kind: American Art Jewelry Today.* New York: Harry N. Abrams, 1994.

Hall, Julie. *Tradition and Change: The New American Craftsman.* New York: E. P. Dutton, 1977.

Hughes, Graham. *A Pictorial History of Gems and Jewelry.* Oxford, England: Phaidon Press Ltd., 1978.

Jazzar, Bernard N., and Harold B. Nelson. *Little Dreams in Glass and Metal: Enameling in America, 1920 to the Present.* Chapel Hill, North Carolina: University of North Carolina Press, 2015.

John Michael Kohler Arts Center. *Remains to be Seen: The Use of Bone, Antler, Horn and Ivory Throughout History and in Contemporary American Art.* Sheboygan, Wisconsin, 1983.

Koplos, Janet, and Bruce Metcalf. *Makers: A History of American Studio Craft.* Chapel Hill: North Carolina: University of North Carolina Press, 2010.

Kristin, Joyce, and Shellei Addison. *Pearls: Ornament and Obsession.* New York: Simon & Schuster, 1993. 206.

L'Ecuyer, Kelly, Michelle Finamore, Yvonne Markowitz, and Gerald Ward. *Jewelry by Artists: In the Studio, 1940–2000.* Boston, Massachusetts: Museum of Fine Arts Publications, 2010.

Levine, Nancy Bruning, ed. *Hardcore Crafts.* New York: Ballantine Books, 1976.

Paris Gifford, Barbara. *Jewelry Stories: Highlights from the Collection, 1947–2019.* Stuttgart, Germany: Arnoldsche Publishers, 2021.

Phillips, Clare. *Jewels and Jewellery.* London: Victoria and Albert Museum, 2000.

Preu, Nancy, Holly Hotchner, David Revere McFadden, and Ursula Ilse-Neuman. *Defining Craft: Collecting for the New Millennium.* New York: American Craft Museum, 2000.

Ramljak, Suzanne. *Crafting a Legacy: Contemporary American Craft in the Philadelphia Museum of Art.* Philadelphia, Pennsylvania: Philadelphia Museum of Art, 2002.

Scarisbrick, Diane, ed. *The Jewelry Design Source Book.* London: Thames & Hudson, 1989.

Spiro Taragin, Davira Jane Fassett Brite, and Terry Ann R. Neff. *Contemporary Crafts and the Saxe Collection.* New York: Hudson Hills Press, and Toledo: Toledo Museum of Art, 1993.

Strauss, Cindi, Janet Koplos, and Susie J. Silbert. *Beyond Craft: Decorative Arts from the Leatrice S. and Melvin B. Eagle Collection.* Houston, Texas: Museum Fine Arts, Houston, 2014.

Watkins, David. *Best in Contemporary Jewelry.* London: Quarto Publishing, 1994.

Wilson, Janet ed. *Skilled Work: American Craft in the Renwick Gallery.* Washington DC: Smithsonian Institution Press, 1998.

Wixom, Nancy. *The Cleveland Institute of Art: The First Hundred Years 1882–1982.* Cleveland: Cleveland Institute of Art, 1983.

ARTICLES

Abatt, Corinne. "Jewelry: The Importance of Interaction." *The Eccentric Newspaper* (Detroit), March 21, 1985.

Addams Allen, Jane. "William Harper: Mythmaker for a Culture." *Metalsmith* 11, no. 1 (Winter 1991).

Adell, Carrie. "William Harper." *Metalsmith* 7, no. 4 (Fall 1987): 54–55.

"An Unusual Piece." *Marietta Times* (Ohio), November 4, 1972.

Anderson, Gwen. "William Harper: Asheville Art Museum, N.C." *Craft Horizons* 31, no. 6 (December 1971): 52.

Apgar, Dorothea T. "Jewels for the Mind." *[Baltimore] News American*, March 2, 1978.

"Baroque Moderne." *Craft Horizons* 34, no. 2 (April 1974): 16–21.

Beckman, Jane. "The Eloquent Object." *American Way*, February 1, 1988.

Benesh, Carolyn L.E. "William Harper." *Ornament* 6, no. 2 (December 1982): 20–23.

Bodine, Sarah, and Michael Dunas. "American Jewelry at the V&A." *American Craft* 45, no. 4 (August/September 1985): 48–53, 69.

Bodine, Sarah, and Michael Dunas. "Is Nothing Precious?" *Connoisseur*, May 1986.

Borsick, Helen. "Previewers Hail 48th May Show as 'the Best Yet.'" *The Cleveland Plain Dealer*, April 19, 1988.

Carr, Carolyn. "Chance to Learn of Distant Crafts." *Akron Beacon Journal*, April 29, 1973.

Cerwinske, Laura. "Mystical Images: Powerful Jewelry by William Harper." *Southern Accents*, 10, no. 6 (November/December 1987): 40, 42–43.

Cetlin, Cynthia. "Multiplicity in Clay, Metal, Fiber." *Metalsmith* 5, no. 1 (Winter 1985): 46–47.

Colby, Joy Hakanson. "Diamonds Aren't This Jeweler's Best Friend." *The Detroit News*, October 30, 1988.

Conroy, Sarah Booth. "Artist Seeks to Evoke Primitive Moods." *Philadelphia Inquirer*, January 5, 1978.

Conroy, Sarah Booth. "Enameled Magic to Touch and to Entice." *The Washington Post*, December 4, 1977: H1.

"Conter l' Email." *L'Evénement du Jeudi,* 23 Juin 1988.

"Craft Alliance Gallery, St. Louis." *Ceramics Monthly* 20 (April 1972): 34.

Cullinan, Helen Brosick. "Harper Dazzles in New York Exhibition." *The Cleveland Plain Dealer*, June 28, 1981.

Davis, Sarah. "Exhibition Review: A Trio of Must-See Exhibitions in New York, Boston, and Providence Highlight Exquisite Designs with Strong Regional Ties." *American Society of Jewelry Historians Newsletter* 33, no. 1 (Fall 2019): 16–21.

Delius, Jean. "25th Ceramic National." *Craft Horizons* 29, no. 1 (January/February 1969).

Donohue, Victoria. "These 3 Artists are So *Au Courant* That 1969 is *Passé.*" *Philadelphia Inquirer*, November 17, 1978.

Ehlers, Sabine. "In Search of a Lost Art." *Tampa Tribune-Times*, November 17, 1974.

"Email." *Gold + Silber, Uhren + Schmuck*, April 1980, Heft 4.

"Enameled Geographies." *Ceramics Monthly* 21, no. 1 (January 1973): 35.

"Enamels 70." *Ceramics Monthly* 18, no. 5 (May 1970): 21–23.

"Famous KSU Artist to Exhibit in New York City Show." *Record-Courier*, September 15, 1972.

Ferrini, Vincent. "Preciousness." *Metalsmith* 5, no. 2 (Spring 1985): 30–35.

"FSU Professor Practices Lost 16th Century Art." *Jacksonville Beach Weekly Leader*, August 1, 1974.

"Giamatti of Yale to Wear a New President's Collar." *New York Times*, May 16, 1982.

Gralnick, Lisa. "The Beautiful and the Grotesque: William Harper at the Cleveland Institute of Art, April 4–June 14, 2019." *The Enamelist Society Newsletter* 17, no. 3 (Fall 2019): 6–9.

Hämäläinen, Helena, and Risoto Laine. "Olisin juuri tallainen." *Me Naiset* 26, 1980: 62–64.

Hammel, Lisa. "Glass Forms of Today Hark Back to Yesterday." *New York Times*, March 9, 1976.

Hammel, Lisa. "Some New Approaches to a Neglected Craft." *New York Times*, December 29, 1976.

Heller, Faith. "It's Jewelry That Fascinates." *Winston-Salem Journal*, July 17, 1982.

Hunter-Stiebel, Penelope. "William Harper: Talismans for our Time." *American Craft* 41, no. 4 (August 1981): 14–17.

Johnson, Barbara Martin. "William Harper, Recent Works in Enamel at the Renwick Gallery." *Washington Review*, April/May 1978.

Kiener, Michel. "Harper the Great, un maître du bijou d'émail." *La Revue de la Ceramique et du Verre*, no. 41 (juillet/août 1988).

"L'Americaine William Harper à la Biennale: Dans l'art, il y est tombe tu petit …" *Populare du Centre*, 6 juillet 1988.

Lebow, Edward. "William Harper/Ruth Siegel Ltd." *American Craft* 48, no. 2 (April/May 1988).

"Limoges al fuego." *Correo del Arte*, juin/août 1988.

Malarcher, Patricia. "Exhibitions: New York: William Harper's 'Saints, Martyrs and Savages.'" *Craft International*, January 1983.

Manhart, Thomas A. "The Art of William Harper," *Art Today*, Summer 1989.

McClelland, Elizabeth. "Enameling on the Upbeat." *Craft Horizons* 31, no. 3 (June 1973): 30–33, 62–63.

Merkel, Katherine W. "The Cleveland Institute of Art Student Independent Show." *Fine Arts* 11, no. 564 (March 28, 1976): 8–9.

Miro, Marsha. "Making the Distinction between Fine and Decorative Art." *Detroit Free Press*, March 19, 1985.

Moehl, Karl J. "Masterworks/Enamels/87." *Metalsmith* 8, no. 1 (Winter 1988): 46–47.

Monroe, Michael W. "Recent Works in Enamel by William Harper." *Goldsmiths Journal*, April 1978.

Perreault, John. "Casting a Spell: The Art of William Harper." *Metalsmith* 33, no. 2 (2013): 40–47.

Peters, John Brod. "Enamels 70." *Craft Horizons* 30, no. 4 (August 1970): 61–62.

"Recent Gift—Soon to be on Exhibit." *Renwick Quarterly*, December 1986, January/February 1987.

Rehne, Af lb. "Gennem ild og jern." *Berglingske Magasin*, July 15, 1988.

Reinhart, Virginia. "Artists and Their Art: Craftsmen." *The Cultural Post/National Endowment for the Arts* 20 (November/December 1978): 10–11.

Revere McFadden, David. "Living with Art: Collector and Visionary, Nan Laitman." *Craft: Archives of American Art Journal* 50, no. 3–4 (Fall 2011): 4–9.

Rubenstein, Betty. "Artist's Jewelry Goes to Big Apple." *Tallahassee Democrat*, May 8, 1980.

"Samples of the Goldsmiths' Craft." *St. Louis Post-Dispatch*, June 16, 1978.

Schiro, Anne-Marie. "Jewelry as Works of Art." *New York Times*, June 1981.

"Showcase: William Harper." *Casting & Jewelry Craft*, November/December 1977.

Stalnaker, Budd. "Exhibition: The Boundless Limitations." *Craft Horizons* 31, no. 2 (April 1971): 49–50.

Stapleton, Constance. "Tomorrow's Antiques: Fine Crafts Can Be a Joy Forever." *The Washingtonian*, May 1979.

Targan, Barry. "To Bear Witness." *American Craft* 44, no. 5 (October/November 1984).

"The Art of Cloisonné." *Ceramics Monthly* 21, no. 8 (October 1973): 21.

The Committee of Religion and Art of America. "Pieces Selected by the Vatican for Their Permanent Collection." *News from Friends of American Art in Religions* (New York), 1978.

Theiss, Evelyn. "Studio Synthesis." *American Craft* 79, no. 5 (October/November 2019): 48–55.

"W. Harper: 'Nous aimons l'invention.'" *Echo du Centre*, 6 juillet 1988.

"William Harper: Ancient Amulets." *Artweek* 7, no. 31 (September 18, 1976).

"William Harper." *Apollo* 114 (Summer 1981): 189.

"William Harper." *Tallahassee Democrat*, December 18, 1977.

ORAL HISTORY INTERVIEW

Harper, William. "Oral History Interview with William Harper." Interview by Harold B. Nelson, Nanette L. Laitman Documentation Project for Craft and Decorative Arts in America, Archives of American Art, Smithsonian Institution, January 12–13, 2004.

ON ENAMELING

Barsali, Isa Belli. *European Enamels.* New York: Hamlyn Publishing Group, Ltd., 1969.

Bates, Kenneth F. *Enameling: Principles and Practice.* New York: World Publishing Co., 1951.

Bates, Kenneth Francis. *The Enamelist.* Middlebourne, West Virginia: Wooden Porch Books, 1991.

Becker, Vivienne. *The Jewellery of René Lalique: A Goldsmith's Company Exhibition, 28 May to 24 July 1987.* London: Goldsmith's Company, 1987.

Clarke, Geoffrey, Francis Feher, and Ida Feher. *The Techniques of Enameling.* New York: Van Nostrand-Reinhold Corp., 1967.

Darty, Linda. *The Art of Enameling: Techniques, Projects, Inspiration.* New York: Lark Books, 2004.

Falino, Jeannine. *Edge of the Sublime: Enamels by Jamie Bennett.* New York: Hudson Hills Press, 2008.

Gentille, Thomas. *Step-by-Step Jewelry.* New York: Golden Press, 1968.

Jazzar, Bernard N. *Painting with Fire: Masters of Enameling in America, 1930–1980.* Long Beach, California: Long Beach Museum of Art, 2006.

Jazzar, Bernard N., and Harold B. Nelson. *June Schwarcz: Artist in Glass and Metal.* Los Angeles: Enamel Arts Foundation/Lucia Marquand, 2019.

Jazzar, Bernard N., and Harold B. Nelson. *Little Dreams in Glass and Metal: Enameling in America, 1920 to the Present.* Chapel Hill, North Carolina: University of North Carolina Press, 2015.

Ogita, Tomoo, and Richard Petterson. *Asian Cloisonné Enamels.* Los Angeles: Dorothy Adler Routh Publishers, 1975.

O'Neill, John Philip. *Enamels of Limoges: 1100–1350.* New York: The Metropolitan Museum of Art and Harry N. Abrams, 1996.

Seeler, Margarete. *The Art of Enamelling.* New York: Van Nostrand-Reinhold Corp., 1969.

Speel, Erika. *Dictionary of Enameling: History and Techniques.* Williston, Vermont: Ashgate Publishing Co., 1998.

Thompson, Thomas E. *Enameling on Copper and Other Metals.* Highland Park, Illinois: T. C. Thompson Co., 1950.

Untract, Oppi. *Enameling on Metal.* Philadelphia: Chilton Co., 1957.

Untract, Oppi. *Metal Techniques for Craftsmen.* Garden City, New York: Doubleday & Co., 1968.

Werge-Hartley, Jeanne. *Enameling on Precious Metals.* Ramsbury, Wiltshire: Crowood Press, 2010.

Zapata, Janet. *The Jewelry and Enamels of Louis Comfort Tiffany.* London: Thames & Hudson, 1993.

BY THE ARTIST

Harper, William. "Cloisonné—Yes, a Contemporary Medium." Forward to *The Art of Cloisonné.* Miami: The Lowe Art Museum, 1972.

Harper, William. "Preciousness." *Precious Objects.* Worcester, Massachusetts: Worcester Center for Craft, 1984. Reprinted in *Metalsmith* 5, no. 2 (Spring 1985): 30–31.

Harper, William. *Step-by-Step Enameling: A Complete Introduction to the Craft of Enameling.* Edited by William and Shirley Sayles. New York: Golden Press, 1973; Paris, 1973; Bruges, Belgium, 1973, Germany, 1974.

Harper, William. "The Magic of Cloisonné." *Craft Horizons* 37, no. 6. (December 1977): 54–57.

Arkansas Museum of Fine Arts, Little Rock, AR
Baltimore Museum of Art, Baltimore, MD
The Butler Institute of American Art, Youngstown, OH
Cleveland Institute of Art, Cleveland, OH
The Cleveland Museum of Art, Cleveland, OH
Crocker Museum of Art, Sacramento, CA
William J. Clinton Presidential Library, Little Rock, AR
Columbus Museum of Art, Columbus, OH
Cooper Hewitt, Smithsonian Design Museum, New York, NY
Dallas Museum of Art, Dallas, TX
Detroit Institute of Arts, Detroit, MI
Hermitage Museum, St. Petersburg, Russia
The Museum of Fine Arts, Houston, TX
Los Angeles County Museum of Art, Los Angeles, CA
Mark Arts, Wichita, KS
Massillon Museum, Massillon, OH
Metal Museum, Memphis, TN
The Metropolitan Museum of Art, New York, NY
Minnesota Museum of American Art, St. Paul, MN
Mint Museum, Charlotte, NC
Museum of Arts and Design, New York, NY
Museum of Fine Arts, Boston, MA
Nationalmuseum, Stockholm, Sweden
Philadelphia Museum of Art, Philadelphia, PA
Orlando Museum of Art, Orlando, FL
Racine Art Museum, Racine, WI
Renwick Gallery of the Smithsonian American Art Museum, Washington, DC
Rhode Island School of Design Museum, Providence, RI
Schmuckmuseum Pforzheim, Pforzheim, Germany
Toledo Museum of Art, Toledo, OH
Vatican Museums, Vatican City, Rome, Italy
Victoria and Albert Museum, London, England
Walker Hill Art Museum, Seoul, Korea
Yale University Art Gallery, New Haven, CT

ACKNOWLEDGMENTS AND CREDITS

ACKNOWLEDGMENTS

Robert Aibel, Moderne Gallery, Philadelphia, PA

Dirk Allgaier, Greta Garle, arnoldsche Art Publishers, Stuttgart, Germany, and Karina Moschke

Kathryne Applegate, Mandy Altimus Stahl, and Alexandra Coon, Massillon Museum, Massillon, OH

William Benjamin-Harper

Ariana Bishop

Jasmine Bruno, Victoria and Albert Museum, London, England

Pauline Cochran, The Georges Borchardt Agency, New York, NY

Lisa Dinhofer

Helen Drutt

Robert Ebendorf

Elizabeth Essner, Marty Stein, Cindi Strauss, The Museum of Fine Arts, Houston, TX

Samuel Everson and Arlie Everson

Christina Ewald, Bruce M. White Photography

Marian Falk

Barbara G. Fleischman

Barbara Paris Gifford

Sarah Grabner, Arkansas Museum of Fine Arts, Little Rock, AR

Cheryl Greenfield

Agnes Gund

Joshua Harper

Meredith Harper

Meritt Harper

Lawrence Hultberg

Carissa Hussong and Laura Hutchison Bhatti, Metal Museum, Memphis, TN

Mackenzie Jones

Sophie Jones, Art Resource, New York, NY

Jan Kaufman

James Kohler, The Cleveland Museum of Art, Cleveland, OH

Riva Ross Margalit

Paul McCoinnaith

Stacy McReynolds, PROCAM, Aurora, IL

Kathleen Mylen-Coulombe, Yale University Art Gallery, New Haven, CT

Harold Nelson and Bernard Jazzar, Enamel Arts Foundation, Los Angeles, CA

Marsha Orr

Rosanna Di Pinto, Vatican Museums, Vatican City State

Logan Recchia and Willow Holdorf, Museum of Arts and Design, New York, NY

Norma Canelas Roth and William Roth

Kim Schwarcz

Jacqueline Simon, Artists Rights Society, New York, NY

Diana Singer

Beth Carver Wees

Jeff Weinstein

Nikki Woods, Cleveland Institute of Art, Cleveland, OH

PHOTO CREDITS / COPYRIGHTS

CREDITS FOR RE-PRINTED TEXTS

AUTHOR BIOGRAPHIES

GLENN ADAMSON

is a curator and writer who works at the intersection of craft, design history, and contemporary art. He has previously been director of the Museum of Arts and Design, New York; head of research at the V&A, London; and curator at the Chipstone Foundation in Milwaukee. Adamson's publications include *Thinking through Craft*; *The Craft Reader*; *Postmodernism: Style and Subversion* (co-edited with Jane Pavitt); *The Invention of Craft*; *Art in the Making* (co-authored with Julia Bryan-Wilson); *Fewer Better Things: The Hidden Wisdom of Objects*; and *Craft: An American History*. He earned his BA in History of Art at Cornell University in 1994 and his PhD in Art History at Yale University in 2001.

ARTHUR C. DANTO

(1924–2013) was an eminent American philosopher and art theorist. A professor at Columbia University and a critic at *The Nation*, he wrote widely on postwar art, focusing particularly on figures like Andy Warhol and Jasper Johns, whom he saw as inaugurating a new relationship between artworks and the domain of everyday life. His most influential idea was that art, which had once been contained in specific genres such as painting and sculpture, had become potentially infinite in its scope. Within this expansive context, art is whatever we decide it is, or in practical terms, whatever an accepted authority proclaims it to be. This "institutional" definition of art has been widely debated ever since, and is seen as a foundational theory of postmodernism. As his essay on William Harper reprinted in this volume (originally commissioned by Peter Joseph Gallery in 1994) suggests, Danto's expansive thought led him to be a critical champion for previously disregarded crafts, including jewelry.

MARY E. DAVIS

is an educator specializing in cross-disciplinary studies of music, fashion, and culture. Her book *Ballets Russes Style: Diaghilev's Dancers and Paris Fashion* earned praise from sources ranging from the *New York Times* to specialized academic journals. Her earlier books include *Erik Satie* and the monograph *Classic Chic: Music, Fashion, and Modernism*. Davis previously served as dean of the School of Graduate Studies at the Fashion Institute of Technology and as professor of musicology at Case Western Reserve University. Before she was a music historian, Davis was a serious pianist. She studied music at St. Mary's College in Indiana and earned a master's degree in performance at the Peabody Institute in Baltimore. She received a doctorate in musicology, writing her PhD dissertation on Erik Satie at Harvard University.

MARTHA J. FLEISCHMAN

is a specialist in American art and a collector. She has been the owner of Kennedy Galleries and publisher of *The American Art Journal*.

TONI GREENBAUM

is a New York-based art historian specializing in twentieth- and twenty-first-century jewelry and metalwork. Along with numerous book chapters, exhibition catalogues, and essays for arts publications, she has written *Messengers of Modernism: American Studio Jewelry 1940–1960* and *Sam Kramer: Jeweler on the Edge*. Greenbaum has lectured internationally at institutions such as the Pinakothek der Moderne, Munich; Academy of Arts, Architecture and Design, Prague; Yale University Art Gallery, New Haven; Cooper Hewitt Smithsonian Design Museum and Museum of Arts and Design, New York; Museum of Fine Arts, Boston; and Savannah College of Art and Design Museum of Art, Georgia. She has worked on exhibitions for several museums, including the Victoria and Albert in London, Musée des beaux-arts de Montréal, and Bard Graduate Center Gallery, New York. Greenbaum is currently a professor at Pratt Institute in Brooklyn, where she teaches the course Theory and Criticism of Contemporary Jewelry.

CYNTHIA HAHN

teaches both early and late medieval art at Hunter College and the Graduate Center, New York. She focuses on issues of production and meaning for both medieval and contemporary makers and audiences, with special attention to issues such as visuality and materiality. Hahn earned her PhD at the Johns Hopkins University and her MA at the University of Chicago. She previously taught at Florida State University, where she was the Gulnar K. Bosch Professor of Art History, as well serving as a visiting professor at the University of Chicago, the University of Delaware, and the University of Michigan. She is best known for her work on reliquaries, which began with the article "The Voices of the Saints: Speaking Reliquaries," *Gesta* 36, no. 1, 1997, which has grown into an examination of the societal, historical, and art historical issues surrounding relics and reliquaries.

UGOCHUKWU-SMOOTH C. NZEWI

is a Nigerian artist, art historian, and curator, currently at the Department of Painting and Sculpture at the Museum of Modern Art, New York. He was raised in Enugu and studied under sculptor El Anatsui at the University of Nigeria, Nsukka, before traveling as an artist and curator. In the United States, he completed his doctorate at Emory University in 2013 and became the curator of African art at Dartmouth College's Hood Museum of Art. In 2017, he moved to the Cleveland Museum of Art. Nzewi has curated the Nigerian Afrika Heritage Biennial three times, the Dak'Art biennial in 2014, and independent exhibitions at Atlanta's High Museum of Art and New York's Richard Taittinger Gallery. Nzewi has also exhibited internationally as an artist and artist in residence.

JOHN PERREAULT

(1937–2015), critic, poet, artist, and curator, was one of the most influential figures in the art world of the past half century. He first established himself as a critic with the *Village Voice*, between 1966 and 1974, and then went on to a multifaceted career including curatorial and leadership positions at the Everson Museum of Art, the American Craft Museum, New York (now the Museum of Arts and Design), and UrbanGlass, New York. In the 1970s, Perreault was among the chief critical supporters of the Pattern and Decoration Movement, taking a leading role in reframing the relationship between craft and fine art, ornament and abstraction. The essay on William Harper included in this volume was written in 2004 at the artist's request, but previously unpublished.

ABRAHAM THOMAS

is the Daniel Brodsky Associate Curator of Architecture and Design at the Metropolitan Museum of Art. Previously the Director of the Sir John Soane's Museum in London, he has also held curatorial positions at the Victoria and Albert Museum and Renwick Gallery, Smithsonian American Art Museum.

BIZARRE BEAUTY
THE ART OF WILLIAM HARPER

EDITORS
Glenn Adamson and Martha J. Fleischman

AUTHORS AND CONTRIBUTORS
Glenn Adamson, Arthur C. Danto, Mary E. Davis, Martha J. Fleischman, Toni Greenbaum, Cynthia Hahn, Ugochukwu-Smooth Nzewi, John Perreault, Abraham Thomas

COPY EDITING
Wendy Brouwer, Stuttgart

GRAPHIC DESIGNER
Karina Moschke, Kirchheim/Teck

OFFSET REPRODUCTIONS
Schwabenrepro, Fellbach

PRINTED BY
Schleunungdruck, Marktheidenfeld

BOUND BY
Conzella, Pfarrkirchen

PAPER
Galaxi Keramik 150 g/qm

COVER MATERIAL
Peyer Duchesse

PROJECT COORDINATION, ARNOLDSCHE
Matthias Becher, Greta Garle

BIBLIOGRAPHIC INFORMATION published by the Deutsche Nationalbibliothek
The Deutsche Nationalbibliothek lists this publication in the Deutsche Nationalbibliografie; detailed bibliographic data are available at www.dnb.de.

ISBN 978-3-89790-716-4

Made in Germany, 2024

Printed with paper from sustainable forestry.